ADULTS LEARNING FOR DEVELOPMENT

Available in the Cassell Education series:

P. Ainley: *Young People Leaving Home*

P. Ainley and M. Corney: *Training for the Future: The Rise and Fall of the Manpower Services Commission*

G. Antonouris and J. Wilson: *Equal Opportunities in Schools*

N. Armstrong and A. Sparkes (eds): *Issues in Physical Education*

L. Bash and D. Coulby: *The Education Reform Act: Competition and Control*

N. Bennett and A. Cass: *From Special to Ordinary Schools*

D. E. Bland: *Managing Higher Education*

M. Booth, J. Furlong and M. Wilkin: *Partnership in Initial Teacher Training*

M. Bottery: *The Morality of the School*

L. Burton (ed.): *Gender and Mathematics*

C. Christofi: *Assessment and Profiling in Science*

G. Claxton: *Being a Teacher: A Positive Approach to Change and Stress*

G. Claxton: *Teaching to Learn: A Direction for Education*

D. Coulby and L. Bash: *Contradiction and Conflict: The 1988 Education Act in Action*

D. Coulby and S. Ward: *The Primary Core National Curriculum*

C. Cullingford (ed.): *The Primary Teacher*

L. B. Curzon: *Teaching in Further Education* (4th edition)

P. Daunt: *Meeting Disability: A European Response*

J. Freeman: *Gifted Children Growing Up*

B. Goacher *et al.*: *Policy and Provision for Special Educational Needs*

H. Gray (ed.): *Management Consultancy in Schools*

L. Hall: *Poetry for Life*

J. Nias, G. Southworth and R. Yeomans: *Staff Relationships in the Primary School*

A. Pollard: *The Social World of the Primary School*

R. Ritchie (ed.): *Profiling in Primary Schools*

J. Sayer and V. Williams (eds): *Schools and External Relations*

B. Spiecker and R. Straughan (eds): *Freedom and Indoctrination in Education: International Perspectives*

R. Straughan: *Beliefs, Behaviour and Education*

S. Tann: *Developing Language in the Primary Context*

H. Thomas: *Education Costs and Performance*

H. Thomas, with G. Kirkpatrick and E. Nicholson: *Financial Delegation and the Local Management of Schools*

D. Thyer and J. Maggs: *Teaching Mathematics to Young Children* (3rd edition)

M. Watts: *The Science of Problem Solving*

J. Wilson: *A New Introduction to Moral Education*

S. Wolfendale (ed.): *Parental Involvement*

S. Wolfendale *et al.* (eds): *The Profession and Practice of Educational Psychology: Future Directions*

Adults Learning for Development

Alan Rogers

CASSELL

PUBLISHED IN ASSOCIATION WITH EDUCATION FOR DEVELOPMENT

To all those—especially Michael—who
have asked me to tell them what I have
learned from India.

Cassell Educational Limited
Villiers House
41/47 Strand
London WC2N 5JE

387 Park Avenue South
New York
NY 10016–8810

Education for Development
Woodmans
7 Westwood Row
Tilehurst
Reading RG3 6LT

First published 1992

British Library Cataloguing in Publication Data
Rogers, Alan *1933–*
  Adults learning for development.
  1. Developing countries. Adult education
  I. Title
  374.91724

ISBN: 0 304 32523 6 (hardback)
      0 304 32420 5 (paperback)

Typeset by Colset Private Limited Singapore
Printed and bound in Great Britain by
Dotesios, Trowbridge, Wilts

Contents

Preface   vii
Abbreviations   viii

    1   Introduction: Adult Education for Development   1

Part I   **Adult Learning and Education**   7
    2   Adult Learning   9
    3   Adult Education: Definitions   19
    4   The Purpose of Adult Education   33
    5   A Changed World   48
    6   Government, Development and Adult Education:
        Ways Forward   64

Bridge   79

Part II **Development**   81
    7   Development: Definitions   83
    8   The Purpose of Development   91
    9   Processes of Development   110
   10   Routes to Change   118
   11   The Five-fold Path   131
   12   Target Groups: Needs, Wants, Aspirations and
        Intentions   146
   13   Change-Agents in Development   159
   14   Barriers to Development   169

Bridge   181

Part III   Adult Education and Development: Re-Orientation   183
    15 Seeking New Objectives   185
    16 Seeking New Target Groups   195
    17 Changing the Role of the Change-Agents   208
    18 Achievements and Outcomes   216
    19 Sharing in Development   226

    20 Conclusion: 'So you think you know better . . .?'   239

Bibliography   242
Index   246

Preface

This book has been written in India on a Rotary International Fellowship 1988–89; but it draws upon thirty years of experience of adult and continuing education in Great Britain and Ireland and in other countries. It is therefore an impossible task to thank all those who have helped to create its understandings. Many people will see parts of themselves in these pages as the result of the discussions, writings and teamwork experiences I have shared with them. I hope that they will feel that the fact that this book has appeared at all is some recognition of what they have contributed.

On the other hand, I must thank those who have had a direct hand in the book's production. In India, Dr L. S. Saraswathi and Rathindra Nath Roy, both field level practitioners of adult education, development and training in Tamil Nadu, and Professor Jayagopal and Professor Sundaram of the University of Madras, read an early draft of this book; the comments they supplied have been most helpful. S. Chandrasekhara of Madras, an experienced and expert industrial and management trainer, became a good friend; much of what is discussed in this book has been influenced by our conversations. Back in England, a number of friends read some or all of what had been written: John Oxenham of the Institute of Development Studies, Sussex, and Peter Oakley and Gwyn Jones, both of the University of Reading's Agricultural Extension and Rural Development Department. The staff of the Education Library of Reading University checked many of the references. To all these people I am grateful for comments both on the general thesis and points of details.

But the views expressed are mine alone, not theirs. And any errors of understanding and of fact which exist in these pages are not their responsibility: they too are mine.

Alan Rogers
Burnham Market, Norfolk
April 1990

Abbreviations

ABE	adult basic education
ACACE	Advisory Council for Adult and Continuing Education
ACRE	Action with Communities for Rural England
AE	adult education
AE	*Adult Education* (UK)
AEF	*Adult Education in Finland*
ALBSU	Adult Literacy and Basic Skills Unit
ARE	Association for Recurrent Education
BHN	basic human needs
BOBP	Bay of Bengal Programme
DES	Department of Education and Science
EBAE	European Bureau of Adult Education
EMD	extra-mural department
EPA	educational priority area
ETA	education and training of adults
FAO	Food and Agriculture Organization (of the UN)
HRD	human resource development
ICAE	International Council for Adult Education
ICEA	International Community Education Association
IJLE	*International Journal of Lifelong Education*
ILO	International Labour Organization
KASUB	knowledge, attitudes, skills, understanding, and behaviour
NFE	non-formal education
NIACE	National Institute for Adult and Continuing Education
NIAE	National Institute for Adult Education
OECD	Organisation for Economic Co-operation and Development
ORT	oral rehydration therapy
PEVE	post-experience vocational education
PICKUP	Professional, Industrial and Commercial Up-dating
REPLAN	programme of AE for unemployed, run by NIACE for UK government
RSA	Royal Society of Arts
UNESCO	United Nations Educational, Scientific, and Cultural Organization
UNICEF	United Nations (International) Children's (Emergency) Fund
UNRISD	United Nations Research Institute for Social Development
WEA	Workers' Educational Association

Chapter 1

Introduction: Adult Education for Development

ADULT EDUCATION IN THE WEST: INDIVIDUALIZATION

Education in the countries of the so-called 'West' has two main characteristics: it is usually seen as a 'good' in itself, needing no further justification; and it is primarily aimed at the individual—personal growth, career development, self-actualization. Both of these are deemed to be self-evident; until recently it has not appeared necessary to educational writers and practitioners to say more precisely what that 'good' is or to argue about the social role of education.

This is particularly true of adult education in the West. Those who provide and those who teach adults in the wide range of formal and non-formal programmes and contexts now available have until the last few years seen little need to justify their activity. What leads to personal self-fulfilment must be good. Even more recent writings on 'adult education for change' and on community education see the process as one aimed primarily at the individual—the provision of learning opportunities, for disadvantaged and other persons and groups to take up if they so wish in order to remedy individual social and economic injustices. This may (indeed, some argue that this *will*) lead to social change, but social change is not the main objective of the programme. Individual growth is the primary purpose of almost all adult learning programmes in the West.

The reason for this is that adult educators in these countries stress the voluntary nature of the adult education process. The key words in the phrase above are 'if they so wish'. Learning opportunities are offered and they may or may not be taken up. Adult education is for those few who come forward, not for the masses. At the centre of this view lies a concept of adulthood which stresses not only the development of the full potential of the individual but also the person's ever-increasing autonomy. Adult education, it is argued, must not deny the adulthood of the learners. Indeed, it should seek to enhance their powers of self-determination, increase the range of choices before them and develop their powers and skills to exercise that choice; it should help to make the people free.

Taken to its logical conclusion, the adult educator will have no goals other than to satisfy the aspirations of the learners, to teach them what they want to learn. In one sense, this is the ultimate of the 'market' approach to education—although we must stress here that we are not talking of a financial market; most adult educators are insistent that no one is to be denied the opportunity of engaging in the form of adult learning they seek simply because they cannot afford it. All people, rich and poor alike (so the ideology goes), should be free to obtain those forms of further learning which most please them.

THIRD WORLD VIEW: SOCIAL RESPONSIBILITY

Education in general, and adult education in particular, are seen in much of the Third World to serve another purpose. Whether narrowly conceived as adult literacy (functional or not), the extension of elementary schooling to the masses, or whether more widely as incorporating extension and post-literacy educational programmes, adult education is based on nationally identified needs rather than on individual wants. People, it is urged, ought to learn to conform, to change their behaviour in ways which will lead to the achievement, more easily or more quickly, of national Development goals. Attendance at educational programmes is not a voluntary option but a social responsibility. The assumption is that we cannot rely upon the people to take the initiative in their own education; persuasion needs to be employed. The education of children, adolescents and adults alike is for social goals. The role of the adult educator is not so much to increase choice as to encourage responsible social behaviour. Adult education in the Third World is for mass education, not for the few.

There are signs that adult education in the West is moving closer to a social responsibility position. In part this is a by-product of the massive upheaval and external pressures which adult education is currently experiencing, for the state is demanding more from it. But in part the change comes from within adult education itself. Evidence of the former is the increasing amount of manpower training programmes for adults which different countries are offering in order to cope with the nation's need for a well-trained labour force; evidence of the latter is the concern of many adult educators with global matters, especially the two over-arching issues of today, the balance between the human population and the resources of this planet (conservation or environmental education), and the need for a peaceful and just society (peace and justice education). The 'global issues' approach to adult education in the West bears some resemblance to the mass campaigns in the Third World; and the manpower training approach has something in common with the 'conformist' view of education in the Third World. Nevertheless, the gulf between the Third World social responsibility view (which can be seen as restricting individual freedom for the sake of nation building) and the personal growth view of Western adult education is still wide.

DEVELOPMENT AND ADULT EDUCATION

It is the thesis of this book that the gulf between the approach of the Third World and that of the West can be bridged, and that the bridge lies in a properly articulated and properly understood concept of Development. The main purpose of this book is to suggest that at the heart of all programmes of adult education in the West should lie the concept of Development. For Development is not a thing which the countries of the Third World alone need; the West needs it just as much. A little thought will convince us that even in the richest of countries, there are regions which are marginalized and underdeveloped, and sectors of society which are disadvantaged. And in the application of the concepts of Development to the West, we have much to learn from the insights and experiences of the Third World.

But if we are to apply these concepts to adult education in the West, we need to see what Development is and what it is not. I argue in this book that Development is not just a matter of planning or technical assistance, of building dams or providing tractors to farmers or new boats to fisherfolk, for example. Just as Development should lie at the heart of all programmes of adult education, so at the heart of every true Development programme there lies a process of educating and training adults.

Some will perhaps see in this assertion a desire on the part of an interested party to promote adult education for its own sake, to secure for it a place in the sun. But the true reason lies in a proper understanding of the Development process. Evaluation has demonstrated that the major barriers to Development lie not so much in the lack of knowledge or skills or resources but rather in attitudes—especially a lack of confidence or an unwillingness to change. And attitudes can only be changed through a programme of education and training. Or to put it another way, the process of changing attitudes as well as providing the new knowledge and skills and understandings which our Development programmes need is what is properly meant by education and training. So that Development agencies in general and change-agents in particular are in fact educators, 'teachers' in the best sense, those who help others to learn, to change.

Put in this way, we can see that education for Development is a matter for the individual, even if the goals are national goals. For although group affiliations assist in the formation and strengthening of new attitudes, nevertheless attitude change is an individual learning process; and the development of confidence and of motivation will, if so directed, lead to both greater social responsibility and to personal growth.

But equally the educator of adults will have goals of his or her own which they will seek to encourage the learners to come to share. For educators of adults are just as much human beings with a sense of social propriety as are the adult learners. Both parties to the educational process need to treat each other equally. The learner should not deny the adulthood of the 'teacher' any more than the 'teacher' ought to deny the adulthood of the learner.

This then is the theme of this book. I am arguing that in the industrialized, technically more advanced, richer, mainly white countries of the world (the 'West') where adult education has been seen as largely either skill training (manpower development) or leisure courses (personal development), a fuller concept of regional and national Development such as has been conceived and executed for many years in Third World countries should lie at the heart of all such programmes. This is not just to argue in favour of adult education for social change; rather it is to assert that adult education in the West is for Development. And in the less industrialized (largely rural), technologically less advanced, poorer and mainly black countries (the so-called 'Third World') where adult education has often been seen as secondary to the national concern for Development, to be done later 'when we can afford it', a proper definition of Development will call for putting the education and training of adults (ETA) at the heart of the Development process itself. Without a full process of ETA, there can be no true Development; without a properly understood concept of Development, adult education will continue to be marginalized; and this equation applies equally to all parts of this 'one world' which we jointly inhabit.

TARGET GROUP

The book is primarily aimed at adult educators, to increase their understanding of Development and to persuade them to put the concerns of local, regional and national Development at the core of their work. Others will also find it useful—extension workers and trainers, to understand their own work better and to justify to others the centrality of their mission; and Development agencies and change-agents, who may be encouraged to give greater prominence to education and training in their programmes.

There are of course dangers in trying to put processes such as 'education' and 'Development' between the covers of a book, for it may lead to the unthinking application of techniques to what are one-off, dynamic, problem-solving events. But the effectiveness of what we do depends not only on the measure of commitment we bring to the task but also on the clarity with which we see the logic-frame of the activity. This book then seeks to provide a framework for a new kind of adult education and a practical programme of reform based on Developmental models. It is not a rationale to justify what we are doing but a manifesto for change. And it seeks to bridge the gap between theory and practice. Development has for many years been evaluating itself, challenging its practitioners to new insights, adopting new approaches. Adult education is now in the same position, facing the same sorts of questions.

The answers will arise more from practical experience than from academic debate. This book has grown out of many years' working as an adult educator in local community development programmes in the West, and several years of visiting India and other countries, participating in programmes of adult learning and Development at grass roots level. My experience abroad led me to move from a university department in England largely concerned with liberal adult education and leisure courses, to Northern Ireland where I saw Development concepts expressed through education and training programmes for adults as essential to the life of the region. Several of my colleagues have asked me to justify my assertion that adult educators in the West have a great deal to learn from those countries which, like India, have for years been working with the realities of underdevelopment. These pages must form part of my response to that challenge. Some have suggested that I have 'gone back on' the ideals they assert I once held in relation to the primacy of the aspirations of the individual learners in adult education. This may, for all I know, be true. All I am sure of is that I have learned so much while working abroad that I find I need new concepts and new terms to express the views I now hold.

Writing in India, talking about the ideas in this book to people, some of whom have a wide experience of Development and of adult education and great fluency in their own tongue but limited proficiency in English (while I, to my shame, have no Tamil and little Hindi), has forced me to try to express myself in basic terms. I am conscious that this can at times sound simplistic and even patronizing. It is not intended to be. Rather it is an attempt to avoid unnecessary jargon and explain as clearly as possible what I mean at every stage. There is nothing more challenging to those of us from the West who engage in verbal games than the straight and sincere question 'What do you mean by . . .?'

DEFINITIONS

It is as well then to deal immediately with one or two definitions to ease our discussions—though some will be discussed in rather more detail later.

Education and training: by 'education' I do not mean the formal system of 'schooling' but all forms of planned learning by which one person directly (face to face) or indirectly (by distance education methods) helps another person(s) to learn something. I see 'training' as a part (but only a small part) of education. Education is wider than training. The distinction is not always clear, and some learners can use a course intended as a relatively narrow training exercise (for example, a language course for company secretaries) as the basis for a wider educational experience (i.e. to expand horizons rather than just to extend competencies). So I use the phrase 'education and training' as a catch-all phrase, to mean all forms of planned learning.

'West' and 'Third World': Some readers will find objections to the terms 'the West' and 'Third World countries' used to express the polarity which exists between the richer and the poorer parts of the world. I share their concern and their views that we live in One World as interdependent members and that the range of variation between countries is much wider than such a two-fold categorization allows. Indeed, this book has been written as one more attempt to build bridges—to share insights, to urge those who live in the richer regions that we have much to learn from the experiences of those in economically and technologically less developed regions, as well as the reverse.

Nevertheless, we need words to express these distinctions. There are two main reasons for using the terms 'Third World countries' and 'the West'. The first is that no set of terms is free from objections. The phrase 'North and South' does not recognize the major role which Australasia plays in world Development; 'economically less/more developed countries' (ELDC and EMDC) lays too much stress on economic and technical rather than social change as the goal of Development; while 'developing' and 'developed' are even worse, for these words imply that the process of Development has somehow ceased in the more industrialized countries, that these regions have no need for further Development. I would have liked to have used the terms 'rich' and 'poor', except that 'poor' carries with it overtones of patronage and fails to recognize the cultural and other wealth of these countries. All such terms have their limitations.

But the main reason I have used these terms is that Developing countries themselves use these words more frequently than any others; and if they choose to adopt 'Third World countries' as a generic term for themselves and see in it no impropriety, I am happy that the phrase will express to at least some of my readers in acceptable language the kind of polarity and interdependence I am trying to discuss.

Finally, the book considers several groups of programmes—those of which I have firsthand experience in the UK and the Indian subcontinent, others in Africa and Latin America through reports from UNESCO and other bodies, and especially a number on the continent of Europe through the papers of the European Bureau of Adult Education and the Council of Europe Community Development Programme. From these, a common thread is drawn: that the West is moving closer to the Third World and is beginning to seek in that part of the world answers to some of its problems.

Part I

Adult Learning and Education

Chapter 2

Adult Learning

Adults learn continuously throughout their lives; they do not stop when they leave school (if they have had any formal schooling, that is).

This is an obvious truth; but it carries with it profound implications. It means that learning is not only associated with schooling, with childhood. And it offers hope to all who need to encourage adults to learn as part of their programme of change. Those who come to these programmes are already engaged in learning; and this natural learning can be built upon to achieve planned learning. It will therefore be useful to look at this continuing learning process more closely.

Learning

Learning means making changes—in our knowing, thinking, feeling and doing. Some of these changes are permanent, others are for a time only.

Learning arises from our experiences. It takes many different forms. One writer suggests that it is possible to have 'non-learning' responses to experience, but it would seem that he is looking for a particular form of learning; it is unlikely that absolutely no form of learning changes will result from our experiences.[1]

And learning from experience means that learning is individual; it is not a collective activity. 'Each individual is processing the experience uniquely for personal use. In learning, the individual is the agent, even though the agent may be subject to the social pressures of the group.' Learning is affected, even controlled to some extent, by society or other collectives, but the learning activity itself—introducing learning changes—is personal.[2]

THE NATURAL LEARNING PROCESS

Intention in learning

There is a continuum of adult learning in relation to intention:

(a) At one extreme there is the haphazard learning which is unplanned. Some learning is very casual; it comes about from the stimulus provided by chance happenings—from seeing roadside posters, from snatches of overheard conversation, from new perceptions of well-known features, from what we read in the newspapers or obtain by accident from the radio/television, from meeting new people, watching films, reading the newspapers and so on. There is in this case no intention to promote learning purposefully either on the part of the adult learner or the source of the new perceptions: it is 'adventitious learning . . . [which] springs from accidental encounters with unintentional sources'.[3]

(b) There is, however, that learning which is purposed on the part of the 'provider'—advertisements, mass campaigns, political persuasion and social propaganda. Once again there is no intention on the part of the learner to engage in learning but there are clear signs in these cases of intended learning on the part of the provider. It may be called *informal learning*.

(c) At other times, learning is more purposeful, designed to meet needs as they arise when facing new challenges or coping with new situations. So that further along the continuum is planned learning: a desire to learn about something will direct the actions of adults at certain times. They will seek out material—watch a particular television programme or search for a book, ask questions of other people, hunt for new knowledge and new skills for themselves. In these instances, there is an intention of learning on the part of the learner, though the intention on the part of the provider may not be equally strong. Material produced for one reason may be pressed into service for another purpose in the desire to satisfy a hunger for learning. Sometimes these learning desires are long-standing interests and of a relatively low level of intensity. At other times, short bursts of intensive learning drives are experienced—creating what have been called 'natural learning episodes'. This kind of intended learning may be termed *non-formal learning*.[4]

(d) And at the far end of the continuum lie those formal learning programmes in which there is a clear intention to engage in learning on the part of both the provider and the learner—when adults attend classes or go back to school or college, for example, or engage in staff training or professional development programmes. On the whole not many adults enjoy such *formal learning* opportunities, and they engage in them for relatively short-lived purposes; but they are increasing both inside and outside the formal education system.

It may be helpful to use a matrix to illustrate these relationships (Figure 2.1). All learning, whether informal or formal, willing or unwilling, will fall somewhere in this matrix.

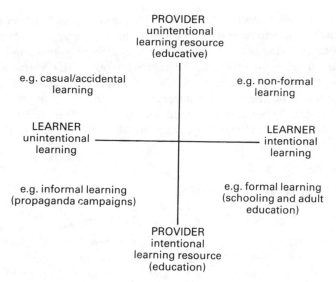

Figure 2.1 Matrix of learning intentions for the provider and learner in adult learning

Reasons for continued learning

Adult learning can be divided into three categories—although it must be stressed that these are not exclusive; they overlap frequently. Adults continue to learn

> in regard to at least three main areas of change with which we all have to cope. Changes in our personal development, our interests, opportunities and abilities all lead to new learning and to new learning needs. Secondly, changes in our occupations, whether heart specialist, historian or housewife, will call for new knowledge, new skills, new attitudes. And thirdly, as each of us enters new social roles or as society redefines the roles in which we find ourselves, so once again some re-learning will take place. Lifelong learning is then for all of us an inevitable reality . . .[5]

(a)   Many adults learn because the *occupation* they pursue requires learning. Whether this occupation is in the home or in the fields or in a place of work (factory, office, school and so on), whether it is paid or not, changes in the work or general environment or in the individual's functions or status will call for new knowledge, new skills and new understandings, for new attitudes and new patterns of behaviour. The 'job' itself, and our perceptions of the job, will change as time passes; and we will be called upon to learn many things. Even the experience of unemployment results in new learning—how to cope, to retrain, to adapt.

(b)   Secondly, as people grow older, they enter into new *social roles*, new relationships which may have little to do with their 'occupations'. They marry, become parents, come to accept responsibility for elderly parents instead of being dependants of those same parents. They adopt new positions in society—as householders or taxpayers or voters and political members of a district, region or state. Moreover, changes in social customs frequently call for a redefinition of these roles: one generation of parents, for example, is not always the model for the next, so that

learning is required as each generation defines and executes these roles for themselves—how to relate to their own children as these grow up, or to the school which
teaches them, or to the politician who demands their allegiance, and so on.

(c) Thirdly, as adults grow older, so their *interests* and their attitudes towards the
world around them change; their focus shifts and their sense of and desire for
meaning alters. And these changed perspectives and concerns will again lead to
learning changes. New interests will emerge as earlier ones decline; beliefs which
once seemed adequate may no longer appeal, while others come to hold their place
with greater or less intensity.

Some characteristics of continued learning

We may note three things about this continuing adult learning:

(a) *Domains of learning:* learning is not just about new facts. Much learning will of
course be concerned with *knowledge*—about people and things, about places and
events, both past and present. Adults continue to garner information throughout
their lives; they increase what they know. But that is not the sole meaning of the
word 'learning'. Adults also continue to acquire and develop *skills*—both intellectual skills, like reasoning and comprehension, and physical skills involved in the
mastery of new tools and new practices: they increase what they can do. They
develop new *understandings*—insights into relationships between facts or concepts, for example; understanding is not frozen for all time at an early stage in life.
They change and increase the range of perspectives. Further, new *attitudes and
interests* are formed. Contrary to some views, appreciation and belief systems
change over time. None of us is completely bound by the sets of values and traditional practices learned in youth, for our culture-set is itself changing, and to a
greater or lesser degree we are free to go with those changes or rebel against them.

The relationship between these four domains of learning is complex. They are
not separate. New knowledge and understandings may lead to the adoption of new
attitudes. Equally, the attitudes and values held will help to determine the new
knowledge and skills developed, and these in turn will bring about *behavioural*
changes. It is rare for 'inner' learning changes not to express themselves in some
form of behavioural patterns (in speech, if not in action): indeed, the only way we
can see that private learning changes have taken place is in the public arena of
behaviour. It is not always easy to distinguish between the various learning components of KASUB (knowledge, attitudes, skills, understanding and behaviour), but
these building bricks of learning do exist.

(b) *Kinds of learning:* the second point to note is that some writers have distinguished
between different kinds of learning. Learning which is directed towards the control
and manipulation of the physical world has been called *instrumental learning*. This
learning can best be expressed in terms derived from stimulus–response and
cognitive learning theories. Secondly, there is that learning which applies to personal relationships (sometimes called *communicative learning*) which may be best
described in concepts drawn from social learning theories. And thirdly, there is that
learning which concerns the learner him/herself (*emancipatory learning*)—personal growth and understanding of self, views of the world, meanings and values

and beliefs—which can best be described in terms drawn from paradigm transformation learning theories.[6]

(c) *Styles of learning:* thirdly, it would seem that people have different ways of learning. Educationalists have categorized learning styles in many ways. No one theory has commanded universal acceptance, though some are more popular as seeming to explain learning processes more satisfactorily than the others. What does appear to be clear is that some adults learn more frequently and more effectively by thinking about things (especially their own experience) and others more by doing (for example, by trial and error); some build concepts and abstractions, others build machines and experiment. There is no single way in which people learn.[7]

Modes of learning

Two main models of natural learning have been identified. They have been called (in technical jargon) 'information-assimilational' and 'experiential',[8] but it would seem better to call them the 'input' and 'action' models.

(a) *Input learning:* in this mode, the learner is relatively passive: he/she responds to new learning from outside. Like a plant, growth depends upon inputs which are controlled by the outsider. Knowledge or skills or understanding is thus said to be 'given' or 'imparted' to the learners. Much formal education is based on this model, but it is also said to apply to the natural learning process—we all learn by new inputs.

(b) *Action learning:* the other mode of learning is one in which the learner is active, searching out the material he/she needs, trying to make sense of their experience. Human beings, it is pointed out, are not like plants; they can decide and take the initiative in their own learning.

REFLEXIVE OBSERVATION ON EXPERIENCE

At the moment, emphasis is laid in current writings on 'reflexive observation' as one of the main tools for active learning. Freire and others have suggested that most learning is accomplished by critically analysing experience. They have spoken of a learning cycle (Figure 2.2) starting with *experience*, proceeding through *reflection* and leading to *action*, which in its turn becomes the concrete experience for more reflection and thus the next stage of the cycle.

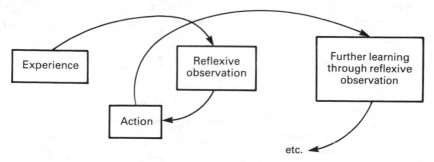

Figure 2.2 The learning cycle: basic features

The reflection stage of the learning cycle is, however, complex. For one thing, as Freire indicates, it includes a judgement, reflecting *critically* on experience. It is not enough just to sit and think about experience: criteria drawn from other sources need to be applied to experience for learning to take place, some input is needed as well as reflexive observation on experience (Figure 2.3). Some writers tend to insist that the main way in which this outside material is fed into the process is through dialogue—dialogical learning is the vogue at the moment; but outside criteria can also come from reading or from films or other media without any element of dialogue, so long as the learner engages with this material.

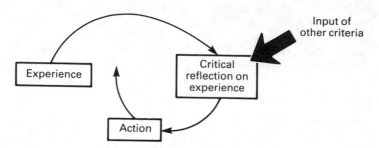

Figure 2.3 The learning cycle: input from outside sources

Secondly, as David Kolb has indicated, reflection will sometimes lead to a stage of creating generalizations ('abstract conceptualization', as he terms it) (Figure 2.4). Hypotheses are formed which are then tested in new situations, thus creating further concrete experience.[9]

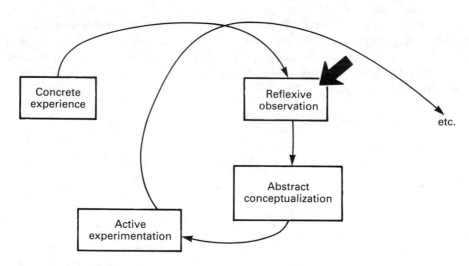

Figure 2.4 Kolb's learning cycle

Styles of learning and the learning cycle

On the basis of this model of reflexive observation on experience as the main approach to natural learning by adults, four main styles of learning have been identified:

1. the *activists*—those who learn directly by involving themselves in the various activities around them;
2. the *observers*—those who prefer to wait and watch what is going on before they decide and act;
3. the *theorists*—those who like to generalize from their experience and to apply what they learn in one arena to another;
4. the *experimenters*—those who like to devise new approaches and try them out to see what happens. [10]

It is important to stress that in this analysis, people are not seen as using only one of these approaches—we all tend to use all of them. Rather, people are thought to prefer one mode of learning above the others; they are stronger at learning through one approach rather than through any of the others. What is absolutely clear is that people learn actively and that they do it in different ways.

Two comments, however, need to be made about this learning cycle. The first is that learning includes goals, purposes, intentions, choice and decision-making, and it is not at all clear just where these elements stand in the cycle. Some decisions are needed before translating reflexive observation into action, before turning from abstract conceptualization into active experimentation; but, equally, decisions and goals occur at other points in the cycle. They tend to be omitted from discussions of this view of natural learning.

Secondly, it is likely that learning styles will vary according to the type of learning being engaged in. Reflexive observation is undoubtedly important for emancipatory learning and no doubt useful in the other kinds of learning as well, and we shall see that it has considerable importance for the educational and training component of Development programmes. But it is not the whole story. A good deal of adult learning does not comprise reflexive observation on experience, setting up hypotheses and testing them out in action:

*   there is the acquisition of facts, information
*   there are those sudden and apparently unassisted insights which we all experience from time to time
*   there is the learning which comes from the successful completion of some task or haphazard experimentation
*   there is the memorization of data or processes
*   there are those changes inspired by watching others

And so we could go on; learning is more than just critical reflection. Probably all adults spend part of their time reflecting on experience but some are more strongly driven in this respect than others. Learning is a varied and complex activity: and the adults who engage in it are very varied and complex also.

'CONCEPT DISTANCE' IN LEARNING

That learning relates to individual experience is now quite clear. Both the ability to learn from experience and the nature of the responses will vary according to the personality and the prior history of the learner. The fact that two persons reflecting on a common experience will derive quite different learning results shows this.

These responses will vary according to what may be called the 'concept distance' of the experience from the central issues and concerns of the person concerned. All persons construct patterns or 'maps' of reality; and they locate all knowledge somewhere on these maps in relation to themselves at the centre of those maps and in relation to other knowledge and events. Some experiences will be 'close to' the learner: they will have many possible points of contact—for example, a task which grows out of one's immediate needs. Others will be more remote, alien to the ways of thought and value systems of the learners. With some the learner will feel more at home, while others appear to be distant from the main preoccupations of the learners. For many people, science and technology lie on the extreme outer parts of their 'map'; they have little in common with these matters. For others, the same may be said of good literature or languages or technical matters such as mending a car or art.

It may be argued that the maps drawn by adults and by children are markedly different. Children draw relatively small maps; they are usually more concerned with what lies outside their maps and are less worried about inconsistencies within their maps; indeed, they seem to expect such inconsistencies to occur. Adults on the other hand are normally less concerned with what lies outside their map ('beyond their ken'); they are frequently more concerned with reconciling any inconsistencies within their maps, seeking to draw the whole together into logical systems which they find satisfying.

Many factors are involved in locating any new material on the map:

(a) how the new subject matter or experience relates to existing experience; things which lie well within the experience of the person are placed close to the centre, matters which lie outside existing experience are felt to be more remote.

(b) whether it is perceived to relate to the current concerns of the learner; even matters which are apparently well outside existing experience will come to be closer if they impinge on the major preoccupations of the person concerned.

(c) how 'difficult' it is thought to be to learn; each of us has a perception of the inherent complexity of some subjects, that they are hard or easy to master, and this will help to determine where we place them on our 'maps'.

(d) whether it is seen to possess internal consistency; issues which have at first sight problems of logic in them will on the whole be pushed further away.

(e) whether it 'rings true', fits in with the general world picture and with other subjects already on the map.

All these play some part in the location of any innovation on the 'map'.

The language in which these 'maps' are described is drawn in part from concepts of distance (things are thought to be 'remote' from reality, for example) and sometimes from personal relations (things are 'alien'). Because of this ambivalence, in an earlier paper on this subject I used the term 'social distance' to express this process of map-drawing, but since this term is used by social scientists to mean something different it seems better to use the term 'concept distance' to express what is going on.

This whole field of the constructs of reality which each individual builds for themselves needs further exploration. But its relevance to our enquiry here lies in the fact that it would seem that more learning changes are made by adults in relation to material which has a close affinity with the learner than in relation to material which is remote. Adults (and it would appear children also) learn more easily material which is not alien to their existing patterns of thinking and their own experience. The process of map-drawing lies at the heart of the way we all learn throughout our lives.[11]

The importance of this for the teacher of adults and for the Development worker is clear. His/her task is to build on this natural learning process by providing a further range of experience not too remote from the learner's existing experience by which the learning goals can be achieved. It is through the construction of new and relevant experiences rather than through the provision of new knowledge alone that the teacher/instructor of adults can help his/her target group to learn.

CONCLUSIONS

Adults then learn throughout the whole of their lives. At times, they will learn slowly, almost imperceptibly, at other times with greater concentration and sense of drive. The process will be uneven and will spring from many needs, some of them perceived, some of them unrecognized, so that in any group of adults there will be a wide range of learning responses, learning styles and learning abilities.

It is not my intention here to go into learning theories in any great detail. My purpose is to suggest that all adults learn, sometimes intentionally, sometimes unintentionally; that they engage in more than one kind of learning; that such learning affects their knowledge, skills, understanding, attitudes and ultimately their behaviour; and that they learn more easily in those areas where the 'distance' between their experience and the new material is not great.

Much of this learning takes place in a haphazard fashion. Some of it is the product of planning on the part of an outside 'agent' but not of the learner, as in propaganda campaigns. But there are for many adults occasions when the learning is intended, when the learner seeks out a helper, a 'teacher' of some kind. It is these episodes which we call 'education'. And it is on these learning episodes that the education and training which is part of both adult education and Development will need to be built.

NOTES TO CHAPTER 2

(1) Jarvis (1987), ch. 2.
(2) Brookfield (1983), pp. 1–4.
(3) Lucas, A.M. (1983) Scientific literacy and informal learning, *Studies in Science Education* **10**, 2–3. See Dave (1976); OECD (1975), p. 6.
(4) Rogers, A. (1986), pp. 68–71.
(5) Rogers, A. (1980), pp. 8–9.
(6) Freire (1972); Habermas (1972); Mezirow, J. (1977) Perspective transformation, *Studies in Adult Education* **9**(2); Mezirow, J. (1981) A critical theory of adult learning and education, *Adult Education* (USA) **32**(1), 3–24; Jarvis (1987), ch. 5.
(7) Entwistle, N.J. (1981) *Styles of Learning and Teaching*, New York; Conti, G.J. (1982) The principles of adult learning styles, *Adult Literacy and Basic Education* **6**, 135–47;

Smith, R.M. (1984) *Learning to Learn*, Open University Press, pp. 168–70, 181.

(8)   Kolb, D.A. (1976) *Learning Style Inventory Manual*, Boston; Kolb, D.A. (1984) *Experiential Learning*, New York.

(9)   See for example Coleman, J.S. (1976) The differences between experiential and classroom learning, in Keeton, M.T. (ed.) *Experiential Learning*, San Francisco: Jossey Bass.

(10)   Outlined in detail in Honey, P. and Mumford, A. (1986) *Manual of Learning Styles*, 2nd edn, London: Peter Honey.

(11)   See Lewin, K. (1935) *A Dynamic Theory of Personality*, New York; Berger, P.L. and Luckmann, T. (1967) *Social Construction of Reality*, Penguin; Schutz, A. and Luckmann, T. (1974) *The Structures of the Life World*, Heinemann; Aslanian, C.B. and Bricknell, H.H. (1982) 'Passages' of adulthood and triggers to learning, in Gross R., (ed.) *Invitation to Lifelong Learning*, Chicago.

Chapter 3

Adult Education: Definitions

The term 'adult education' means many things in different contexts and different periods. Adult education today is not the same as in earlier years; and the words as used in Third World countries do not mean the same thing as they do in the West. UNESCO noted: 'in essence, adult education is so closely related to the social, political and cultural condition of each country that no uniform or precise definition can be arrived at'. Even within one country, different writers can use the term to mean different things.[1]

For inherent within the concept of adult education are many ambiguities. In order to grapple with these, a number of different titles have been coined—Continuing Education, Recurrent Education, Lifelong Education, the French term *éducation permanente*, Non-Formal Education, and so on. These differences, adding richness to the concept, do not perhaps matter too much, except that some persons approaching adult education for the first time find it all very confusing. So it seems desirable to try to define how the term 'adult education' will be used in this book—what is included and what is excluded and why.

Adult education is not just literacy

Adult education is not simply the provision of elementary education (literacy, numeracy and social skills—i.e. those parts of cultural initiation which a child often gets at school) for those adults who have never been to school or who for many different reasons did not learn adequately while in school. We need to make this clear because in some countries, 'adult education' is seen to be synonymous with remedial education for adults, especially adult literacy, so that other forms of adult learning (such as health education, income generating programmes, agricultural extension, professional development or vocational training) are often excluded from 'adult education'.

There is a simple reason why it is unsatisfactory to equate adult education with learning literacy. Initial education is largely intended to induct young people into the society to which they belong. It aims to do more than this of course—to help children to find and develop themselves, for example. But much of its time is devoted to socialization and other normative skills and attitude development. Adults on the other hand, whether literate or illiterate, have by definition already become established in society; they do not need to be 'brought in'. So that adult education is not 'schooling for unschooled adults', even though it will include the provision of some form of literacy and numeracy and basic coping skills for those who need them. Adult education covers the teaching of literacy to adults but it is much wider than that.

Adult education is the provision of educational opportunities for adults. It covers more or less all forms of planned and systematic learning which adults experience in the process of living their lives. But this too needs further elaboration: we need to look more closely at what we mean by 'education' and what we mean by 'adult'.

Education

The term 'education' is used in three main senses—to indicate a *process*, a *system* and a *goal*. In general, I prefer to see education as a *planned process of purposeful learning*. This process is often carried on *within* a system; and many people speak of education as if it were that system (for example, when saying that the government spends money on 'Education'). But that system itself is not 'education': it is a system designed to promote the process of education, an 'educational' system. It is only too possible to have the system but to have little or no education taking place, and equally some of this process of education (planned learning) takes place outside the educational system. Education is also sometimes seen as the goal of the process: schools and colleges exist to lead to 'education', students attend to 'acquire education'.

ADULT EDUCATION AS PROCESS

In discussing education as process, we need to distinguish between 'education' and 'learning'.

> Sometimes disputes about such issues as this get tangled because the words 'education' and 'learning' are used as though they were interchangeable, and the argument slides from one to another as is convenient. So it is perhaps worth making the point initially that these are different things. . . . Learning is a pretty basic characteristic of living tissue and it normally goes on . . . throughout life. Education involves processes of learning which are planned— usually planned by somebody to be followed by somebody else (though the planner/tutor may be dead and may communicate with the learner/student through such media as print, film and the like). . . .
> [Education then is] planned processes of learning undertaken by intent; the sort of thing that commonly (though by no means always) goes on in classrooms and that involves some who are teachers and some who are taught. In much discussion of adult 'education' the word is used much more loosely. Thus in much French writing about *éducation populaire*, it seems to be used so as to include the whole range and apparatus of leisure-time activities— cinemas, libraries, television and sports clubs—on the grounds that these exert an educative influence on people who use them and are therefore aspects of education. Certainly there is a sense in which anything that happens to us, from getting drunk to listening to Beethoven, may be said to be 'quite an education'; and certainly we learn . . . from our experiences, including those of our leisure. But such learning is unplanned and largely unintended: we do not go into either the pub or the concert-hall with a primary intention of learning. If we intend to learn we behave differently: we join a class or a correspondence course, we hire a

tutor or buy an instruction manual; we adopt the role of student and submit ourselves to a planned process of tuition.[2]

Education then is concerned with learning but it is not simply the same as learning. *Learning*, as we have seen, is a process of making changes in knowledge, skills, understandings, attitudes and value systems, and in behaviour. Some of these changes are intended, others are not intended. And learning continues throughout the whole of life; it is part of the process of living. *Education* on the other hand consists of episodes of *planned* learning. For most adults, this is a voluntary activity, one which they willingly adopt in order to achieve a goal. For others, it may be somewhat less voluntary, and the purpose may be less clearly seen or even imposed on them. But it is a piece of systematic, structured learning with a purpose, 'sequential learning experiences planned and monitored by an agent for a learner'. Education (and this includes 'training') can be seen as an intended intervention into the natural learning process in order to give this informal learning a direction, increased impetus and some structure.[3]

We need to note certain things about this process of education as purposeful learning. First, planned learning implies that there is a *planner* (who may or may not be the same as the teacher) and a *learner* or a group of learners. Someone is helping the learner(s) to learn. The planner(s) may be removed far from the learner(s) or immediately available, or a combination of both of these; and the teacher/planner and the learner(s) may co-operate in the planning process. The means of learning (the teaching–learning materials and the curriculum of experiences devised by the planner) may be in the form of a self-instructional tool, a book (manual), film or radio programme, etc., or a class (lecture, demonstration, etc.). But whatever the form, there is in education an agent and one or more learners. The planner/teacher will be concerned both with the immediate provision of materials and experiences for the learner(s) and also with the whole of the learner's social and physical environment (including the existing informal learning) so that this becomes a support system rather than an obstacle to the process of learning.

Secondly, purposeful learning implies that there are *goals* to be achieved. These will often have been set by the teacher or planner(s), in which case they need to be accepted and internalized by the learner(s) before learning can be effective; but in many forms of education for adults, they have been set by or in collaboration with the learners. There are a wide range of learning goals: some are narrow—to learn how to sew, for example; others are more open-ended—personal growth or enhanced awareness. The process of identifying and promoting the goals of learning is one of the tasks of the planner(s).[4]

Thirdly, planned learning which is education will be concerned with *all the domains of learning*—with increasing knowledge, with developing skills, with the formation of attitudes, with gaining insightful understanding, and with changes in patterns of behaviour. The aim of the educational process is to help the learners to make more or less permanent changes in all of these areas of learning.

But this process of encouraging learners to bring about learning changes directed to an agreed goal is far from being a mechanistic activity; for the planned learning process is *a dynamic relationship*. Education is not the same as manipulation—as indoctrination, for example. It is a 'meeting' between people—a living encounter with a purpose. Adult education is thus a dynamic and normally willing encounter of adult with adult.

Who is an adult?

Definitions of who is an 'adult' will again vary in different contexts and in different periods. Clearly some age factor must be included in our concept of being an adult. Some countries, following UNESCO, speak of adults as being those aged between 15 and 35, but clearly the term includes those older than this upper age limit. I mean by 'adult' anyone who has reached a certain stage of development normally associated with an appropriate age and recognized in each social context as being definitive, someone who by virtue of that stage of development both thinks of themselves as adult and has been accorded adult status, usually indicated by legal rights and duties; he or she has taken their place in society. In most societies, an adult is someone who has a measure of internalized independence in decision-making, no longer being under someone else's authority. A young person who is earning his/her own living is not necessarily an adult until they can show that they possess the standard of development, maturity and experience, the status given by society at large and the independence of action which traditionally go with adulthood within their own culture. They have assumed the responsibilities of adulthood.

So we need to settle for some definition, such as all men and women over a certain age (in some societies 15, in others 18, etc., but with no upper age limit) and who (for our purposes alone) are not still attending their first school or college. An adult is someone, who has finished initial education, seen as preparation for living (provided, that is, that he or she ever attended school) and who has started the process of 'living'. Adults may return to the educational system or engage in other forms of education and training full-time or part-time, but they will have had a break from their introductory education.

There are still many difficulties about this definition. In some societies, for example, many women who would be seen in every other society as adult are denied most of the expressions of adulthood and apparently do not see themselves as 'adult'—they willingly accept that others will necessarily be involved in decisions relating to habitual behaviour; and many men live within an extended family, and their role, although it allows them autonomy in day-to-day matters, does not include much in the way of personal responsibility in certain areas of decision-making. Are these adults according to our definition above? Each society must make its own judgement about the nature and extent of adulthood. It will, however, be useful to point out that adulthood is an ideal state: none of us reaches it in full. We are each limited to some extent in our autonomy; the extent to which others are involved in an individual's decision-making will vary from culture to culture.

Education and adult education

Is it necessary to stress the 'adult' dimension to adult education? Why cannot we just speak about 'education' as applying to children, college students and adults? There is after all much in common within the processes of planned learning of all groups, and the links between the education of adults and the education of children have been noted on several occasions. It must therefore be asked whether what is distinctive about adult learning is sufficiently important to require a specific category of education to itself.[5]

Although there is much in common in all forms of education, it has been recognized for many years that it is helpful to clear thinking and to devising educational programmes to make distinctions within the whole educational enterprise in at least two ways: (a) the special characteristics of teaching different subject areas—history or music or science or agriculture or literacy, for example; and (b) the special characteristics of helping particular categories of learners (very young children or adolescents, for example) to learn. We are not asserting the primacy of any one form of education, merely trying to understand more fully what is going on.

Put in this way, we can note that it is becoming increasingly understood that adults learn—and study in order to learn—in different ways from children and young people (college students), and that these differences need to be reflected in the educational processes offered to them. Just as one does not treat a fifteen-year-old student like an eight-year-old, so one does not treat an adult learner like a child or a college student if we are to be effective in the education we seek to promote. Within the general category of adults, there will be many different groups, and their differences need to be allowed for in devising planned learning programmes for them. So that adult education is itself not a single undifferentiated whole: it is a complex of educational opportunities to meet the particular needs of different sets of people. Nevertheless, when contrasted with provision for younger learners, certain approaches seem to be common to all forms of adult learning.

The differences between adult and younger learners are many and have been explored elsewhere.[6] Here we need to note that they relate primarily to the following:

(a) The *experience* and thus the *expectations of learning* which adults bring with them; these are different from the experience and expectations which children and college students bring to their education. It is agreed in all forms of education that the effectiveness of the learning process depends on the way the materials and activities used to bring about the learning relate to the existing experience of the learner(s). Adults will inevitably have a larger range of experience and will have developed different approaches to the process of assessing this experience.

(b) Their *orientation to learning*: the intentions and focus which adults have towards their education are distinctive. For children and college students, the education they are receiving tends to be their primary concern at that stage in their lives and is seen by them and their teachers to be preparatory for some future way of life. For adults, the education they undertake is on the whole secondary to the process of living itself, although at the same time it is more directly related to that process of living. For unlike younger learners, most adults come to their education with specific life-related intentions of their own and a determination to do something about these intentions. Adult learners are 'political' persons in the sense that they can act immediately in relation to the learning they are pursuing.

(c) Their *ways of learning*: by the time adults come to their educational experiences, they have established learning strategies of their own. Even illiterate adults have been learning all sorts of things for many years and have developed effective ways of learning. These individual learning styles need to be discovered and used in the process of planning purposeful learning for adults.

There are other features of the way adults learn which call for distinctive approaches within the common framework of education. Taken together these characteristics mean that it is helpful to distinguish adult education from primary or secondary or higher education, to treat adult learners differently from children or college students. This is not of course always done: much education for adults in practice treats the learners in the same way as children are treated; their experience and expectations, their intentions and purposes, their particular learning styles are ignored or even denied.

Education and training for adults

Are all learning opportunities for adults then 'adult education'? For example, if an adult goes back to school or college, is he/she in adult education? Or is adult education only the provision of learning opportunities *outside* of the formal system? What about professional career development courses or industrial training, including those courses which some employees are compelled to attend (e.g. staff training sessions for shop workers, etc.)? In other words, is adult education the same as all forms of education and training for adults?

Wiltshire excludes from his definition of adult education not only 'casual learning that is incidental to other activities' but also those

> recreational activities in which there is no commitment to learn (even though these may take place in an educational institution); education done under compulsion; and education that belongs to the period of tutelage and preparation for occupation (even though this may for some individuals in some societies extend beyond the age of legal independence and on into the twenties or early thirties).[7]

His approach argues that where adults are compelled to attend particular forms of education or where adults continue to attend educational programmes within the formal system as part of their initial education, they are 'not in adult education'.

Here we need to look at two things, the relationship of adult education with continuing education, and equally its relationship with non-formal education.

Continuing education

Some people distinguish between adult education and continuing education. A number of writers in Third World countries use 'adult education' to mean the provision of basic education (especially literacy) for the post-school population, and 'continuing education' to mean post-literacy and all other forms of education and training which build upon this initial education. In the West, the term has come to have a more restricted meaning with a particular ideology—the continuation of formal schooling into adulthood, more of the same sort of education as already exists for older learners. So that today some people define adult education as liberal education for personal development, and continuing education as courses of further professional training and development. In both sets of countries, continuing education, because it is largely vocational in nature and mostly within the formal system of education, is often thought to be separate from and outside of adult education.

But if it is true that adults learn in different ways from younger persons whatever the context of their learning, because their experience, intentions and learning styles differ from those of children and adolescents, then adults learning in continuing education will be characterized by adult learning processes. Continuing education consists of planned learning opportunities for adults which, like all other forms of education and training for adults, need to take the special characteristics of adult learning into account when the learning experience is being constructed.

Adult education thus embraces continuing education. Some people attempt to indicate the differences of emphasis by employing the phrase 'adult and continuing education'; but adult education is used in this book as an all-embracing term, inclusive of continuing education.

This means that not all adult education is voluntary. The term covers what has been called 'mandatory continuing education',[8] those more or less compulsory programmes such as doctors' refresher courses, unemployed training schemes and bank staff training days. The learners in these programmes are adults, even though they are less than voluntary; and they need to be taught as adults. Appropriate methods of teaching-learning need to be adopted in these cases as well as in the more voluntary learning activities of other parts of adult education. Much continuing education takes place within the formal system of education—in schools, colleges, polytechnics and universities; can this be called adult education or is it a case of adults joining the formal system of education?

Nevertheless, all forms of education which take account of the distinctive learning processes of adult learners would seem to be covered by the term adult education. Continuing education, whether inside or outside the formal educational system, in order to be effective, needs to treat the learners as adult learners and not as child or adolescent learners, taking full account of the learners' intentions and experience. So that the definition of adult education as 'all those forms of education which adults experience excepting that which they pursue full-time or part-time directly following the period of their compulsory education'[9] would seem to indicate that when a person stays on at school beyond the age of compulsory schooling or goes to college straight from school, they are not in adult education; if they go back to school or college after a break, then it is arguable that they are in adult education.

Non-formal education

This discussion would seem to provide at least part of our answer to the second question, the relationship between adult education and non-formal education. Non-formal education has been defined as all education provided outside of the formal system, whatever its purposes, target groups and providers.

Non-formal education is often seen to be a radical alternative to formal education in at least two ways, in its organization and in its methods.[10]

Formal and non-formal education organization

Formal and non-formal education can be distinguished in terms of organization and content in several respects:

(a)   Non-formal education is open to anyone, irrespective of their former educational level, whereas formal education is highly selective, dependent on prior success in educational terms, rejecting the many and selecting the few to continue their studies further. Because of this, formal education is strongly organized; we can speak of a formal education system. Non-formal education on the other hand has no clear pattern, no structure; we can only speak of non-formal education programmes.

(b) The content of non-formal education tends to be concrete, life-related, constantly changing to meet new needs, to deal with real issues of current (and to some extent passing) concern, whereas formal education is based on a fixed body of theoretical, textbook, compartmentalized knowledge of more permanent interest. Non-formal education is personal in nature, formal education is more impersonal. In a way, this distinction is reflected in the kind of buildings used—formal education usually takes place in special buildings, out of the community, dedicated to one function alone, i.e. education; non-formal education takes place in a variety of settings within the community.

(c) Non-formal education tends to be for immediate application in day-to-day life, not (as with most formal education) to prepare for some future purpose.

(d) Non-formal education is a continuing process, not a once-for-all occasion. Unlike schooling, non-formal education allows the learner to go back time and again for more. Non-formal education is available in many different forms during the whole of life. Formal education on the other hand is usually available only for the young and is terminal: the learner knows when he/she has finished it (usually by passing or failing an examination). Non-formal education is usually validated by the learner's experience of success, formal education by external standards set by the teacher or other educator.

A useful illustration of the difference between the two may be drawn from the differences between modern athletics and the public marathon. In athletics, only those who qualify can compete, only a very few 'win'; the race is competitive and exclusive. In the public marathon, all may join in, the standards are set by the runners—each one competing against themselves, not against the others (to finish or to finish in a better time than last time, etc.)—and the race is collaborative—each person helping the other to further endeavours—and everyone wins.

Table 3.1   *Formal and non-formal systems of education compared*

	Formal	Non-formal
Goal:	To prepare for life To maintain status quo Impersonal	To help with living now To change society Personal
Content:	Fixed Compartmentalized	Changing Integrated

Structure:	Selective entry
	Located in special
	  institutions
	Terminal
	Divided into rigid
	  sectors
		Open entry
		Located in the life-site
		
		Continuing
		Not organized

Evaluation:	Self-assessing	Validated by change

Formal and non-formal methods

Sometimes the terms formal and non-formal are applied to teaching–learning methods. In brief, non-formal methods consist of discovery learning, of active learning processes, while formal methods include more of presentation and demonstration modes, one-way communication, from teacher to learner. Non-formal teaching–learning methods tend to be controlled by the learners, formal teaching–learning methods are hierarchical, controlled by the teacher.

The relationship of non-formal and formal education

What then is the relationship between formal and non-formal education?

1. We should not see non-formal education as simply the opposite of everything the formal educational system stands for. It is not just a reaction against something, a negative concept. Non-formal education is a positive approach to teaching and learning which stands in its own right and which challenges the formal system.

   Nevertheless it is realistic to note that non-formal education is and probably will remain a lesser partner in the educational enterprise. It cannot be regarded as a genuine alternative to the formal system in the education of young people because of parental and political aspirations; so that non-formal education is under pressure from the formal system. It is in danger of being either formalized (made to look like the formal system) or marginalized (because it is different, it is regarded as being unimportant). Because of this, many people see the future of non-formal education as resting with the education and training of adults where there is less pressure from the formal system, rather than with out-of-school youth. Even here, it may be regarded as an alternative (second chance) means of entry for disadvantaged adults into the formal system rather than as an educational programme with its own mission. On the whole, it would seem clear that the formal system will influence non-formal education more strongly than non-formal education will affect the formal system.

2. The distinction between formal and non-formal systems and formal and non-formal methodologies is useful. There is no inevitable relationship between the formal system and formal methods or between non-formal programmes and non-formal methods. Many schools and colleges inside the formal system have devised patterns of teaching–learning which display characteristics of non-formal methodologies, in which the learners control the aims, content and processes. It is perhaps in the field of teaching–learning methodologies that non-formal education has begun to influence the formal education system more strongly. On the other hand, many non-formal organizations use remarkably formal teaching–learning methods. This relationship may be represented by a matrix as shown in Figure 3.1.

This distinction between organization and methodologies enables us to see more clearly the overlap between the formal system of education, non-formal education and adult education. Some people write as if non-formal education and adult education are the same thing, but I do not think so, for two main reasons:

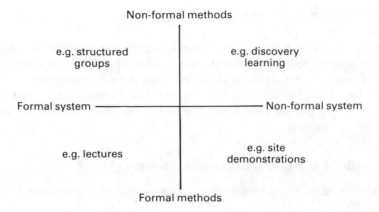

Figure 3.1 Matrix illustrating the range of methodologies used in formal and non-formal systems

(a) Some non-formal education is offered to out-of-school children. This is clearly not adult education for it does not call for adult learning methods, it cannot treat the learners as adults. Non-formal education, although it includes some forms of adult education, is wider than adult education.

(b) Secondly, some education inside the formal system is directed towards adult rather than younger learners and uses adult teaching–learning methods; it treats the learners as adults. Although this cannot be called non-formal education, it can be included in our definition of adult education. Adult education is both narrower than non-formal education, in that it excludes the provision for school-age learners, and wider than non-formal education in that it includes some parts of formal education. The two overlap but are not the same, as illustrated in Figure 3.2.

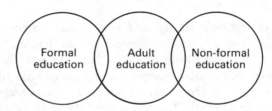

Figure 3.2 The relationship of adult education to formal and non-formal education

What is adult education?

My definition of adult education then is as follows: *all planned and purposeful learning opportunities offered to those who are recognized and who recognize themselves as adults in their own society and who have left the formal initial educational system (or who have passed beyond the possible stage of initial education if they were never in it), whether such learning opportunities are inside or outside the formal system, so long as*

such learning opportunities treat the learners as adults in decision-making, use appro-
priate adult learning methodologies and styles and allow the learners to use the experi-
ence for their own purposes and to meet their own needs.

Such learning opportunities will include a wide spectrum of activities—vocational programmes, career and professional development, leisure and hobby pursuits, personal and social growth programmes, specific training and general interest courses. One UK list puts it: 'literacy classes, postgraduate courses, driving instruction, Bible study, technical training, dancing tuition and university extension courses' (National Opinion Research Centre 1963). The range of such learning opportunities will vary greatly from country to country and from period to period.

Adult education in Third World countries thus covers not just literacy campaigns but also community and environmental health education, nutrition, income-generating programmes, agricultural extension, women's programmes, social forestry, vocational skill training—in short, any form of education and training for adults; and in the West, it covers all that normally goes under the title of adult education, adult training and continuing education, both inside and outside the formal educational system. Wherever adults decide either separately or in groups to learn something under guidance, there we have adult education; and the most appropriate methods to be used in all forms of education and training for adults are those methods which treat the learners as adults, not as children or younger persons. The term cannot be restricted to any one kind of adult learning programme; it comprises all efforts to offer to adults the systematic learning experiences which they need to cope with their current and changing 'life-site'.

ADULT EDUCATION AS DELIVERY SYSTEM

Adult education then is a *process* by which adults, who are already engaged in continuous learning, adapting to changes in their circumstances, engage in more structured programmes of learning in a planned and purposeful way at different times throughout their lives.

But the term 'Adult Education' has on occasion been used in a narrower sense to mean a series of *provisions* made by a range of bodies, some formal, some non-formal. 'Adult Education' then can refer to the collection of agencies which provide these learning opportunities for adults.

'Adult Education'—a system?

When we look at adult education as a provision in any country, we see a very diffuse and complex system. We cannot speak of adult education in the same way as we speak of primary or secondary or tertiary education, for these are formal and contained systems. We need to view adult education differently.

(a) First, purposeful learning opportunities for adults are provided by a host of *agencies*—state, para-statal, voluntary and commercial. Banks offer training to their staff, private institutes offer languages to specific target groups or to the general public, management consultancies offer advancement programmes to narrow bands of clients. Most governments offer learning opportunities to adults; but unlike formal education, educational and training programmes for adults are not under one single ministry. They are to be found in departments such as Agriculture, Commerce, Fisheries, Food, Industry, Labour, Manpower Development or Human Resource Development, Rural Development, Social Welfare—the list is almost endless. In a recent survey in one state government,[11] twelve departments were found to have units created to offer 'extension' to adults. There are educational institutions like schools, universities and colleges which open their doors to adults for a first, second or further chance. There are the increasing numbers of voluntary bodies and interest groups like churches, charities and political parties; there are informal agencies such as libraries, museums, theatres and concert halls, etc. There are those who seek to earn a living by providing education and training for adults. And beyond all of these, there are self-help groups, providing a chance for their members to learn from each other and in other ways.

But within this wide spectrum of learning opportunities for adults provided in many different locations and by many different formal and non-formal agencies, it is possible in most countries to see a distinction between, on the one hand, those bodies which are specifically charged with the provision of education and training courses for adults (adult colleges or institutes, the Workers' Educational Association (WEA), open universities and university extra-mural departments, folk high schools, etc.) or which provide education for younger groups but include some provision for adults in their programmes (community schools, polytechnics and universities, etc.), and, on the other hand, those agencies which provide such educational opportunities incidentally to other non-educational activities (libraries, museums, churches, community groups, etc.). The former constitute a more formal element within the wider field and they have a greater control over their own destinies, for they can influence the policies which direct their activities. 'Adult Education' (used with capitals) in this book refers to these special agencies; 'adult education' (without capitals) refers to the wider more informal field of learning opportunities for adults.

(b) The *means* of adult education and training are more varied than in schooling. Correspondence courses, open learning systems, daytime or evening courses of varying lengths, shorter more intensive residential courses, self-study packs, the media—the formats in which these programmes are offered and the modes of teaching–learning available to adults are legion.

(c) The *teachers* have varied roles and relationships with the learners, in part indicated by the different names used—instructors, trainers, extension workers, animators, promoters, facilitators, tutors and so on. Many of them are part-timers, non-educationalists (in a formal sense, for they are rarely trained and qualified for their educational task). The number of full-time professional educators and trainers of adults, except in the agricultural and health extension services, is small, and most of them organize as well as teach. Most teachers of adults are practising professionals of one sort or another who are willing, persuaded or even sometimes compelled to pass on to others some part of their expertise.

Diversity, coherence and change

The significant thing about this 'diverse constellation of opportunities'[12] is that decision-making in adult education is not centralized or direct; it is heterogeneous, complex and diffuse.

In this adult education is similar to Development. But adult education is more culturebound and less international in character than Development. The pattern of Adult Education as provision has grown up in each country over many years. Sometimes a particular form or organization will have been transplanted from one country to another—university extra-mural departments, for example, or community colleges or folk high schools from the West to Third World countries;[13] but the mix in every country will differ. The possibilities of specific interests, governmental or non-governmental, influencing this adult education network, seeking to change its direction or purpose or to focus its efforts onto particular activities, will be few and difficult to exploit.

This being so, it is something of a paradox that adult education is more influenced by general climates of opinion than is the formal system of education. Schools and colleges respond but slowly to the demands of the nation or changing general concerns. Adult education provision on the other hand tends to adapt itself more rapidly and directly in response to general changes in culture. Over the years that adult education has been a feature of Western societies, it has shown many and remarkable changes of emphasis, ideologies, forms of provision and learning methods, some of them resulting in controversies and conflicts. The emergence of the concept of continuing education is one such example.

But despite this, there has been in many parts of the West some sense of coherence in this diversity. It has been pointed out, for instance, how similar the programmes of liberal adult education of different providing bodies are and how resistant to change they are.[14] Adult educators talk a language of their own. It is only in the last few years that this coherence has fallen apart with the appearance of new forms of provision, new matters of concern. Nevertheless, we must remember that in adult education as elsewhere, older fashions do not die away with the advent of newer ones; the later find a niche alongside the earlier, and so the network becomes ever more complicated.

Perhaps the most striking example of this incrementalism is the question of the purpose of adult education—what it is all for. It is to this we must turn for the next stage of our argument.

NOTES TO CHAPTER 3

(1) Lowe (1975), ch. 1.
(2) Wiltshire, H. C. in Rogers, A. (1976), pp. 132 and 137.
(3) OECD (1975), p. 6. On training, see Lawson, K. H. (1983) Lifelong education: concept or policy? *IJLE* 1(2), 97–108; Paterson (1979); Magee, S. R. and Alexander, D. J. (1986) Training and education in continuing education, *IJLE* 5(3), 173–85.
(4) Rogers, A. (1986), ch. 4.
(5) Thompson (1980), pp. 48–54.
(6) Thorndyke, E. *et al.* (1928) *Adult Learning*, New York; Kidd (1959); Miller (1964); Knox (1977); Rogers, J. (1979); Lovell, R. B. (1980) *Adult Learning*, Croom Helm; Rogers, A. (1986); Brookfield, S. (1986) *Understanding and Facilitating Adult Learning*, Open University Press.

(7)   Wiltshire, H. C. in Rogers, A. (1976), p. 137.

(8)   Brookfield (1983), pp. 30–4.

(9)   Strategy Report (1980), p. 2.

(10) On non-formal education, see Coombs, P. H. (1968) *The World Educational Crisis*, New York; Coombs and Ahmed (1974); Srinivasan, L. (1977) *Perspectives of Nonformal Adult Learning*, New York; Sheffield, J. R. and Diejomoah, V. P. (1972) *Non-Formal Education in Africa*, New York; Evans, D. R. (1972) *Non-Formal Education*, Amherst; Evans, D. R. (1981) *Planning of Nonformal Education*, Paris: UNESCO; Bock and Papagiannis (1982). On the relations between formal and non-formal education, see the final report of the UNESCO International Symposium on the *Co-ordinated Planning of the Development of Formal and Non-Formal Education*, Paris, 1987. It should be noted that almost all writers and policy-makers in relation to non-formal education are the products of the formal educational system, not of NFE.

(11) State Resource Centre, Tamil Nadu, Madras, unpublished survey.

(12) McIlroy and Spencer (1988), p. 127.

(13) Townsend Coles, E. K. (1977) *Adult Education in Developing Countries*, 2nd edn, Oxford: Pergamon.

(14) '. . . there is . . . a surprising consistency in the provision of a common core curriculum in institutions of all types. The impression is of a broad national consensus about what kinds of things adult education ought to offer. . . .' Mee, G. and Wiltshire, H. C. (1978) *Structure and Performance in Adult Education*, Longman, p. 110.

Chapter 4

The Purpose of Adult Education

Before discussing differing perceptions of the purpose of adult education, two matters need attention—the debate about the purpose of education in general, and the relationship between adult education and the formal systems of education.

THE PURPOSE OF EDUCATION

Discussions over the nature and purpose of education in society have revealed four main clusters of ideas:[1]

(a) that it has a *technical* function, to provide a trained labour force, to promote the skills and knowledge required by a modern industrialized society to acquire greater prosperity; education gives capabilities.

(b) that it *establishes status*. Education is a process of jostling by which an individual achieves a role and thereby a set position which he/she occupies for the rest of life. In this 'meal-ticket' view of the function of education, the constant battles between groups to control different social and economic resources spill over into the schools and colleges. Education follows the changes in society.[2]

(c) that its main effect is to *reproduce* social structures and cultures, preventing change taking place so that the individual is adapted to the dominant social and cultural norms; education instils respect for the existing elites.[3]

(d) that if it is effective, it is a *revolutionary force* for both individual (providing mobility) and society (promoting development). It enables the learner to reflect critically on the reality around and to co-operate with others to change that reality.[4]

There seems to be a general consensus that education cannot be neutral: it either confirms or seeks to change the existing reality.

ADULT EDUCATION AND EDUCATION

These debates have spilled over into discussions about the role and purpose of adult education. They have, however, been complicated by another question, the relationship between adult education and the formal educational system. This has been seen to be of two kinds:

(a) Adult education exists to extend formal schooling to those who 'missed out', who failed to get what the more fortunate got through formal education (whether that fortunate group is a majority as in many countries in the West or a minority as in most Third World countries)—what is called a 'remedial' view.
(b) Adult education exists as something quite different, performing functions which formal schooling could never perform—what may be called a '*sui generis*' view.

In practice, adult education performs both roles in varying degrees and is subject to both forms of policy. It provides new forms of initial education and special programmes for adults in a series of lifelong learning opportunities.[5]

This two-fold orientation of adult education does not help for clarity of thought in the debate about the purpose of adult education, and there has been and still is much impreciseness and confusion in the terms used and the arguments put forward. Nevertheless, there has grown up in the West a general consensus about the nature and purpose of adult education which centres on two main points:

• that it is for the individual
• that it is for those who attend voluntarily

Recently that consensus shows signs of dissolving, but before we can examine this in detail, we must look more closely at these two points and at the way in which this consensus has been arrived at.

The development of adult education in the West

Thinking about adult education in the West over the last 150 years has undergone significant changes, and many different positions have been adopted. Two main strands have persisted throughout this period, the liberal education view and the social change view. They have existed alongside each other, each interrelating with and borrowing from the other.

The nineteenth century saw the emergence of a number of programmes of both kinds, although those directed towards social change tended to predominate—Sunday schools for the masses, for instance, or mechanics' institutes or trade union education, which represented an intention in a new wider democracy to 'educate our masters', to provide learning opportunities appropriate for a society in which all of its adult (male) citizens should participate fully. Most of these programmes, however, expressed their goals in terms of individual growth, so that both strands today claim the same movements as antecedents for their particular approaches and philosophies.

But during the twentieth century, the liberal approach has predominated. The stress since the 1930s has been on individual growth. Such an approach characterized all parts of the educational system in Western societies; how far its origins lie in the latent but powerful philosophies of Aristotle or in nineteenth-century pragmatic and entrepreneurial attitudes, or indeed in the successful completion by most of the West of its ambitious programme of universal elementary education, is hard to determine.[6]

Lifelong learning and lifelong education

The years after the Second World War saw enormous strides in understanding of adult education. It was at this time that the concept of lifelong learning and of lifelong education—which had emerged before the war—was clarified and refined:

> it is ridiculous to suppose that schools can provide all the learning needed for life, especially in its vocational aspect: those who work on that assumption (as Sir Richard Livingstone put it) 'behave like people who would try to give their children in a week all the food they require for a year: a method which might seem to save time and trouble but would not improve digestion, efficiency or health'.

This is true not only of technologically changing societies but of all parts of the world:

> Life is such an endless research problem that no student can ever come out of any educational institution with ready-made solutions to it. The best a student can hope to come out with are the techniques of learning and thinking about any problem life might present.

What came to be called 'the front-end loading' or 'banking' models of education were increasingly considered to be inappropriate for a rapidly changing and uncertain world. 'Learning later' became one of the keynotes of discussions. One result of this emerging understanding of lifelong learning was the view that everyone should have the opportunity to participate in planned learning at any stage in life when their individual needs required and when their desires were aroused. Schooling remained the main form of education, but it needed to be supplemented by lifelong education.[7]

The way such lifelong learning needs and desires were to be met varied according to the social structures, culture and understandings in each country. Different responses were given to the call from UNESCO in the early 1960s for a coherent programme of education continuing throughout life from childhood to old age. Faced with a policy decision as to whether to integrate adult education into a single educational system or to keep it discrete, three main polarities emerged.

(a) Some governments urged the adaptation of the existing formal system to cope with new groups of learners. In America, the community colleges and other educational establishments became the focus of a new approach towards helping adults to learn purposefully through the existing or a new kind of formal educational system; and in other countries, 'community education' called for the integration of child and adult learning opportunities and the use of nationally provided educational facilities by and for the whole community, which had after all paid for them. It was out of this strand that Continuing Education came—the continuation of formal education which follows on from, accepts the premises of, and cannot criticize initial formal education. This approach sought to open up formal education to meet the needs for lifelong learning rather than change it altogether.

(b) At the opposite extreme, the French and the Council of Europe called for *éducation populaire*, building various life-related activities in society and new agencies into an informal pattern of education for continued learning (*formation*) rather than using the formal system of education to meet learning needs which sprang as much from cultural as from economic and technological changes: thus 'paid educational leave' prescribed by statute encouraged the growth of private providers of adult learning programmes, including continuous vocational training (*éducation permanente*). This approach left the formal system untouched.

(c) The Organisation for Economic Co-operation and Development (OECD), on the other hand, advocated 'Recurrent Education', a refocusing of the formal system so as to allow 'adults who want to resume their education' access to 'formal and preferably full-time education' in a nationwide and lifelong pattern of provision which would give them the opportunity to go in and out whenever they needed to. This was seen as a new strategy, radically changing the schools and colleges to the new insights of lifelong education, incorporating the formal and informal adult education agencies into one single educational system. It was seen to be a matter of entitlement to education, especially in relation to the needs of work. But Olof Palme of Sweden gave a particular thrust to Recurrent Education when he urged that it should be used to redress educational inequalities, and the UK's Association for Recurrent Education also took this line: those who were earlier denied their opportunity for whatever reason should if they so wish have the right to recover the ground they had lost to more fortunate persons. Recurrent education was seen as a strategy for implementing the whole of lifelong learning at childhood and adult stages by transforming the educational system through political action.

Uncertainty in practice

Although the above 'doctrinal' positions were taken up, in practice more mixed approaches were adopted. Most countries drew 'a sharp distinction between vocational and non-vocational education, the first being equated with "training" rather than the cultivation of the mind or education for self-fulfilment which has been regarded as the primary aim of education'; or between a narrow view of vocational training as skills development and the formation of compliant attitudes on the one hand, and a wider view which 'aims at the growth of the personality as a whole and which should be of assistance in regulating the development of production in such a manner that it serves in the realization of basic human values and adapts itself to the preservation of the balance of nature' on the other hand. Systems were built to institutionalize these distinctions. Special institutions (like the folk high schools of northern Europe and the Workers' Universities in Yugoslavia) and special activities (like the Scandinavian study circles) were created to promote increased adult learning opportunities. In the UK, adult education was at first added as an appendage to existing formal educational establishments (universities, colleges of further education or some schools) or provided by non-governmental agencies; it was only later that special public Adult Education Institutes were set up by local education authorities. The term 'adult education' joined 'primary', 'secondary' and 'further/higher' education, striving for an equality of acceptance alongside but separate from these other sectors of the whole educational service.[8]

The reasons for this lack of consensus are many and probably derive from the dilemmas of pluralism inherent in Western democratic societies. But in large part they spring from tensions within education itself, tensions, for example, between spontaneous learning and stimulated learning which were more acutely felt in adult education with its emphasis on the autonomy of the adult learner, tensions which in turn reflected the differences between the two main strands of adult education, the social change and the liberal ideologies.

It is not surprising then that the terms used in these discussions were often confused and vague in meaning. Lifelong learning, lifelong education, continuing education, permanent education, recurrent education were all mixed up, often in the same document. 'Continuing Education' was for a time the favoured term to express the whole of (educational) life after school. This certainly was how the UK Advisory Council for Adult and Continuing Education (ACACE) used the words. Sometimes the phrase was employed in an even wider sense, to mean all education from the cradle to the grave: an Oxford conference saw 'lifelong education' as synonymous with 'continuing education', and as late as 1983 the two terms could be employed interchangeably, with a note that 'the social policy of continuing education has evolved from the liberal-democratic tradition of adult education'. 'Continuing Education' then had no value-laden connotations such as it has today; indeed, 'continuing education' and 'liberal adult education' were on occasion used to cover the same field of adult education, contrasted with 'recurrent education' which was seen as 'radical' education.[9]

The learner-centred approach

Behind all this diversity, the unifying theme was that adult education was for the individual. Both the social change and the liberal tradition views of adult education were agreed that the individual learner was the prime concern of the programme. The study of 'andragogy'—how adults can best be helped to learn while respecting their adulthood—which was more advanced in the United States than in Europe, stressed the student-centredness of adult education—the development of the whole person, the individual's motivation, freedom of choice and participation in the learning process, the achievement of goals set by the learners themselves. 'Adults should learn what they want to learn, when they want to learn it, at their own pace, in their own location and for their own purposes' was the slogan of bodies like the WEA. 'Individuals . . . have *the right to choose* their own provision for their own purposes' [original italics], to 'exercise a real choice about the sort of learning experience they choose to undergo.'[10]

The end result of this learner-centred approach was the view that adult learners should come to control their own education. The overriding aim behind all educational provision for adults is to help the learners to become independent, so that the planner/teachers will become redundant as the learners plan and carry out their own purposeful learning. And if the objective of adult education is to end outsider-led education and training and to create self-directing learners ('to enable the students to think and work independently' as the Russell Report phrased it), then the planner/teacher will encourage the learners to engage in the exercise of autonomy during the educational process itself.[11] We cannot teach about democracy without practising democracy in our teaching; we cannot teach on equal terms without exercising equality.

Demand-led provision

The demand for this kind of adult education was seen to come from the learner. Programmes of education for adults had to be based on what the learner(s) wanted to learn, not on what the planner/educator decided the learner(s) should learn. It is something of a paradox that these learners' desires were often expressed in the language of needs rather than wants, for needs and wants are not the same: 'needs are prescriptively defined by the educator in terms of the educator's perception of those needs'.

Various writers explored this in depth. Some, like Carl Rogers, saw these learning needs in terms of adulthood—drives towards more and more autonomy and maturity. Others, like Maslow, saw different levels of needs—for self-actualization, once the prior and 'pre-potent' needs for food, shelter and safety, and then for love and belonging, recognition and esteem from others, had in large part been met. Still others have sought to express these needs for learning in terms of a search for meaning, each adult interpreting reality in an attempt to make sense for him or her self. The area of learner needs is perhaps the clearest indication of the individualistic approach to adult education in the West.[12] Wiltshire proclaimed this most expressively when he saw the pressure for adult learning as arising from 'a sense of dissatisfaction with oneself' and the task of adult education as 'not socialisation, not vocational training but something which may perhaps be described as individuation—self discovery and self development voluntarily undertaken'. Self-actualization became an essential part of liberal adult education: 'All forms of education are a means to an end . . . the end of personal development, of an awareness of oneself or one's society.'[13]

The private wants of the learners then, rather than public needs, became the touchstone of adult education, and it was increasingly set against Continuing Education, which was coming to be seen as almost exclusively vocational in nature, denying individual growth and expression. The recent British Labour Party statement that the first aim of adult education is the promotion of 'personal development and self-fulfilment' repeats what has been the text of most providers from Mansbridge with his 'right of the [class] members to decide how, why, what or when they wish to study' and the 1909 Report, *Oxford and Working Class Education*, to the Russell Report of 1973 and other governmental, para-statal and non-governmental statements.[14] Similar views were posited by adult educators in other countries.[15] As Raymond Williams pointed out, such a 'doctrine [was] based on individualist theories of man and society' rather than socialist views.

The purpose of education then was seen to be individual growth and self-development through enhanced experiences at the instance of the learner(s). And the result of this emphasis on providing programmes to meet the wants of the learners was 'the learning contract'. Provision was seen to be the subject of negotiation between the provider/planner/teacher on the one hand and the learner(s) on the other. 'The ideology of adult education achieves for practitioners a promise to their clientele that their primary concern will be with students' needs and interests.' In practice there was little real *negotiation*. What the learner wanted was king: the adult education agency was not supposed to provide anything which the adult learner(s) did not want. Despite the language used, demand, not need, became the criteria for provision; it was to be 'designed in the simplest possible way to respond to demand'. The aim was to 'attract participants'; and it followed that if no one turned up to the programme, this merely showed that the adult education agency had 'got it wrong' in their planning—the *right* kind of learning opportunities to meet the learners' wants were not being provided.[16]

Special needs

Such an approach presupposes that demand is pre-existent and articulated by those who are educationally aware. But if everyone was to have these opportunities, there would have to be special provision for groups which were specially disadvantaged. Many people, even in the affluent West, were too poor or too poorly prepared educationally to be able to take advantage of what was offered to them; others were living in places not yet reached by the provision of adult learning programmes. So picking up on the work of writers like Paulo Freire (the new guru of adult education), Ivan Illich and others who pointed out that educational 'drop-outs' were not so much failures as casualties of the educational system, programmes and resources for EPGs (Educational Priority Groups) and EPAs (Educational Priority Areas) and other special sectors abounded.[17] The largest set of programmes was for the largest disadvantaged sector—women. Many adult education agencies sprang to the rescue once the *Feminine Mystique* was revealed and the invisible became visible (though it is significant that many women's movements kept themselves aloof from the various colleges and education bodies which provided New Horizons, New Opportunities for Women, Wider Opportunities and other special programmes 'for' women). But there were also programmes and pressure groups for other interests—the physically handicapped, the elderly, the retired and retiring, the unemployed, the immigrant, the inner city resident, the itinerant, the mentally impaired, and so on. This was the time when adult literacy agencies were established in industrialized countries after the discovery that illiteracy existed in societies which possessed universal compulsory free education, when coping and survival education for adults was developed, when English as a Second Language (ESL) was found to be a major need, when pre-school groups, playgroup classes and mother-and-child programmes were launched.

Many will argue that the purpose behind these programmes was to bring about structural change, to alter the balance between the dispossessed and marginalized on the one hand, and the educated and powerful on the other. As one engaged in some of these initiatives in the heady 1960s and early 1970s, I can only say that at the time it did not feel like this. We hoped that the process of widening opportunity for education to persons hitherto excluded would result in profound social change. But we were naïve in assuming that our small pittance of effort would bring about the mass conversion of the West; we underestimated the numbers needed to achieve social revolution. We did not, many of us, consciously drive towards a set goal, a specific desired change. Our role was permissive rather than persuasive: to help our students 'to understand and *perhaps* change society'. Social change was incidental to our activities: the primary purpose was individual growth. Even some of the overtly 'social change' and community development programmes of the time were based on a concept of education as personal development, on desires for greater individual freedom and individual learning changes. The New Communities Project in Hampshire (UK), for example, was aimed at providing an 'education for individual self discovery and self development . . . to encourage growth in human personality, character and creativity . . . greater confidence in their own ability and potential', not for radical change. The education provided could be used by the learners for their own purposes—for personal interest (though stopping short of increased earnings) or greater participation in democracy: the choice would be theirs.[18]

Certainly, we failed to appreciate that 'the logic of class or group interests is different from the logic of individual interests', that escape for a few from a particular class or group did not mean any change within that class or group as a whole. And so we continued to help some few individuals to increase the range of their choices, to come to have a greater measure of control over some larger or smaller part of their own lives. Choice was our watchword; and our success stories were those who were enabled to improve themselves rather than improve their social environment. Our doctrine was one of liberation: freedom for the individual to choose and to participate. T. Ten Have summed up our philosophy even when we had not heard of Ten Have himself:

> adult education is that process within an individual by which he/she comes to a better understanding of oneself and of reality, to a critical evaluation of both, and to a conscious and direct handling of the possibilities offered within the social reality.

The more abstract (some would say abstruse) conceptualization of this point came in the work of Habermas, though this did not percolate to some parts of the adult education scene in the West until the end of the 1970s.[19]

THE MARGINALIZATION OF ADULT EDUCATION

In practice, then, the philosophy underlying the considerable increase in adult education provision in the 1960s was individualistic—that everyone had a right to education throughout their lives. Access programmes for mature students, Return to Study courses, the Open University and its successors, the University of the Third Age and community colleges all emerged from the commitment of the practitioners. The specific needs of those adults who did return to study were researched, new programmes of learning and new formats were devised, new delivery systems were developed and experimented with. The search was on for an alternative to the formal system, open to everyone who wanted to join irrespective of their wealth or poverty, irrespective of their previous educational experiences and qualifications. Throughout the West, the winds of change were felt in adult education; even in the Soviet Union, where pleas for a closer relationship between the world of work and the world of education seem to have been heard rather earlier than in the rest of Europe, new initiatives were launched. Some even went so far as to assert that institutionalized adult education itself was denying to its clients self-reliance and responsibility for their own learning. They sought to develop open networks of learning and self-instructional resources, relating life and learning in spontaneous self-learning processes rooted in everyday life, so that each person could plan his/her own learning.[20]

Disillusionment with the formal system of education, felt by many educators (themselves often the successful products of it), had another result. Some of this provision of new modes of learning for adults, accepting as it did the analysis of formal education as having failed these adults badly and as continuing to bar their way into further learning, was opposed to certification or at least sought new and more appropriate forms of recognition such as certificates for the learning achieved through life experience. The great debate on non-vocational liberal adult education continued to animate the providers of adult educational programmes for many years after it had ceased to fill the pages of the journals. Adult education was to be an open-ended process in which individuals enriched themselves.[21]

The result was that this programme was seen by governments and by many educationalists as being merely of personal value, 'dominated by concepts of leisure time satisfactions'. Adult education thus came to suffer from 'crippling marginality', not just in terms of society or governmental interest but also in terms of the educational system as a whole. More than 90 per cent of the spending of the UK government on education has been devoted to those under the age of 25. The recent emergence of new programmes of continuing education, such as PICKUP and PEVE, and especially employment training provided by the Manpower Services Commission and its successors in the UK and by similar bodies in other countries in the West, has resulted in some redistribution of resources towards the older age groups. Nevertheless these programmes—in societies which increasingly attach significance to paid employment and to education as building up a trained workforce for such paid employment—have themselves helped to confirm the apparent irrelevance and low status of liberal non-vocational adult education until, in the end, attending adult education classes has come to be regarded not so much as preparing for a better use of leisure but as a leisure activity in itself. Adult education has been increasingly marginalized—the last item on the educational agenda, on the back pages of the educational journals.[22]

Voluntaryism

But adult education became marginalized for another reason—it reached only a small audience; it was not a mass programme. There were, it is true, claims that adult education programmes were 'for all people', 'to enable every person to develop their full potential', 'a body of provision for all sections of the population', a programme in which 'all manner of people from different levels of society are . . . integrated into a liberal informative educational world' [which] 'offers a broad curriculum to a broad cross-section of the population' and so on. But such claims were unrealistic. Although the aim was that everyone was to be able to continue and advance their learning, the doctrine of meeting learner demands meant that programmes were designed to appeal only to those who were already interested, those who possessed the motivation to take advantage of them and the ability to articulate their wishes, not to those who failed to see or refused to listen, who would not take up the opportunities provided for them. The principle of voluntaryism underlay both the liberal tradition and the emancipatory philosophy of the liberation theologians amongst adult educators.[23]

Adult educationalists institutionalized this voluntariness. They targeted 'those who wished to take courses designed to meet their needs'. Even those who worked with disadvantaged or action groups (residents' groups, amenity societies, community associations, etc.) worked with those parts of the urban conglomerations where a response was apparent and ignored the rest. There was an elitism of motivation. Adult educators in the West did not on the whole have to struggle with the problem which continually faces extension workers and development change-agents in Third World countries, how to motivate reluctant learners. There were some exceptions, but in general if programmes did not appeal and recruit, they were simply closed and often not offered again. As training courses for tutors began to stress student-centred active learning methods, participatory processes and respect for the adults' adulthood and autonomy, so the selectivity of adult education programmes became more marked. The concentration of those who were concerned with working-class education on education for leadership led to similar forms of elitism.[24]

In speaking of elitism, I am not talking of the fact that, despite the commitment of most adult educators to narrowing the gap between the educational haves and have-nots, the programmes actually increased this gap, so that the more education one had the more one wanted and the more one got, until adult education has become 'mainly a middle-class phenomenon'. 'There is overwhelming evidence that the more initial education people experience, the more they wish to continue with their education in later life.' Nor am I speaking of a financial elitism, though over the years the financing of adult education programmes has tended to increase that tendency. For both of these are forms of elitism which adult educators have resisted strenuously.[25]

Rather the elitism I am talking of is one which adult educators have connived at. It springs from voluntaryism. The result of relying upon the learners to articulate their demands has been that adult education has reached only 'a small and socially discrete' sector of the population; 'it performs [its] functions for a small minority of the population'. Adult education is seen to be irrelevant to the large majority of the population.[26] The low participation rates in many countries show this. The diffuse nature of adult education and the differing interpretations of what is and what is not adult education mean that it is virtually impossible to obtain accurate statistics, but the general picture is clear. Few countries can boast the levels of participation of some of the Scandinavian nations (Finland 25 per cent, Norway 27 per cent, Sweden 40 per cent). In the UK a survey in 1980 suggested a participation rate of some 16–20 per cent of the adult population over a three-year period. A parallel survey in the Irish Republic (1982) produced a figure of some 11 per cent in one year and 16 per cent over the previous three years. In the United States, a survey taken by the National Center for Educational Statistics in 1982 indicated a take-up rate of nearly 13 per cent per annum. Comparative work done on a number of industrialized countries using other methods of analysis reveals much the same (Table 4.1).

Table 4.1   *Annual participation rates for adult education by nation*

	%
Australia	13
Canada	23
Denmark	17
France	7
Soviet Union	31
West Germany	11
United Kingdom	15
USA*	27

* Higher than the 1982 survey finding mentioned in the text.

One reason for such rates is clear: as a recent survey of adult students in London (UK) indicated, the role of the adult education service is still seen to be '. . . meeting the educational needs of those who, for whatever reason, failed to benefit from initial education *and are motivated* in later life to make up' [my italics]. [27] Adult education is intended only for those who want to come.

Individualism and social change

There were of course exceptions to this 'voluntary elitism': the older social tradition did not completely die away. A strand of adult education seen as a 'national necessity' and committed to the development of an informed and participatory democracy continued, helping to create, form and direct the working-class movement. The calls of bodies such as the National Council of Labour Colleges (1909) and the early WEA for social reform through education rather than through revolution were renewed: 'every adult educationalist is an agent of change and is committed to social change in so far as he [*sic*] works for the dissemination of educational values'. But the fact that these voices were exceptions stresses the general truth, that adult education in the West was aimed more at the advancement of the motivated individual than at the 'Development' of society as a whole. From government and practitioners alike comes overwhelming evidence of this. The Adult Education Act of 1976 in Norway puts it well:

> [adult education] is to help the individual to obtain a more satisfying life. This act shall contribute to providing adult persons with equal opportunities to acquire knowledge, understanding and skill, which will improve the individual's sense of value and personal development and strengthen the basis for independent achievement and co-operation with others in working and community life. [28]

What is more, the doctrine of individualism held sway even in many of these apparent exceptions. Most socially purposive adult education programmes were still at heart voluntaryist and individualistic. The Liverpool EPA programme, held up as the model of social change adult education, reported that it proceeded by 'conducting a house to house survey of adult education needs and then organizing activities *for those expressing interest*' [my italics]. This was not an alternative approach to individualism; it held both concepts of self-actualization and social change in the same basket. From Freire with his discussion of individual development and collective consciousness, to Russell ('the value of education is . . . measured . . . by the quality of life it inspires in the individual and generates in the community at large'), it was felt to be possible to speak of the two goals in the same breath, of 'greater social and political awareness as well as intellectual enlightenment'. Individual development leads to social equality as well as to economic growth; growing individual awareness will bring about social transformation, 'enabling people to understand and even challenge their own organisational culture'.

Some it is true found it hard to reconcile individualism with social structural change: 'for the individual, basic education may offer rewards, for the disadvantaged as a group it offers very little that can ameliorate the circumstances . . . or the conditions which produce them'; 'to the individual working-class person, mobility in this society may mean something; . . . to the class or group . . . however, mobility means nothing at all. The only true mobility at this level would be the destruction of the whole class society.' But these are few. For most adult educators, when they borrow the language of radicalism, social change will be brought about through voluntary individual development. 'If education is . . . related to consciousness, the learning becomes a "social" as distinct from a purely "personal" activity; a liberal progressive movement for educational change . . . could be a primary factor in reshaping the world for the better . . . [it would] promote equality' [here, the sentiments are influenced by American writings where 'liberal' is seen to be synonymous with 'radical']. For those adult educators in the late 1960s who possessed a social purpose, large-scale structural change would come about through the increased awareness and decisions of individuals.[29]

The trouble with this position is, however, that more than a century of adult education in the West has not in fact led to any form of social change.

NOTES TO CHAPTER 4

(1)   Halsey *et al.* (1961).
(2)   Tyler, W. (1977) *Sociology of Educational Inequality*, Methuen; Berg, I. (1973) *Education and Jobs: the Great Training Robbery*, Penguin; Cousin, B. R. (ed.) (1972) *Education: Structure and Society*, Penguin; Simkins, T. (1977) *Nonformal Education and Development: Some Critical Issues*, Manchester: Manchester University Press.
(3)   Brown, R. (ed.) (1974) *Knowledge, Education and Cultural Change*, Tavistock; Bowles and Gintis (1976); Bowles, H., Gintis, S. and Simons, J. (1976) Impact of education on poverty: the US experience, *International Development Review* 18(2), 6–10; Bourdieu, P. and Passeron, J. (1977) *Reproduction in Education, Society and Culture*, Sage; Griffin (1983); Althusser, L. as cited in Thompson (1980), pp. 35–6.
(4)   *AE* 51(4) (1978), 257; Curle, A. (1973) *Education for Liberation*, New York; Charnofsky, S. (1971) *Educating the Powerless*, California; Wren, B. (1977) *Education for Justice*, London: SCM; Kindervatter (1979).
(5)   See for example Lindeman, E. (1938) Preparing leaders in adult education, reprinted in Brookfield (1988), pp. 93–4.
(6)   For the individual in the West, see Macpherson, C. B. (1973) *Democratic Theory*, Oxford: Clarendon: 'man is free when he is proprietor of his own person'; Macfarlane, A. (1979) *The Origins of English Individualism*, Oxford: Blackwell; Allen, C. K. (1943) *Democracy and the Individual*, Oxford: Oxford University Press; Thompson, D. F. (1971) *The Democratic Citizen: Social Science and Democratic Theory in the Twentieth Century*, Cambridge: Cambridge University Press. In much (but not all) of the thinking in the West, the state is seen to be made up directly of individuals (Toynbee called such Western democracies 'universal churches'); in much (but not all) of the thinking in Third World countries, the state is thought to be made up of collections of collectives.
(7)   Rogers, A. (1980), p. 11; Kabuga, C. (1977) Why andragogy? *Adult Education and Development* 9 (September), 1–3. For lifelong learning and education, see Parkyn, G. W. (1973) *Towards a Conceptual Model of Lifelong Education*, Paris: UNESCO; Lengrand (1975); Cropley, A. J. (1977) *Lifelong Education: a Psychological analysis*, Oxford; Cropley, A. J. (1981) *Towards a System of Lifelong Education: Some Practical Considerations*, UNESCO; Gelpi, E. (1985) *Lifelong Education and International Relations*, Croom Helm; Dave (1976). For an early statement, see Yeaxlee, B. A. (1929) *Lifelong Education*, Cassell.
(8)   Chickering (1981); Schuller, T. and Megarry, J. (eds) (1979) *Recurrent Education and Lifelong Learning: World Yearbook of Education*, Kogan Page; OECD (1971) *Equal Educational Opportunity*; Houghton, V. and Richardson, K. (eds) (1974) *Recurrent Education*, Ward Lock; OECD (1973); OECD (1975); Himmelstrupp, P., Robinson, J. and Fielden, D. (eds) (1981) *Strategies for Lifelong Learning I: a Symposium of Views from Europe and the USA*, ARE; Legge, D. (1982) *The Education of Adults in Britain*, Open University Press.
(9)   See Wiltshire, H. C., Second thoughts on continuing education, in Rogers, A. (1976), pp. 132–5; Jessup, F. (1969) *Lifelong Learning: a Symposium of Continuing Education*, Pergamon; Griffin, C. (1983) Social control, social policy and adult education, *IJLE* 2(3), 219; Griffin, C. G. (1978) *Recurrent Education and Continuing Education: a Curriculum*

Approach, ARE, p. 3; Boyle, C. (1982) Reflections on recurrent education, *IJLE* 1(1), 5–18. The Russell Report, p. 16, uses an Anglicized version of the French term as 'permanent education', as does the Council of Europe report *Permanent Education* (Strasbourg, 1970).

(10) *AE* 60(3) (1987), 281; McIlroy and Spencer (1988), pp. 99, 147, 158: '[educators] should leave the specific choice of provision to those intended to benefit from it. . . . whatever the student wishes to choose . . . .' For andragogy, see Knowles, M.S. (ed.) (1978) *The Adult Learner: a Neglected Species*, Houston; and Knowles, M. (1975) *The Modern Practice of Adult Education: Andragogy Versus Pedagogy*, New York; Ingalls, M. (1973) *A Trainer's Guide to Andragogy: its Concepts, Experience and Application*, New York.

(11) Russell Report, para. 108; Wright Mills, C. (1959) *The Power Elite*, Oxford: Oxford University Press, p. 318: 'the end product of such liberal education of sensibilities is . . . the self educating self-cultivating man and woman'.

(12) Rogers, C. (1969) *Freedom to Learn*, Columbus, Ohio; and Rogers, C. (1961) *On Becoming a Person*, Boston; Gould, R.L. (1980) Transformations during early and middle adulthood, in Smelsen, N.J. and Erikson, E.H. (eds) (1980) *Themes of Work and Love in Adulthood*, Mass.; Maslow, A.H. (1954) *Motivation and Personality*, New York; Lengrand (1975), p. 139: 'the real educational process concentrates not on a body of knowledge . . . but on the needs of the human being, his [*sic*] aspirations and the living relations he maintains with the world of objects and persons'. For needs in AE, see Hirst, P.H. and Peters, R.S. (1970) *The Logic of Education*, Routledge and Kegan Paul; Wiltshire, H.C., The concept of learning and needs, in Rogers (1976), pp. 145–8; Armstrong, P.F. (1982) The myth of meeting needs in adult education and community development, *Critical Social Policy* 2(2); Armstrong (1982); see ACACE (1979), para. 5: 'we are concerned all the time with individuals and individual needs'. Mee seems to confuse 'demands' and 'needs': he writes that a comprehensive educational service for adults designed to meet 'whatever the demands they would make on such a service' would need 'to uncover adults' educational needs': Mee (1980), pp. 100–3.

(13) Rogers, A. (1976), pp. 138–9; Flude, R. and Parrott, A. (1979) *Education and the Challenge of Change: a Recurrent Education Strategy for Britain*, Open University Press, p. 91. Jarvis (1987), pp. 98–9, talks of a break in 'cognitive harmony', and this 'imbalance' produces a desire for learning. Mezirow, J. (1977) Perspective transformation, *Studies in Adult Education* 9(2); Mezirow, J. (1981) A critical theory of adult learning and education, *Adult Education* (USA) 32(1), 3–24.

(14) *Education Throughout Life*, p. 9; Mansbridge, A.E. (1920) *An Adventure in Working Class Education*, London, p. xviii; Newman (1979), p. 35; McIlroy and Spencer (1988), pp. 3–14; the 1909 Report; the 1919 Report: 'it seems to us vital to provide the fullest opportunities for personal development. . . .' The reports of the DES, the UGC and other bodies reflect the same position. See the speech of the Chief Inspector of Training of the former Manpower Services Commission at the May 1988 London Conference of ALBSU, criticizing Further Education for 'failing to address individual's needs', *AE* 61(2) (1988), 146. For a recent example of the individual emphasis in AE in the West, see Boud, D. and Griffin, V. (1987) *Appreciating Adults Learning: From the Learner's Perspective*, Kogan Page. Thompson (1980), p. 14, draws a distinction between individual intellectual needs and collective economic and social needs; but Boone, E.J., Shearman, R.W. and White, E.E. (1980) *Serving Personal and Community Needs through Adult Education*, Jossey Bass, sets out to explore community/collective needs and sees all needs which AE addresses as individual: 'sense of self, of professional growth, opportunity, sense of community, experimentation': adult educators are 'leaders of the effort to facilitate the continuing self-development of adults' (p. 8). See Rogers, J. and Groombridge, B. (1976) *Right to Learn*, Arrow.

(15) See for example Jobert (1988), p. 2: education 'can become a time for self-reflection and questioning one's immediate field of perception . . . to help him/her develop a project based on . . . his/her interests and resources'.

(16) Keddie (1980), pp. 45–7, 62; Strachan, R., Brown, J. and Schuller, T. (1988) Adult education and scientific literacy, *AE* 61(2), 109; Armstrong (1982).

(17)   Crombie and Harries-Jenkins (1983), p. 101. This theme is an old one. The WEA movement in its early days spoke of the 'educational inexperience' of most adults, of their impoverished initial education, and built the tutorial system to cope with these needs: see Harrison (1961); Jennings, B. (1979) *Knowledge is Power: a Short History of the WEA 1903–78*, Hull; Mansbridge, A. (1913) *University Tutorial Classes*, London; Lovett (1975); Midwinter (1972). For the de-schoolers, see Illich (1970); Reimer, E. (1971) *School is Dead*, Penguin. See Firth, S. and Corrigan, P. (1977) Politics of education, in Whitty, G. and Young, M. F. D. (eds) *Society, State and Schooling*, Falmer Press.

(18)   McIlroy and Spencer (1988), pp. 70, 139; Lindeman (1926), pp. 8–9: 'in adult education, the curriculum is built around the students' needs and interests . . . The approach to adult education will be via situations, not subjects.' See Thompson (1980), p. 100: 'The libertarian solution of the de-schoolers is to disestablish the professions and deinstitutionalize society *on behalf of individual freedom*' [my italics]; Fordham *et al.* (1979).

(19)   Willis, P. (1978) *Learning to Labour: How Working Class Kids Get Working Class Jobs*, Saxon House, as cited in Thompson (1980), p. 62; T. Ten Have quoted in Leirman (1987); Habermas (1972).

(20)   See for example Clyne (1972); Newman (1979); Jackson (1970); Kirkwood (1978).

(21)   Borzak, L. (1981) *Field Study: a Source Book for Experiential Learning*, Sage; Boydell, T. (1976) *Experiential Learning*, Manchester: Manchester University Press; Keeton, M. T. *et al.* (1976) *Experiential Learning: Rationale, Characteristics and Assessment*, Jossey Bass; Moon, R. and Hawes, G. (eds) (1980) *Developing New Clienteles of Adult Students*, Jossey Bass; Brookfield (1983), pp. 167–72. See publications of the Learning from Experience Trust (UK) and the Council for Adult and Experiential Learning (USA).

(22)   Hutchinson (1978); Harries-Jenkins (1983); McIlroy and Spencer (1988), pp. 56, 123; Clarke, M. (1958) *The Marginality of Adult Education*, Jossey Bass; Thompson (1980), pp. 12–13. *AE* **60**(3) (1987), 284: AE is 'not being starved to death, merely neglected as being of no significance whatever'.

(23)   OECD (1973); OECD (1975); McIlroy and Spencer (1988), pp. 99, 147; *AE* **60**(3) (1987), 236–7.

(24)   *Education Throughout Life*, p. 8; Harrison (1961), p. 268. 'The WEA and the Labour College classes have trained successive generations of leaders for the trade union and Labour movement'—Griffiths, J. (1969) *Pages from Memory*, London, p. 48.

(25)   OECD (1975), pp. 3, 8.

(26)   Harries-Jenkins (1983); see Adequacy of provision, *AE* **42**(6) (1970) and *AE: Adequacy of Provision*, Leicester: NIAE, 1970.

(27)   See figures in EBAE (1988); Petersen *et al.* (1982); OECD (1975), p. 4, gives 20 per cent for Germany, 34 per cent for Sweden, 10 per cent for USA. See ACACE (1982), p. 52; *Lifelong Learning: Report of the Adult Education Commission, Republic of Ireland*, Dublin, 1983, p. 88; *Adult and Continuing Education Today* 12 (June 1982), 49. A recent survey from Scotland suggested a total of 42 per cent of the adult population had participated at some stage, but an annual participation rate is not given: Munn, P. and MacDonald, C. (1988) *Adult Participation in Education and Training*, Edinburgh: Scottish Council for Research in Education, p. 9. For ILEA survey, see *AE* **60**(3) (1987), 215. For social bias, see McIlroy and Spencer (1988), pp. 129, 137; Taylor, R. and Ward, K. (1986) *Adult Education and the Working Class: Education for the Missing Millions*, Croom Helm; *AE* **60**(3) (1987), 287, 294–5; OECD (1975), p. 8.

(28)   McIlroy and Spencer (1988), p. 2; 1909 Report; Lovett (1971), p. 25; EBAE (1988) Norway. Baroness Hooper, one of the UK Ministers for Education addressing the annual conference of NIACE at Loughborough (UK) in May 1988 spoke of the essential character of education as providing for personal growth. The President of the Austrian Adult Education Association, Mrs Frölich-Sandner, spoke in August 1988 of adult education helping individuals to cope with change rather than to direct it, of 'adult education being free from party politics and oriented towards the individual and his or her educational needs': *AE* **61**(2) (1988), 150; *AE* **61**(3) (1988), 256; Council of Europe (1984), p. 27. Lawson (1977) writes of the 'traditional role [of education] . . . general

cultural diffusion and personal development'.

(29)   *AE* **61**(2) (1988) 121; Newman (1979); Thompson (1980), pp. 9, 107; Jackson, K. and Lovett, T. (1971) Universities and the WEA: an Alternative Approach, *AE* **44**(2). Dave (1976), p. 34, describes lifelong education as 'a process of accomplishing personal, social and professional development throughout the lifespan of individuals in order to enhance the quality of life of *both* individuals and their collectivities' [my italics]. See Finch, J. (1984) *Education as Social Policy*, Longman, p. 94: 'education for both individual development and social purpose'. Russell Report: 'Traditionally the WEA has believed that much of its work in general education was directed to greater social and political awareness as well as intellectual enlightenment'; 'it seems to us vital to provide the fullest opportunities for personal development and for the realisation of a higher standard of citizenship'. Lovett (1971), p. 13: 'As far as individuals are concerned, success can be reckoned . . . in terms of . . . [various competencies and attitudes]; but in the most important sense, success will depend on the extent to which adult education contributes to the process of social change'; and Lovett (1980), p. 155, speaks of adult education as 'meeting a variety of needs and interests among the working class, encouraging personal growth and development, and supporting greater community awareness and involvement'. See Keddie (1980), pp. 62–3. Fletcher (1980) distinguishes between *liberal* and *liberating* interpretations of adult (community) education, but others hope to reconcile the two, e.g. Brookfield (1983), pp. 66–70. In the USA, Bowles and Gintis wrote that a liberal view of education provides the means of furthering personal benefit and fulfilment, whilst at the same time promoting social justice, equality and the integration of the diverse interests of different groups in society. See Clarke, M. (1978) Meeting the needs of the adult learner: using non-formal education for social action, *Convergence* **11**, 3–4; O'Sullivan, D. (1981) Adult education, social change and the interpretive model, *Aontas Review* **3**(1), 57–70, which argues that social change springs from individual learning.

Chapter 5

A Changed World

The student riots in France and elsewhere in the late 1960s, coupled with the reactions in the United States and other countries to the Vietnam War, marked a distinct change. How far the re-emergence of social conflict at this time derived any inspiration from those programmes of adult education which had been designed to alleviate the worst aspects of disadvantage is not clear. The de-schoolers and the liberation theologians had taught us to view the disadvantaged as oppressed victims rather than as handicapped, and the systems as partial, not disinterested, and the UNESCO Report *Learning To Be* (1972) showed a possible new educational future. Some educators had come to see that self-fulfilment adult education had not led and probably never would lead to the massive and urgent social reconstruction which was necessary to achieve social justice. So the questions were rewritten: how could society be changed in the direction of a wider-based democracy, and what if any were the parts to be played, respectively, by (adult) education and/or direct action?[1]

The student riots failed, or so many judged at the time. But the climate had been changed irrevocably in at least two ways. First a sense of internationalism and collective responsibility had grown. We now saw ourselves as part of an interdependent 'global village'. The language was colourful ('spaceship earth', for example) but the sentiments were real and pressing. Adult education felt these changes. UNESCO international conferences on adult education began in 1972, with their consequential redefinition of the term and the loosening of the close links between adult education and local cultural value systems. The International Council for Adult Education was established in 1973 and other international bodies in distance education and university adult education followed. Adult educators began to visit Third World countries from the early 1970s, following the Development trainers and extension workers who had gone ahead but who did not talk to adult educators of what they learned from these visits. The 1976 Declaration of Nairobi was issued, though like the Fauré Report in practice it fell on largely deaf ears in the West.[2]

The second change was the emergence of an era of gloomy futurology, ranging from *Future Shock* and *Silent Spring* to the Club of Rome reports from 1972 onwards. The pressing need now was not so much to advance the cause of particular disadvantaged groups (though this was still important) or even to cope with a world undergoing accelerating comprehensive change, as to address global problems.

In this emerging sense of crisis, the question was asked whether education had a role to play. A new set of objectives began to be discussed—not just to promote personal growth but to use education to ameliorate some social condition or to solve some social problem, to undertake a task set by the state (a health campaign, for instance) or by a concerned constituency (to mobilize support for environmental conservation, for example). Even some of those who saw adult education as the provision of learning opportunities for those who wanted them were no longer willing to wait for clients to present themselves: the needs of this new (pessimistic? realistic?) world were so pressing that agencies, they urged, should seek to persuade those who did not want to learn to take action through education and to urge those who were abusing the natural and manmade environment to change their attitudes and behaviour. The oil crisis sealed the old world off from the new for ever: what was at stake was not just the welfare of some individuals or groups of people but of society itself. A new meaning was given to the phrase 'survival education': it no longer applied just to helping those who were struggling within an oppressive world to make their voice heard and to take control over some part of their own lives, but to the survival of the human race on this planet.[3]

DEVELOPMENT IN THE WEST

For gradually the peoples and governments in the West have come to realize that their societies have problems in many ways similar to those of Third World countries, and that part of the answer lies, as in the Third World, in programmes directed towards nationally set goals. Now, I do not want to be misunderstood. The Developmental needs of the Third World countries are of such an immense degree that they must always be in a class of their own. And to urge that the West has similar needs must not be seen as in any way weakening the demands which the Third World countries can legitimately make on the rich countries of the West.

At the same time, as we begin to look at our own societies through Third World eyes, we are learning much about ourselves. Western societies have, for example, come to recognize that they have a literacy problem, and national goals have been set, national programmes launched. Growing awareness of other issues has resulted from the unremitting pressure of non-governmental interest groups such as CND, Amnesty International, Friends of the Earth and Greenpeace, and from some para-statal bodies such as the UK Health Education Authority. Belatedly, the media and governmental agencies have joined in. These new concerns are increasingly being expressed in Developmental terms (see, for instance, the language used by the European Community), and the goals of the new programmes are remarkably similar to those of Third World countries—national integration and communal harmony; help for the unemployed and under-employed, especially in an age of new technologies; justice for women and other sectors particularly disadvantaged or marginalized (immigrant or itinerant groups, for example) and so on. Most Western cities have urgent housing and inner city regeneration needs, opportunities for formal education are not yet universal; and concern is increasingly expressed about such matters as population growth, resource depletion and the arms race, the health and nutritional status of many sectors, pollution control and the care of the environment, widespread poverty, the abuse of children, the care of the elderly, poisoned industrial relations, rural deprivation and the collapse of a sense of local community.[4] All these are areas of concern in which Third World Development programmes have devised strategies which are of relevance to the West.

Sustainable Development

To these concerns may be added the emergence of the concept of 'sustainable Development': 'an approach to progress which meets the needs of the present without compromising the ability of future generations to meet their own needs' (Tokyo Declaration). The concept of 'sustainable Development' is built on the premise that one of the most pressing world problems is the current use of the earth's resources in such a way that they will no longer be available for future generations. Growth which fails to 'respect limits to environmental resources' is no longer acceptable. Such a doctrine applies to all countries, not just to the poorer nations in the Third World:

> . . . we are talking here not just of the economic development of developing countries but of all development—of human progress, if you like. It is 'development' in its broadest sense; and the requirement that it be 'sustainable' is an injunction to all countries and all people. The ability of future generations to meet their own needs can be compromised as much by the excesses of industrial and technological development as by the environmental degradation of under-development.

Indeed, it is urged, this new insight should strike home first in the West:

> responsibility for global environmental management must rest with developed countries since, in general, the industrialized countries have higher levels of resource use *per capita*, fewer unmet needs and a greater capacity to deploy resource-saving and new anti-pollutant technologies . . . 'sustainable development' is . . . not . . . a new approach to development in developing countries but about sustainability at a global level.

The ideas contained in this new vision of sustainable Development are spreading gradually throughout the world. Combined with other pressures for change, they are helping the West to see, slowly, too slowly, that it too has Developmental needs and must therefore adopt Developmental approaches to meet those needs.[5]

What we are seeing is the beginning of a new approach to Development, 'alternative Development'. Views from the old dogmas persist; some Western politicians can still repeat that 'what is part of our lives today are the ambitions of the Third World tomorrow', but others have come to see that 'the criteria of progress are changing'. Development is coming to mean not so much adjustment to an industrial way of life (which some Third World countries have in fact made relatively easily, using both old and new technologies) but a question of resource management. It is to the world as a whole that we need to turn to find the solutions to the world's problems, not just to the West.[6]

REACTIONS TO CRISIS: EDUCATION AND THE ECONOMY

In the search for answers, some people came to see education—especially adult education, free from what were regarded as the irrelevancies and corrupting influences of the formal schooling and university systems—as one vehicle for helping to address these problems. Not only can education help societies to adapt to a 'critical present and an uncertain future', to 'train people to tolerate uncertainty'; it can also directly help with the solution of non-educational problems, including social transformation. Universities, for instance, can 'serve the nation's needs'; they have a Developmental role in view of current levels of unemployment, violence, social conflict and economic decline. And governments in some cases have directly asked the educational agencies to assist in relation to these problems.[7]

The aspect of Development for which education is seen to be of direct relevance is economic revival. Since knowledge is taken to be the basis of economic growth, in an age of new technology, education is 'an engine fuelling the economy'. Universities and colleges exist to promote human resource development, especially in relation to the community which stands around them; they are increasingly being called upon to make their teaching and the fruits of their research available to others. Formal education is 'given the central role of providing the skilled labour power by which technology [can] be translated into greater material wealth'; and if schooling failed to develop human talent adequately, then continuing or adult education must do this: in Spain, 'vocational training, technical innovation and adaptation to new needs in production among groups most disadvantaged by the changes in industry' [received most attention]; 'adult education was placed low on the list of priorities'. 'It is likely that in the future all adult education will be geared more to vocational needs' [Scotland].[8]

A third strand (economic growth) then was added to the two (personal development and social change) which have already been identified as central to the role of education in the West. The strand is not of course new; the need for vocational training had been heard in the nineteenth century and persisted throughout the succeeding years. But it now received new emphasis alongside the other two. Sometimes all three were combined together: the OECD asserted that adult education was 'designed to fulfil three general tasks, to improve competencies, to promote self-fulfilment and better inter-relationship within society, and to enhance social action', and it saw Recurrent Education as a strategy to 'create better opportunities for individual development *and* greater educational and social equality *and* play a role in generating economic growth' [original italics]. More frequently, economic growth was combined with personal development: in the UK, for example, the Department of Education and Science considered 'higher education valuable for its contribution to the personal development of those who pursue it, at the same time valuing its continued expansion as an investment in the nation's human talent', while the Universities Grants Committee saw 'higher education attempting to meet both the needs of the economy for highly skilled manpower and the aspiration of individuals for an educational experience which will provide for personal development'.[9]

The role of adult education in Development in the West

Education then was seen to have a role to play in settling some at least of the Development issues which faced Western governments from the early 1970s. But when it came to Adult Education, government attitudes were more ambivalent. On the one hand, traditional adult education was seen to be ineffective, irrelevant to such social and economic needs and therefore marginal. So new instruments were devised in many countries. In the UK, the Manpower Services Commission, established in 1974, declared itself to be 'in the business of opening up an alternative education and training system alongside the existing [adult education] system', because 'the latter is not attractive to customers'. On the other hand, in countries like Germany and Finland, 'government looked to Adult Education to provide programmes that can demonstrably contribute to its short and long-term social, economic, political and cultural objectives', as well as maintaining its traditional role. The role of adult education was reviewed: commissions were appointed in Ireland, England and Wales, Scotland, Finland and the Netherlands, and many special sector committees were set up; a number of countries legislated for adult education (sometimes for the first time)—France 1971, Denmark 1975, Norway 1976, the USA 1976, etc.[10]

The aspect which governments called upon adult education agencies to assist with most was unemployment. Adult education was seen as a major tool to retrain the unemployed or keep them quiescent: 'when the new jobless move on to different work or remain unemployed, the responsibility for them is almost always left to the educational system' (Finland); 'it is essential that basic education should be available to counter the loss of personal dignity, the waste of human resource and the vulnerability to political extremism that hopeless unemployment can bring', wrote the UK's ACACE with uncharacteristic prejudice; while in Norway, adult education was seen to exist as much 'for the sake of stimulating the economy and adapting the workforce to the changing employment market . . . as a way of providing as many as possible with a chance for self-development and self-fulfilment on their own terms'.[11] But there were other approaches: in Germany, when the Ministry of Health or other government body wanted local-level agencies to participate in some social programme, for example an anti-smoking campaign, they funded them through the German Adult Education Association.

But in many cases, this call fell on deaf ears. Most adult educators failed to respond or resisted the re-orientation required. The offering of learning opportunities to some 10 per cent of the adult population who were already motivated for self-actualization continued; indeed, this is still the fundamental objective of most of the programmes of adult education offered in the West today. Although many agencies have stressed that the two basic needs of today's world, to secure an equilibrium between the world's human population and its natural resources, and to secure a just and peaceful harmony between peoples, are so urgent that adult educators should no longer ignore the 60–75 per cent of adults who even in educated Western democracies have participated in no form of planned continued learning since they ended their initial education, such pleas still remain unheeded as far as the majority of adult education providers in the West are concerned or have become the subject of rhetoric, not practice.

University Adult Education in the UK and change

University Extra-Mural (or Adult Education) Departments (EMDs) in the United Kingdom provide one example of this more general refusal to listen. Over the last ten to fifteen years, these departments have come under increasing pressure from three main sources. First, central government has called for some say in what is done, asserting that as publicly funded servants, the universities should engage in publicly demanded tasks. Secondly, pressure for Continuing Education (seen mainly as professional development courses, vocationally oriented) has arisen both within and without the university. And thirdly, there has been a growing sense of unease amongst some departmental staff at what they see as the apparent irrelevance of the programmes being offered—that they are not contributing significantly to the real advancement of the region in which they stand.

But despite these pressures, many university EMDs were slow to adapt to the changes demanded of them by the rest of the university and government alike. Many have taken their stand on the defence of the liberal tradition. They have failed to identify clearly what is essential in their ethos and what are their greatest strengths: first, the successful approach to access to higher and advanced learning which they can offer to those who have traditionally been excluded from it; secondly, their insistence that education means the education of the whole person, not just narrow vocational training; indeed, that vocational training in knowledge and skills is most effective when combined with wider education in understanding and attitudes and personal growth; and thirdly, the belief that the teaching of adults calls for special expertise and approaches and therefore for some full-time specialist staff—and to insist upon taking these with them into the new world they are urged to enter. With these in their armoury, EMDs can enter these new fields and yet retain their distinctive contribution to education as a whole.[12]

It may be argued that the record of EMDs in access to higher education is not remarkable; that they compartmentalize as much as any other university department; and that they are themselves not always very good at teaching adults. They have not yet been able to persuade their university colleagues, let alone their governmental masters, that they are doing a good job in any of these respects. But there is much experience and conceptual understanding (if not practice) in these departments, and the pressures for change are irresistible. And a number of these departments, while attempting to preserve some or all of the ground won over so many years, are now beginning to change rather than cling to traditional forms without substance for the sake of their cherished beliefs. Higher education as a whole needs the values which adult educators bring with them.

The same is true of other parts of the adult education spectrum in the West. The world has changed, and adult education is faced with a challenge: either to change with it, preserving and utilizing the essential characteristics of adult learning in the service of new needs; or resist the change, insisting on older individualistic models and thus remaining marginalized, effective with the few rather than the many. There is a good deal of awareness of the fact of change. 'Adult education in Finland is at the moment in a phase of great change and development'; 'provision for adult learners in England and Wales is undergoing rapid structural change at present', are only two of many remarks in national reports. Most countries can speak of 'the last decade's upheavals'.

Some adult educators have realized the need for new approaches: 'developing adult education quantitatively and especially qualitatively is such a huge task that it is no longer sufficient to organise it in traditional ways', as Finland reported. New philosophies and structures are needed because the problems which adult education now addresses are no longer specifically educational.

Faced with unemployment, changes in industry, the introduction of new technologies and regional development, training seemed to the political powers that be [in France] one of the

means of coping with these social problems . . . education is no longer the central figure
. . . original educational answers have to be found as traditional 'courses' rarely provide a
relevant answer . . . non-pedagogic criteria for evaluation, particularly economic, will
serve to measure the effectiveness of the training initiative; . . . the division between general
education and vocational education . . . should be replaced by an integrated concept of
these two ideas.[13]

But reactions have not always been as forward-looking as these remarks suggest.
Although there are increasing signs of a willingness to respond positively, a majority of
adult educators have chosen to resist the pressure for change; and the result for them has
been and will continue to be marginalization, financial cuts and increased competition
from other bodies.

Two examples may be provided.

Local authority provision: a rural example

The published programmes of 803 courses offered in 1988–89 to the population of a
large section of the rural county of Norfolk, UK, by the Local Education Authority
(excluding the WEA and the University of Cambridge) reveal the nature of existing
provision (Table 5.1). Few of these programmes may be termed Developmental apart
from the health programmes. None of the crafts was intended as income-generating
activities, though some of them may have been used for this purpose. Only one 'social
roles' course was provided, for parish councillors. The language courses were mostly
non-certificated though some could lead to an examination. Second chance courses in
mathematics and English were provided only on a small scale. Employment skills
included typing, with some shorthand and computer courses, most of them intended for
home rather than business use: only seven courses were offered for small businesses. The
small (less than 20 courses in all) multiple category of 'personal and social skills'
included personal beauty, creative writing, assertiveness, communication skills, personal development through groups, mathematics for worried parents, caring for the
elderly, parents and children, playgroups, and sign language for the deaf.

In answer to the charge that the people of this rural English county are not being
offered much that will lead to the social, economic or political development of that

Table 5.1   *The range of adult education courses offered by Norfolk LEA 1988–89*

Arts and crafts 30%	Painting and drawing 4%; flower arranging 4%; dressmaking, etc. 5%; drama 5 courses; music (all forms) 15 courses
Cooking 19%	Including cake icing 8%
Health 18%	Including keep fit 6%; sports 10% (mainly swimming and badminton); health diets 6 courses
Employment skills 8%	
Academic courses 8%	Mainly languages 6%
Other outdoor activities 5%	
Second chance 6%	Including basic skills, school leaving certificates
Other indoor activities 3%	Mostly bridge; do-it-yourself and decoration 6 courses
Personal and social skills 3%	

region, except in health, the agencies may well respond that they see the provision of learning opportunities for Developmental tasks as the responsibility of other bodies such as the Manpower Services Commission (now the Training Authority), the Agricultural Training Board, the Rural Community Council and even the Women's Institute. Adult education agencies in Norfolk set themselves a strictly limited task—to meet the leisure-time requirements of a small section of the adult population of that county. Even those programmes which could be said to be contributing to the cultural development of Norfolk—for which adult education would claim to have special concern—are directed mainly towards individual self-gratification. There is no sign that Norfolk is part of a multicultural society (only one English as a Second Language course). One course exemplifies this attitude of non-involvement: domestic poultry keeping ('Discover the joys of keeping hens at home hygienically and economically') in a county noted for its poultry. We must not of course underestimate the ability of adult learners to take from these courses what they want—to use 'Making the most of your knitting machine' for income-generating activities, for example; but there is apparently no *policy* to promote income-generating activities in a region which despite its wealth has substantial pockets of poverty.

For adult education agencies in Norfolk base their programmes on those subjects which experience has shown the learners will come to; they 'seek to do no more than satisfy articulated demand', as the OECD put it. The agencies plan with a particular target population in mind; they have apparently ignored or overlooked other target groups within the region. They either have not surveyed the needs of the region as a whole or have decided to leave the meeting of those needs to others. Even when the programmes of the University of Cambridge Extra-Mural Board and the local WEA are added, there are few signs that adult education is 'exploring the reality [of Norfolk] critically' which its defenders claim to be adult education's ultimate justification. Where, for instance, are courses for the large and small farmers in this rural region; for the many local councillors or school managers; for the small business community or professional groups, shopkeepers, parents of young children in a rural environment, the unemployed (the experimental Hunstanton Local Development Project which ran for one year 1986–87 under the auspices of REPLAN pointed the way to possibilities in this area), or young persons starting in their chosen career? Where are there any courses on what it means to live in a rural area in the 1980s and 1990s—in Europe, for example? Adult education is still—as judged by this and many other examples—concentrating on its traditional clientele, the leisured and relatively well educated and on the whole wealthy seeking activities to fill their spare time. If these adult education programmes were closed down tomorrow, the impact on the Development of the Norfolk region would hardly be noticed. There is nothing here which will lead to any understanding of, let alone change in, Norfolk society.[14]

Local authority provision: an urban example

Much the same can be said of Adult Education Institutes in urban areas, although there are significant differences especially in programmes relating to minority communities and local associations, to which some urban adult education centres are more responsive than most rural agencies. An example from London (Wandsworth and Putney 1988–89) indicates this. The published programme of 813 courses[15] is summarized in Table 5.2. Out of a total of 813 courses, a third (272 courses) were in the appreciation and practice of art and crafts (of which drawing and painting and courses relating to clothing were the largest categories). Other creative arts—writing, music and drama—were represented in another 8 per cent (66 courses, of which dance accounted for 24). Health programmes, including keep fit, diet, first aid and yoga, accounted for 70 courses (8 per cent).

Table 5.2 *The range of adult education courses in Wandsworth and Putney 1988–89*

Arts and crafts 42%	Including dressmaking 8%; drawing and painting 8%; dance 3%
Academic courses 10%	Including European languages 7.5%
Health 8%	
Second chance 8%	
Personal and social skills 8%	
Sports 6%	Mainly swimming
Other indoor activities 5%	
Employment skills 5%	Including home computing 3%
Other outdoor activities 3%	
Cooking 3%	

Programmes designed to help with vocational concerns (small businesses, computing —though most of the 26 courses in this category were for home users—and typing) were only 39; languages courses totalled 64 and were mostly European (French 27, Spanish 12, German 10, Italian 8). Academic-type interests—history, sociology, politics, philosophy and religion, film, literature, the environment and Third World issues—numbered 32 courses, some of them in association with London University. Programmes aimed at special groups were varied more than numerous: 4 per cent were specifically for women (assertiveness, self-defence, massage, etc.), though other programmes (e.g. keep fit) were listed as being directed at women. Mother, parent and family education received special attention in 20 courses. There were 68 basic education and English language courses at various levels. Training for workers in the community (playleaders, etc.) was provided in five courses.

Certain comments are needed on this list. First, (as with Norfolk) these courses are of different lengths, from very short to much longer. Some are for certificated programmes, some not. A number are for untutored groups (club classes) meeting to practise their activities. So that not all are of equal educational significance. Secondly, a particular feature of this programme is the imaginative way in which categories are combined, so that there may be some repetitions in the analysis above. Thirdly, the analysis is based on the advertised courses alone: various community groups hold meetings (many of which are concerned with social and political matters) in this Adult Education Institute.

Nevertheless, the conclusions are much the same. Allowing for the fact that there are other agencies engaged in the Development of this part of London, formal Adult Education (and this includes the WEA and the University Extra-Mural provision) concentrates its resources on the cultural and non-vocational interests and concerns of the neighbourhood. It offers more than Norfolk but still relatively little towards the economic, social and political Development of the area in which it stands.

The liberal backlash

Indeed there is a backlash in favour of a non-vocational concept of adult education. The 'high calling' of Tawney and the strong words of the 1919 Report have been reasserted:

education (as the Russell Report in 1973 put it) is 'not for economic purposes alone'. 'State-sponsored economicism . . . the kind of education blessed by government' is rejected on various grounds—not least the fact that the direct link between education and economic growth is not proven, and that educational provision of itself does nothing to generate jobs—in favour of one or both forms of liberal education, personal growth and/or social change: 'those forms of study which are undertaken for the love of God and for the development of the personality' on the one hand, or learning opportunities which become 'a means of liberating the working classes from the bondage of capitalism's culture' on the other.[16]

Liberal adult education today has widened its brief. It has gathered to itself much of what it formerly despised, namely social purpose, partly because it sees itself as equally threatened by the vocationalism of Continuing Education, partly because the new programmes of education for the unemployed are stimulating an interest in wider approaches to social education. Borrowing concepts and language heavily from its equally beleaguered partner, social change adult education, it claims for itself a monopoly of educational virtues, and to speak for all true educators. The advantages of 'liberal adult education' (however defined, for the term is used loosely to cover many different forms of education to suit the purposes of those who employ it) have been frequently rehearsed in sharp contradistinction to the drawbacks of continuing education/vocational training (Table 5.3).

Table 5.3 *A summary of contrasting phraseology used to describe liberal adult education and continuing education/vocational training in the recent literature*

Liberal adult education	Continuing Education/Vocational Training
Critical and liberating	Limited and externally controlled
Deals with ends and means	Deals with means only
Deals with broad issues	Deals with immediate problems only
Aims to produce thinking critical citizens	Aims to produce efficient conventional technicians, producers of profit
Open-ended; arguments for and against	Utilitarianism
'Really useful knowledge' calculated to make one free	'Merely useful knowledge' which limits, controls and anaesthetizes
Means of personal development	Servant of specific conceptions of economics
Stimulus to enable students to choose own paths	Helps students to adapt to prescribed social change
To help students to understand and perhaps to change society	Tool of manipulative technicians of a fixed social order
Liberating	Not liberating
Creates awareness of issues of individual change	Training for political control and economic reproduction
Addresses issues	Addresses techniques and skills
Internally determined goals	Externally set purposes
Aimed primarily or even exclusively at facilitating the development of the person as a whole and in accordance with his or her own background and wishes or at giving people increased confidence in themselves and their abilities	Aimed at good marks, the development of computer technology and computer science, the fight against inflation and an effort to make products more competitive on world markets . . . it gives a quick clearly identifiable return on the investment in an occupational and career context

Note: this list has been compiled from recent European and North American writings in which liberal adult education has been contrasted with Continuing Education or vocational training; the weighted language is that of the originals, not mine; the aim is to demonstrate the negative approach to Continuing Education which currently exists among many adult educators. It can be extended with many other examples.

Liberal adult education has always been, and still to some degree is, considered to be in competition with adult vocational training; thus there is a certain amount of tension between liberal adult education and adult vocational training with the result that . . . it is not always possible to establish co-operation:

so writes a leading adult educator from Finland. In Scotland, 'liberal adult education has been threatened; the attitude of the [government] is that adult education should be vocationally oriented and entrepreneurial'.[17]

Clearly much of this is partial. For one thing, the picture drawn of continuing and vocational education is inaccurate and unsustainable; and even if it were to contain the 'errors' listed, it is surely not impossible for those who believe otherwise to redeem Continuing Education from these faults.

But equally seriously, the claims made for liberal adult education are excessive and unrealistic. Liberal adult education, it is alleged, is 'flexible, responsive . . . closer to the market place, relevant to the majority of the community'; 'it is a means of increasing social equality', 'able to voice the educational requirement of local communities', to provide 'an education which helps citizens to understand, control and change their lives'. Such goals are praiseworthy: they are exactly the same goals as Development agencies set before themselves. But there are few signs that adult education in the West in fact achieves any of these aims.

Indeed, these and the other claims which liberal adult education makes for itself are not just unproven: they are in many cases patently untrue. It clearly is not 'open to all', however much this is urged to be the case. Its assertion that its 'democratic dialogue, rigorous pursuit and critical probing' help to make people more critical cannot be seen to be correct, for no evaluatory tests which can assess the validity of these claims have been devised and utilized. Many practitioners realize the falseness of such claims, though where it fails, they protest the *potential* of liberal adult education to achieve these goals.[18]

So that it is all the more serious to note that such claims suffer from a logic gap. How can it be urged that liberal (non-vocational) adult education 'facilitates the development of the person as a whole', 'developing the total personality of their students', when it ignores all that part of an adult's life which is devoted to earning a living? The advocates of liberal adult education admonish vocational training for 'attempting merely to develop people into narrow half-humans who can only adapt themselves to the demands of work'; but by omitting any form of vocational enhancement, liberal adult education is itself 'dividing up the person', is itself helping to 'develop people into . . . half-humans'.[19]

NEW APPROACHES

Such criticisms of liberal adult education are not often articulated. Nevertheless, some are aware of them. And thus while a number of committed adult educators, deeply concerned, 'cling courageously to the old faith, . . . continue to meet on the margins of a decaying educational system to practise the ancient rituals of reading, discussing and exploring the links between experience, knowledge and the social order', others have turned away from what they see as such a 'bland and neutral liberal approach' to 'something more committed'. For them, 'intellectual satisfactions alone', 'academic parlour games', are not enough. There are some exceptions to the rejection of the demands which national bodies are now making in the West that adult education should help in the task of social and economic renewal.[20]

A number of adult educators then are seeking purpose in their work beyond the self-gratification of the individual adult learner in a series of responses which are now more varied and complex. Some have found it in a positive, even enthusiastic, response to the emergence of Continuing Education, whether it comes at the instance of government, of commercial and industrial interests or of the professionals themselves. Some have looked for it in political involvement, in action groups. Some are trying hard to persuade new groups to come in, identifying new audiences, experimenting with new formats, taking education and training to the people (for example, 'tutors-in-residence' schemes).

Socially purposive adult education

Others have found such purpose in reinterpreting their liberal adult education to give it a social purpose. Thus, for example, local history courses are for some tutors and providers no longer seen simply as a self-fulfilling hobby like stamp collecting for a small number of activists, but as part of a process of strengthening social identity and local pride, rebuilding local communities as concerned entities, and as such they are of value to *all* members of those local communities, not just to a few. History itself is seen 'as a collaborative process of reconstructing the past in which non-professionals must play a crucial part'. Genealogy has similarly become family history, a search for roots and understanding; natural history has become natural resource development and conservation; literature has become creative writing as well as a search for understanding human relationships. Adult basic education is now seen not just as the development of individual competencies but as a means 'to put the people in the way of perceiving social ills more clearly'. These adult educators have followed the same path as those 'concerned scientists who have crossed disciplinary boundaries and have integrated their specialist knowledge within a broader morally oriented framework'; their programmes are infused with a social sense of purpose. In these ways, they have sought to demarginalize themselves and their field of activity—and at the same time to increase participation in their programmes.[21]

Social action

Liberal adult education thus sometimes talks like social change adult education. Nevertheless, the congruity between the two is not a happy one. For although 'collective goals can be deduced from theoretical reasonings by educationists', at root the social change strand has always been hesitant about the individualism which lies at the heart of most adult education (even socially purposive adult education) in the West. Pioneers like Raymond Williams in the UK and Coady and Horton in North America and their successors identified individualism with middle-class competitive culture in opposition to what they saw as the more co-operative working-class and community cultures. They decried efforts which were oriented to changing individuals rather than the real causes of their problems—economic and social structures and unequal power relationships. The basic approaches of these two strands of adult education are opposed to each other over the central issue of individualism. And these voices, which had been few and marginalized within adult education itself, have now been strengthened. After 1968, there was a new age of questioning, and the failure of adult education to bring about the desired and necessary social restructuring was attributed to the narrow and exclusively educational goals which liberal adult education set for itself; what was needed was social action.[22]

But such voices, although growing in number and confidence, are still relatively few in Western adult education. The main thrust remains to give to those individuals who want it their rightful educational opportunity; the rest can be ignored. Most of the newer forms of 'social change adult education' are equally based on individualism. Some even regard the social change strand as the main guardian of individualism. For although many writers have argued that liberal adult education is essentially based on individualism, it has been suggested by others that liberal adult education might even reduce personal growth; only socially committed adult education directed at social change can develop true individualism.[23]

> Education—of adults as well as young people—is to help to make everyone aware of the realities and problems of the community and to permit the free development of personality and thus the acquisition of a sense of individual identity, collective identity and responsibility and to permit the exploitation of local skills and the ongoing learning of new skills, which implies the endowment of each individual with maximum capacity for adaptation and innovation.[24]

The central goal, then, has been only slightly redefined: 'to enable adults to obtain better insight into their personal and societal situation and to foster within them the skills to act upon that situation'. The focus remains the same, the needs of the individual learner in society. And this is taken to imply a rejection of state-set goals; the essentially non-governmental role of adult education is reiterated in many countries in the West.

Nevertheless, the calls of the state for help with Developmental issues will not go away: nor can they be ignored. Roger Boshier has put the problem clearly into perspective when he suggests that instead of continuing to provide programmes which have a high utility for the individual but low utility for the state ('where the starting point and long-term goal . . . concerns the need and desire to facilitate the self-actualization of individual learners' as opposed to societal-centred adult education 'conducted because education can be instrumental in ameliorating or changing some social condition or problem' such as the need of some local inhabitants to use a new water supply or of a whole nation to save power or to cope with an outbreak of disease such as AIDS) (Figure 5.1), the time has come to seek programmes which have a high utility for both the individual and for society.[25] This is the challenge which faces adult education in the West today arising from new perceptions of developmental needs and new demands from governments for help with new tasks.

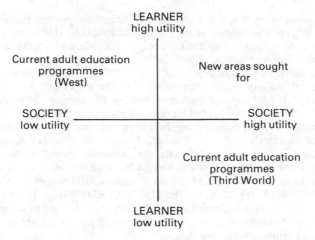

Figure 5.1 Matrix illustrating the range of utility for learner and society of adult education programmes

NOTES TO CHAPTER 5

(1) Fauré, E. (1972) *Learning To Be: the World of Education Today and Tomorrow*, Paris: UNESCO: it is noteworthy that this report relatively rarely appears in bibliographies of adult education in the West and is even more rarely cited.

(2) Jackson, B.W. (1966) *Spaceship Earth*, New York; Jackson, B.W. and Dubos, R. (1972) *Only One Earth: the Care and Maintenance of a Small Planet*, New York; Ackhoff, R.L. (1974) *Redesigning the Future*, New York. UNESCO Declaration reprinted in Rogers, A. (1984). See Lowe (1975). The 150 Hours Movement in Italy is, however, one example of an educational movement which grew out of the student unrest and industrial action in 1969: see Yarnit (1980b).

(3) Dumont, R. (1973) *Utopia or else . . .*, New York; Brown, L.R. (1978) *The Twenty-ninth Day: Accommodating Human Needs and Numbers to the Earth's Resources*, New York; Laszlo, E. *et al.* (1977) *Goals for Mankind: a Report to the Club of Rome on the New Horizons of Global Community*, Dutton; Peccei, A. (1977) *The Human Quality*, Pergamon.

(4) For illiteracy in the West, see for example Velis, J.-P. (1979) *La France illettrée*, Editions du Seuil; St John Hunter, C. (1979) *Adult Illiteracy in the USA*, New York; *Illiteracy in Industrialized Countries: Situation and Action* (special edition of *Prospects* 17(2), UNESCO, 1987); *Literacy in the Industrialized Countries: a Focus on Practice* (special edition of *Convergence* 20(3–4), 1987). For an itinerant programme in Denmark, see Council of Europe (1984), p. 20.

(5) See Brundtland (1987); quotations come from speech of Shri Sonny Ramphal to Royal Society of Arts, UK, printed in *RSA Journal* 135 (November 1987), 882–3.

(6) The speeches were those of Mrs Thatcher and Mr Gorbachev, repeated in a BBC broadcast, *The Greatest Challenge*, November 1988; I am grateful to the BBC and the producer for permission to quote from this broadcast.

(7) Arocena (1986), p. 2; *AEF* 25(3) (1988), 4; King, E.J. (1976) *Education for Uncertainty*, London: King's College. Denmark (like other countries) reports 'a governmental invitation to do experimental work', Kandrup (1988); in Spain, 'political priorities were focused on . . . vocational training, technological innovation and adaptation to the new needs in production among groups most disadvantaged by the changes in industry': Luna (1988), p. 2.

(8) Gerver (1988), p. 1; *AEF* 25(3) (1988), 4; McIlroy and Spencer (1988), p. 35; Luna (1988), p. 1; Keir, C. (1963) *The Uses of the University*, New York: 'the basic reality is the

widespread recognition that new knowledge is the most important factor in economic and social growth'; see also Halsey *et al.* (1961); Edwards, E. (1982) *Higher Education for Everyone*, London: Spokesman Books. See quotations from DES (1972) and UGC (1984) cited in note 9 below. See also DES (1980), p. 1: the central purpose of university continuing education is 'to promote growth'; DES (1985), p. 1: 'Higher education must contribute more effectively to the improvement of the economy'. Many universities have followed this line: McIlroy and Spencer (1988), p. 16, quote a University of Manchester paper of 1986: 'it is the social duty of higher education to commit part of its resources to . . . [the development of a] high technology base in the regional economy [and] a highly trained labour force constantly updated'. Tapper, T. and Salter, B. (1978) *Education and the Political Order*, Macmillan, p. 149, cite the prevailing view that 'education is fundamentally an economic resource which should be employed in a way which maximises its contribution to the development of Britain as an industrial nation'.

(9)   OECD (1973); OECD (1975), p. 8; DES (1972); UGC (1984), p. 1: see UGC (1984), p. 2: 'although our case for the development of continuing education is largely founded on considerations of employment and economic prosperity, we do not overlook the importance of social, cultural and other factors'.

(10)   OECD (1975), p. 8; see EBAE (1988) *passim*; Peterson, R. E. *et al.* (eds) (1980) *Lifelong Learning in America*, Jossey Bass.

(11)   *AEF* 25(3) (1988), 3; ACACE (1979); Kandrup (1988).

(12)   McIlroy and Spencer (1988), p. 156, illustrates this complacency but does not use the term itself. For universities and AE, see Ashmore, O. (1982) University adult education, in Costello and Richardson (1982); Ellwood, C. (1976) *Adult Learning Today: a New Role for the Universities*, Sage; Groombridge, B., Rogers, A. *et al.* (1991) *Universities and Continuing Education: into the 1990s*, New University of Ulster; Jennings, B. (1981) Can universities meet the challenge of Continuing Education? in Sockett (1981); Draper, J. (1986) Universities and non-formal adult education, *Convergence* 19(3).

(13)   EBAE (1988) France 3 pp. 1–2; EBAE (1988) England and Wales, p. 1; Green (1977), p. 41; *AEF* 24(2) (1987), 2; *AEF* 25(3) (1988), 6; *AE* 61(2) (1988), 98; *AE* 61(3) (1989), 227.

(14)   Norfolk County (UK) published AE programmes 1988–89; REPLAN (1987) *Rural Needs Bulletin* 1, 2–3.

(15)   Published programmes of Putney and Wandsworth AE Institute, London, 1988–89.

(16)   McIlroy and Spencer (1988) *passim* is the most recent example of this 'backlash', and it summarizes many recent writings in this topic.

(17)   EBAE (1988), Finland; *AEF* 25(2) (1988), 3; Gerver (1988), p. 1; see also EBAE (1988) France 3, which distinguishes between general education and vocational training; EBAE (1988), Norway; Rogers, A. (1983) Research and development in adult education, in Wallis, J. V. (ed.), *Papers from Scutrea 13th Annual Conference*, Nottingham University, pp. 1–15.

(18)   Raybould, S. (1951) *The English University and Adult Education*, WEA; McIlroy and Spencer (1988), pp. 51, 88–9, 103–4, 111, 114, 154; 1909 Report, p. 83; Kandrup (1988), p. 1; ACACE (1979). Other examples can be cited: e.g. AE is 'the motor force behind progressive social awareness and responsibility': OECD (1975), p. 8, etc.

(19)   *AEF* 24(2) (1987), 31.

(20)   *AE* 61(3) (1989), 227; Ryan (1971); Clyne (1972); Thompson (1980), pp. 13–14: 'the problem with most liberal adult education since the Second World War is that it has concentrated on satisfying intellectual need alone . . . it has been too far removed from the processes by which ordinary men and women can meet their collective economic and social needs'.

(21)   ACACE (1979); Thompson, P. (1978), p. 11. See Yarnit (1980a), pp. 185–7; Rogers, A. (1977); Rogers, A. (1966) The teaching of local history in adult education, *Bulletin of Local History, East Midlands Region* 1, 3–9, University of Nottingham; Rogers, A. (1977) Communities past and present, *Architecture East Midlands* 70, 29–31; Leirman (1987).

(22)   See Thompson (1980), pp. 11, 20–21, for example. 'I do not think we shall succeed in developing adult education unless we make it more social'; Livingstone, R. W. (1941) *The Future in Education*, Cambridge: Cambridge University Press, p. 52. See Lawton, D.

(1973) *Social Change, Educational Theory and Curriculum Planning*, University of London; Paterson, R.W.K. (1973) Social change as an educational aim, *AE* **45**, 353–9; Lovett, T. (ed.) (1988) *Radical Approaches to Adult Education: a Reader*, Croom Helm; Laidlaw, A.F. (1961) *The Campus and the Community: the Global Impact of the Antigonish Movement*, Montreal; Lotz, J. (1973) The Antigonish movement: a critical analysis, *Studies in Adult Education* **5**(2), 97–112; Crane, J.M. (1983) The Antigonish movement: an historical sketch, *IJLE* **2**(2), 151–62; Adams, F. and Horton, M. (1975) *Unearthing Seeds of Fire: the Idea of Highlander*, N Carolina. Lindeman (1938), reprinted in Brookfield (1988), p. 95, put this point in characteristic biting form: 'Adult education, wherever it has become a live issue and wherever it has succeeded in something more than a quantitative sense, has been thought of and pursued as an instrument for social change and not merely as a means for increasing the efficiency or the smartness of a few selected individuals.'

(23) See Keddie (1980), p. 54: 'individualism tends to produce uniformity rather than diversity'; King, R. (1978) *All Things Bright and Beautiful*, cited in Keddie (1980); Paterson (1979).

(24) Council of Europe (1986b), p. 9.

(25) Boshier, R. (1979) Adult education issues in the future, in Burch, W.R. *Readings in Ecology, Energy and Human Society: Contemporary Perspectives*, New York, p. 180.

Chapter 6

Government, Development and Adult Education: Ways Forward

In view of the reactions of most adult education agencies, it is no matter for surprise that many Western governments, as they became aware of pressing social issues, rejected traditional adult education as the vehicle for their newly discovered national Development goals. For their need was not how to provide purposeful and planned learning opportunities for a few seekers after truth and freedom, but how to provoke and equip all members of society to play their part in solving the problems which faced them. Every adult, not just the few, needed to learn essential life skills to live in this modern world; and governments could no longer wait until the sleepers awoke, until the people demanded learning opportunities for themselves.

CAMPAIGNS AND TRAINING

It was not that governments were blind to the fact that what they needed were *educational* programmes for Developmental purposes. Launching a campaign against heart disease in the UK, the Minister for Health recently said that 'government is not contemplating any legislation . . . we prefer to follow the line of education and more information for the people'; and the metrication programme in the 1970s was seen as a major educational programme for all adults. The education of adults is recognized as the main route to Development.

But in meeting these needs, governments, aid agencies and voluntary bodies very rarely turned to Adult Education for assistance. Health matters like smoking, alcoholism, drugs, heart disease and most recently AIDS (with one or two notable exceptions) have been treated as mass campaigns, ignoring adult education agencies. Large-scale training programmes for the nation's manpower needs in the light of new technologies and new industrial structures have been entrusted to bodies specially created and not tainted by motivational elitism. That some of these programmes have not been a success is no cause for rejoicing; to a large extent it highlights the failure of the adult education agencies to play their part in meeting the nation's needs. And in other cases, they have been successful; for while it is only to be expected that governments will tend initially to treat these Development issues as bureaucratic or technical matters requiring regulation and narrow training inputs, nevertheless (to the chagrin of some adult educators) governments and their agents have often learned quickly that appropriate adult teaching–learning methods are necessary for the successful attainment of their objectives, the solution of Developmental problems.[1]

The same is true of the increasing number of para-statal bodies, independent non-governmental agencies and special interest groups which have come to press for Developmental goals and to adopt Developmental strategies to attain their ends. One example will suffice. The farming interests in the UK declared 1989 as British Food and Farming Year. Their objectives were clear, 'to increase awareness and understanding of farming and food issues in the public at large and to change patterns of behaviour in these fields'—goals which by any definition are educational in character. Those responsible 'developed a very successful primary and secondary level educational programme' and prepared a schools' teaching–learning pack and a teachers' handbook. They launched a programme with museums and other agencies; they built a model farm at one of the country's major tourist centres, arranged events with county local history societies and other bodies, and organized a fair in London in association with one of the major food retailing firms. They pressed the libraries, art galleries, the media, the Post Office into service; and they mounted their own touring exhibition. 'Through other means such as a best-selling cookery book, in-store promotions, etc., we are endeavouring to reach the housewife direct.' But those responsible for these initiatives had no contact with those who argue that they have the greatest amount of experience and expertise in helping adults to learn, i.e. the adult education agencies; and these agencies showed little interest in this campaign. It is arguable that some involvement of adult education would not only have helped to make the programme more effective but would also have ensured that the end result was increased choice on the part of the consumer rather than propaganda, and this would have been in the best interests of those whom adult educators claim they exist to serve.[2]

Developmental responses from adult education

Some adult educators have, however, seen and responded to these challenges; the climate in adult education in the West is beginning to change. Contact with Third World countries by individuals at grass-roots level and by organizations through international bodies and conferences has created a new interest in the connection between adult education and Development. Articles on this subject have appeared over the last few years in most countries in the West, and writers like R. H. Green and Ettore Gelpi have begun to explore the implications of this relationship.

These new insights are creating new local responses to government requests and pressures. Certain countries have gone further along these lines than others: as UNESCO noted, 'in some states there is a strong tradition of voluntary effort . . . and so . . . adult education stems from the work of non-state agencies. In others, adult education has become a means of propagating views having official approval.' Thus in Spain, efforts have been made 'to link up the programme of Adult Education to the process of . . . development of the community'; neighbourhood projects related to drugs and to prisons have been devised, while in Aragon a crafts training project has been launched through one of the People's Universities. Portugal has the Algarve project for participatory development; in France the Le Creusot programme used local history material as a basis for the development of new economic activities; and in Italy the Prato project aims 'to start a process which will lead to the reconversion, recomposition, quantitative and qualitative development of infrastructures and to educational and cultural intervention'. Other examples include some of the west coast programmes in Ireland, and the ambitious projects in Greece 'contributing to socio-economic and cultural development, especially in the most disadvantaged regions through integrated regional projects'. All these examples show how far some countries are mobilizing state and private adult education agencies towards the socio-economic, cultural and political Development of the region within which they stand, and equally how easily the language of Development sits with the language of adult education.[3]

In addition to responding to outside pressures, various sectoral programmes inside adult education are encouraging new attitudes. Programmes of education for the unemployed have prompted a more thorough exploration of social education. The women's movement has from the start been a missionary programme, seeking to share a new vision of the world and to create a new society through structural change and the promotion of a new *mentalité*, while at the same time being concerned to avoid 'invading the person' by imposing knowledge and thought patterns on others. Educational guidance services for adults reveal a similar tension—whether to be responsive to motivated individuals or proactive, reaching out to the unmotivated: this issue is brought to the surface regularly in the current debates on these services.

But these programmes have tended to remain separate entities, divorced from each other; they have not been integrated into a total concept of balanced Development. And they have left the mainstream of adult education largely untouched, being regarded as exceptions, as interesting and pioneering ventures. The need for environmental, and justice and/or peace education as part of adult education has on the whole remained in the realm of theoretical propositions, the fashionable themes of conferences and publications, slogans to be attached to existing programmes rather than the basis of a radical rethinking of the nature and purpose of adult education. Such propositions do not in practice seem to have had the power to become an awakening and redirectional force; certainly so far they have not made practical contributions to the construction and implementation of educational programmes for adults.[4]

COMMUNITY EDUCATION

Some have seen this integrating role being played by the concept of Community Education. Community education, embracing schooling as well as adult education, tends to mean many things to many people. At least four main strands may be detected:

1. community (especially parental) involvement in children's education, even the day-to-day running of schools (this was how the Plowden Report in the UK used the term);
2. the school as a unifying force for, not just a social institution in, the community (this was how John Dewey saw community education);
3. the use of the school to help reconstruct society (this was how Henry Morris saw his Village Colleges);

4. rather wider than the schools, a network of educational and social services: 'the aim of community education is community development. It is a social rather than an academic conception of education, one which is intended for all the people for their social life of work, leisure and citizenry' (this was how Eric Midwinter defined it).[5]

In relation to adult education, two main strands can be discerned. On the one hand, community education may be seen as wider than adult education, embracing the formal as well as the non-formal systems, seeking to mobilize all forms of education, especially the primary and secondary schools, into the service of the whole community: hence the village college and community school movement, mainly in the rural areas, seeking to link the local community to governmental resources. But rather later a more radical urban-based approach to community education emerged, more exclusively connected with adult education. This emphasized action by the local community, the opposition of community and government, the utilization of the resources which lie within the community itself rather than dependence on outside services. It was, and still is, more overtly political in nature. Some projects like the Sutton-in-Ashfield (Nottinghamshire) Community School sought to bring both of these strands closer together; but the majority of those who today adhere to the community education movement do not subscribe to the radical doctrines of the minority.

The less radical strand of community education draws a distinction between community education on the one hand and community work, community action and community development on the other hand. Community development (they argue) seeks to affect the course of social change in local communities by analysing social situations and by forming relationships with different groups and services to bring about desirable change. It is the aim of community development to involve the people in deciding, planning and playing an active part in the operation of those services which affect their daily lives. The democratization of community services and action by local citizens for the improvement of their own communities are the main purposes of community development. Community development programmes then serve as a bridge between people and services; they seek to encourage local communities to participate, and planners and providers of services to be more sensitive, more open to popular involvement.

Education is one such service. Community education serves as a bridge between the community and the providers of educational programmes. It aims to encourage the people to influence and to use the educational programmes which are provided for them, and at the same time it seeks to press these programmes into the service of the people. Community educators thus work with the providers of educational services, to open up provision at all levels (schools, colleges and adult education), to make it more relevant; and they work with the people, helping them to influence and eventually to come to control the educational services which operate in their local communities to achieve their own self-fulfilment needs. Community development and community education then (for these people) are similar but not the same thing: community education is one tool to lead towards community development.

The more radical wing of community education, however, does not draw a distinction between community development and action and community education. The advocates of this form of community education see the achievement of personal satisfactions as being brought about mainly by an increased awareness of belonging to a community. They view adult education as existing not primarily for the individual but for strengthening community identity and community bonds. Community education in this form attempts to use education (especially adult education) to support the local people in their efforts to play a positive role in issues which affect their daily lives. It seeks to do this through locally sited, integrated, issue-based programmes, breaking away from the more compartmentalized, subject-based provision of traditional adult education housed in dedicated educational institutions. Community education of this variety takes community issues for its subject, leading to community action.

There are of course variations within these two main strands. In the radical strand, for example, some see community education as being synonymous with working-class education. They adopt the view that the 'culture of silence' which is ignored by those who wield power in today's society needs to learn to speak, to value itself for what it is. Others, fearing the divisiveness of this, replace class consciousness with neighbourhood consciousness or interest-group consciousness (community education for the disadvantaged).

The two strands of community education live uneasily together. The difference lies in their attitude towards the formal system of education. Those who follow the line of community schools are not hostile to governmental resources and provision but seek to secure popular control over what are seen as community (not government) resources. Those who follow the more radical line are more hostile; they would wish to devise new approaches and new systems. The former hope to change and to press the existing system into the service of the local community; the latter wish to bring about structural change. For the former, the education provided is the important thing. For the latter, the main aim is not the educational process but the social change which education will bring—the adult educator is more than an educator, he/she is an activist.

Community education now enjoys increasing popularity in the West; but it has not come to hold that central position in adult education which will help forward the re-orientation required. For one thing, community education, like liberal adult education, is hostile to those forms of continuing education which are strongly vocational in nature; it cannot easily embrace continuing education within itself. Moreover, the anti-government stand of much community education, seeking new forms of educational organization, alternative routes to Development and alternative structures, prevents many of its adherents from wholeheartedly contributing to nationally set Developmental goals. Although its attachment to the formal education system of schools and colleges has helped to reduce the marginality of the less radical form of community education, nevertheless within the field of adult education, community education is itself marginal: community educators often see themselves to be out of the mainstream of adult education. With its strong interest in child education through the schools, community education does not always see the distinctiveness of adult learning—although the radical strand is more clear on this. But the radicals set themselves apart from the rest of adult education because of their ideology.[6]

DEVELOPMENT AS A NEW LOGIC FRAME

Community education, with its emphasis on community development, cannot itself provide, though it may point the way to, a new over-arching concept which can preserve the best in traditional adult education, make sense of the surviving strands of socially purposive adult education, harness the newer energies of continuing education, and help adult education respond to the new challenges which government and non-governmental agencies alike are throwing down.

That concept can be provided by Development—national and regional Development as well as local community Development. Development is increasingly a matter of concern in Western societies. Western governments have widened their agendas to include matters which formerly were the concern of adult education, and agencies are being created to offer programmes to the same people who are the concern of adult education, especially the deprived, the disadvantaged and the marginalized. Development is already congruous with the concerns of adult education, especially in its current emphasis on participation; and its concepts and practices are well understood, tested and proven to be relevant. A balanced programme of Development which embraces not just economic growth but also social development, cultural enrichment and wider political participation would seem to offer to adult education agencies some logic frame in which to set their concerns and programmes.

We need to be clear what we are talking about, because continuing education has increasingly adopted the language of Development for its own forms of programme. It talks in terms of relating to nationally set objectives, of promoting regional development and of being responsive to local needs, of being an assistant to government. But the concerns of continuing education are limited: when it speaks of regional development and local needs, it is concerned for *economic* development and the needs of local employers. The language of Development is used in continuing education solely in terms of economic growth and the economic and industrial needs of the nation. Even when continuing education speaks of 'social and economic' needs, it is clear that its primary focus is on economic growth, not social change. Continuing education confirms rather than challenges the existing status quo; it promotes technical, not social or cultural change. Despite the language which it often uses, continuing education cannot provide a fully balanced programme of Development education—social, economic, cultural and political—for the nation or for the region.[7]

The mission of adult education

If then community education cannot offer a full philosophy for all forms of education and training of adults because it omits the interests of professional groups and others who are not working-class or disadvantaged; and if continuing education cannot provide it because it is mono-centric, concentrating on economic growth and unable to embrace social, cultural and political change, we need to turn back to adult education to see whether it can cope better with such a fully integrated concept. Adult education, with its experience of and expertise in all forms of adult learning, is free to embrace within itself both continuing education and community education. It already has a wide base incorporating much cultural, some social and (in principle at least) political programmes—although traditionally it has left out most forms of economic growth programmes.

Adult education is today faced with the question of deciding what its mission is. So far it has tended to operate on short-term goals—to help individuals and groups to solve particular problems or to develop particular interests. And the agenda has tended to be set by the formal system of education—the universities, colleges and schools. Adult education has to a large extent not been free to set its own goals in relation to society at large; today there is an opportunity for it to define its own long-term goals.

The ambivalence within adult education

There is, however, some reluctance to face this issue squarely. This is understandable, for there is at the heart of present-day adult education an ambivalence, an uncertainty as to the way ahead.

Provision

On the one hand, adult education in the West has a concern with a range of provision, defined either in terms of subject areas or target groups. It is never quite sure exactly as to the nature of those subject areas or target groups, or where the limits between what is and what is not appropriate for an adult education body to provide lie, but there is some recognition that those limits do exist. The Northern Ireland Strategy Report made one attempt to define those limits by saying that courses which *exercised* rather than *developed* skills, knowledge and understanding further can hardly be called educational, so that the Badminton Club supported by the Adult Education Institute is not appropriate, whereas a beginners' class in badminton is. Others have explored other sorts of limits: non-vocational adult education, for example, or adult education for special groups (the unemployed, ethnic communities, etc.) or for different phases of adult life (mothers with young children, pre-retirement, etc.) or for social and political roles (planning committee members, members of school governing bodies, voluntary body leaders, etc.). Almost all adult educators are agreed that some subjects are best done by adult education and others best left to other agencies; they are aware that there are many other bodies engaged in providing programmes of education and training of adults, and that it is incumbent on adult education to establish its own distinctive niche. Adult education agencies then are responsible for the provision of some but not all forms of education and training of adults.[8]

Process

On the other hand, adult education has a concern for methodology, for developing understanding and good practice of the most effective teaching–learning approaches for adults as distinct from younger learners. And this concern extends to *all* education and training for adults, not just to the provision made by the adult education bodies themselves. There is perhaps rather more consensus on this question of process than on the question of content, though debate still persists.[9]

The choices

Some agencies have chosen to go along the path of process, engaging in academic study and offering training courses to other providers of education and training of adults. Others have chosen to pursue the path of provision, offering programmes to the general public or specific target groups, separate from the other providers. Still others have tried to combine both approaches, though often holding the two sectors in separate departments or divisions (an Adult Education 'Training' Division inside an Adult Education Institute, for example). There is some uncertainty as to which role will most help to diminish the marginality and irrelevance with which adult education is often regarded today in the light of the new Developmental concerns.

To pursue the path of provider of programmes alone, to carve out its own peculiar niche, would make adult education merely one among many such workers in the community. This path would leave the provision of some or all health education programmes, for example, or social welfare information programmes, poverty relief, religious education and environmental enhancement programmes to other bodies. It would be to place adult education *alongside* these other providers, on the same level. The defence of liberal education as the *raison d'être* of adult education will inevitably mean that adult education agencies will be limited to narrower and narrower fields of provision as more and more alternative agencies appear or are created to join the army of providers. Such a role is unlikely to reduce the marginality of adult education significantly. In an increasingly Developmentally-minded world, the justification for such programmes would lie in the necessity to make provision for cultural Development alongside social, economic and political Development—and it has been convincingly argued many times by adult educators that cultural Development is traditionally the most neglected of all Developmental fields and needs a special guardian.

A way forward

There is, however, another path. Motivated by a concern for a fully balanced national, regional and local Development programme, adult education would be willing to join with other agencies, bringing to bear its special insights, experience and expertise (for example, the training of part-time workers, participatory approaches to adult learning) and above all its concern for individual growth and attitude formation which these other agencies will need if their work is to be fully effective. At the same time adult education can add to the total stock of provision its special concern for cultural Development within the region which no one else can offer. In this way, adult education would become both a specialist and a provider, a link worker and assistant within the community to some of the many Development agencies which are outside the region, and at the same time a provider responsible for maintaining one sector of Development which is its particular concern.

We must not of course arrogate to adult education (or indeed to the process of education itself) a centrality which it does not possess. Many have noted that education is an inefficient tool of social engineering, speaking of the 'insignificance of schooling . . . in its capacity to promote major changes'; 'nor is it claimed that education can solve all social ills'. This particularly applies to adult education: the divided and isolated nature of much adult education and its general ethos, an in-built respect for the viewpoints of others, are thought to make it especially ineffective in promoting change unless backed up by a large-scale movement. Nevertheless, education (including the education of adults) is an essential component of programmes of social change; any society engaged in a planned process of Development needs a healthy educational system to complement the other agencies of change it uses. Thus adult education needs to play its part by joining with other agencies in promoting planned change (Development) rather than stand aside or attempt this task on its own. In following this path, it can learn much from Third World countries where adult education has played this role for many years.[10]

ADULT EDUCATION IN THE THIRD WORLD

Adult education is growing in importance in the Third World, for many see it as a valuable tool for social and economic Development. On the whole, there is little sense of a movement for adult education: the impetus comes not so much from below, from those seeking initial or additional education and training, as in the West, but more from above. Priorities are determined—agricultural extension, literacy and fundamental education, family planning, health, school leaving certificates, and so on—and target groups established—women between the ages of 15 and 35, backward classes, low income groups, mothers with very young children, out-of-school youth, illiterates, itinerant communities, small and marginal farmers and so on. Some programmes are directly under the Ministry of Education (whatever its title), but vocational training and social programmes are run by other government departments or national bodies supported by government. Although there are many variations from country to country (for example, some countries have large numbers of voluntary, non-statutory organizations offering adult learning programmes, while others have very few), in several countries something approaching a national adult education system or 'pattern' may be seen to be emerging from the structures which are growing up, helped and encouraged by the government to implement government Developmental programmes.[11]

Adult education then is seen by many in the Third World as a bridge between the desires of some to achieve a higher income and social status on the one hand and the Developmental goals of government. Mostly it is a tool of government. Voluntary umbrella associations have emerged in almost all countries, keeping alive the flame of independent criticism and value judgements, but these are strictly limited by their resource base. For, despite the greater social role which governments in most Third World countries envisage for it, adult education is still severely under-resourced; even if governments wished to expand their adult education provision, political realities restrict the freedom to move resources from the formal to the non-formal sectors of education.

The two purposes of adult education which we identified above can both be seen in Third World countries. Adult education offers to many adults that initial education which they were unable to obtain in childhood; and at the same time it offers opportunities of learning which could not be provided through the schools or colleges. Adult education (or its counterpart, non-formal education) exists in most countries because of the high cost and low performance of the formal system of education; but equally it exists to help promote centrally planned Development policies. It underpins most government programmes. Few Third World countries would dream of launching a major campaign (for example) for national integration and communal harmony or health or family planning without pressing into service adult education agencies as well as formal educational institutions such as the universities. Thus both voluntary and statutory adult education agencies in the Third World tend to act as co-ordinating bodies, using the various government programmes to create an integrated Development programme for the area which they serve.

In this way, adult education directly confronts poverty and injustice in a way that it does not in the West. It is true that more emphasis is given to teaching literacy (sometimes with some post-literacy) and to vocational training in skills and knowledge, either for employment or for self-employment, than to political or participatory education, even by the voluntary bodies, for most of these rely upon government support or aid from international welfare agencies and this limits their active involvement in radical social change programmes. Nevertheless, national economic growth and the relief of suffering are the main goals of adult education in Third World countries, and they press into service all the resources they can muster.

There are of course critics of this kind of adult education, both in the Third World countries themselves and in the West. Perhaps the voices in the West are loudest, because a good deal of this Third World adult education does not conform to Western or a priori theoretized models of participatory adult education. Much adult education in the Third World is ineffective or affects the lives of individuals but leaves the systems they live in untouched, enabling a few of the poor and illiterate to escape from their poverty and illiteracy, sometimes at the expense of the communities in which they formerly lived (this is not always true: many neo-literates continue to live in their communities and contribute to them); but then so does much adult education in the West. It is not helpful to make such judgements; better to try to understand what is happening and what is being attempted.

Adult education agencies in Third World countries then (a) have wider goals and programmes than in the West; they (b) relate to and draw upon the resources of the programmes of many different government and international agencies; and above all they (c) seek to work in a directive way with larger sections of the population, not waiting for voluntary learners to materialize in their programmes but going out to persuade the target groups to learn what they do not always want to learn. In these three respects, at least, the contrast between the West and the Third World could not be more marked.

ADULT EDUCATION AND DEVELOPMENT

But there are possible grounds for congruence. The value of adult education serving as a focus of 'inter-agency co-operation' as practised in Third World countries has already been recognized in the West. It is not only in community education that the necessity for adult educators to 'involve [themselves] with the work of voluntary agencies . . . and to strike constructive and fruitful alliances with colleagues in the related fields of health and housing', is being urged—'adult educators will themselves learn a great deal from association with such programmes'. The 'grey area' between adult education and social work (including the statutory bodies) has long been a matter of concern: 'both could profit considerably if the relationship were fully explored'.

Some writers, such as Illich, are suspicious that co-operation would mean accepting the ideologies of these state-led agencies. But others have recognized that 'it is both unwise and unnecessary to ignore the possibilities of using the resources of the state' for a programme of adult education for social change: 'the adult educator needs to learn to change from being a lone ranger to being part of a collective'. In Greece, for example, the General Secretariat for Adult Education 'pursues non-formal education activities in co-operation with providing institutions in other areas of intervention—e.g. the Ministries of National Education, Culture, Agriculture, Employment, Health, Social Security and the Environment' and with other state and para-statal organizations concerned with youth, foreign affairs, trade and industry, insurance, tourism, small businesses, radio and television, and with the police, local government and cultural associations both public and private.

Co-operation goes further than merely sharing resources and ideals: it relates to a common Developmental plan for the region in which adult education has a full part to play. In Italy, rather than 'scattered intervention' by the adult education agencies, programmes seek to ensure that 'public institutions, special bodies and cultural associations will be called upon to contribute to the realization of a plan . . .'. But co-operation of this kind is not well known in other countries such as the UK.[12]

Adult education then is one among many agencies engaged in the Development process. It is not of course the only body in the field. But it is the only agency capable of adopting this co-ordinating role in relation to Development:

- because adult education is not just an administrative body but has direct experience of teaching adults
- because adult education has developed specialisms in helping adults to learn which these other bodies need
- because adult education is dedicated (at least in theory) to helping its participants to examine reality critically
- because adult education with its concern for holistic education is general in approach, not limited in its concerns as are other Development agencies such as the health and manpower training services

This last point suggests the true basis on which adult education can enter Developmental programmes devised by others. Adult educators have insights and experience which will enable them, in association with the local community, to help write the Development agenda. It is not a case of merely accepting the goals set nationally or regionally. The centrality given to adult education by its special expertise in helping adults to learn will enable adult educators to contribute to determining not just the processes but also the objectives. The holistic approach of adult education is both its claim to a central role in local Development and also its special contribution.

Under such a model, adult education agencies would direct their provision to the Developmental needs of the region or community within which they are located; they would determine for themselves what those needs are; they would forge alliances with some or all of the increasing number of statutory and non-governmental bodies created to help meet those needs and to use their resources, financial and other; they would set Developmental goals for themselves or accept the goals of others; and they would seek to bring those goals to all the people of the locality, not just a few.

This will mean: working in a new way with less direct provision and more training of local Development workers within the community; assisting other agencies; full-time staff spending more time in promoting areas of work in the community and less on face-to-face teaching of small self-selected groups; looking at achievements and outcomes in terms of local Development rather than individual learning satisfactions.

Such a model is I believe not only possible; it is both desirable and necessary for today. The concept of Development is the only concept which would seem to offer to adult education any hope of making sense of its position and its special expertise and experience.

Two factors call for the inevitable involvement of adult education agencies in the growing Development programmes in the West:

(a) It is increasingly being realized that there can be no effective Development without there being a process of education and training of adults at the heart of it. It follows that adult education agencies must either provide that essential ingredient on the grounds of their expertise in adult learning, or stand on one side, allowing others to provide it, thus being excluded from Development programmes and further marginalized.

(b) Secondly, if adult education sees itself as helping others to examine reality critically and to explore ways of changing that reality, this must lead us to look critically not just at the reality which surrounds each of the individuals in our classes and programmes but also to look critically at the reality of our own adult education and our own society. This will impel adult education programmes into dealing directly with the major problems which face Western societies today.

Ultimately our response is a question of belief. If we believe that education and training for adults is important and should reach the widest possible group of people, we can no longer ignore the three-quarters of the adult population who have never come to our programmes. It is not enough to continue providing opportunities for a few individuals to advance their own careers and enhance the quality of their own lives. Instead we must play our part in mobilizing the whole of society in a joint drive towards a Developmental programme involving environmental enhancement and social harmony on a basis of justice and peace. These are surely not unworthy goals for adult educators to offer to the society they seek to serve rather than personal self-actualization.

But the implications of this for our programmes are profound. The criteria for mounting programmes will cease to be student demand but the Developmental needs of the nation and/or region or local community. There will of course be opposition from existing adult education agencies to such ideas. Some see Development as centrally planned, state controlled and directive, and their anti-government stance is long-standing. Others will oppose measuring the achievements of adult education by pre-set goals; yet even those engaged in liberal adult education with their emphasis on developing a critical spirit and greater democracy have such pre-set goals for themselves and their learners, so that the setting and accepting of national, regional and local Developmental goals for adult education programmes can and should hold no terrors. Adult education 'is not an end in itself, but it is an excellent way of solving a great many problems'.[13]

It may be too strong to assert that to reject such a path is to side with the existing structures: 'refusal to take sides in the conflict of the powerful with the powerless means to side with the powerful, not to be neutral'; 'no matter if we are conscious or not as educators, our praxis is either for the liberation of men, their humanisation, or for their domestication, their domination'. Adult education does have a choice: it can find other roles for itself in this new world. But the road leading to national, regional or local Development in partnership with others would seem to offer most.[14]

In accepting such a role, adult education in the West will need to become more like adult education in Third World countries, where it is seen as intervention, not simply responding to requests but taking the initiative, and long-term, not simply a series of one-off events like a class. It will seek to promote social goals amongst more or less reluctant target groups rather than teach voluntary learners. And it will no longer be acceptable to point to one or two 'success stories' of individuals who have used adult education as a ladder to climb from humble origins to professional competence. Adult education seen 'as a safety valve to channel off the most able of the deprived and create an illusion of opportunity for all' merely confirms the basic premises on which society and its formal education systems are founded. Rather, success will be indicated by the extent to which mass mobilization of whole peoples behind targets set by some and internalized by the many has been achieved. Evaluation of adult education will be 'in terms of social and economic effectiveness'.[15]

We shall explore some of these implications and criteria in more detail, but before we do this, we need to examine what is meant by Development. This we shall do in Part II.

NOTES TO CHAPTER 6

(1) The new prominence given to education in development in the West is illustrated by the statement of the European Commission, May 1986: 'consumer education is now increasingly accepted as an essential element in the education of every citizen of every modern state'. See also statement by the UK Urban Regeneration programme co-ordinator, J. Lunday: 'urban regeneration is primarily an educational task', Civic Trust Educational Group, unpublished paper (April 1989); etc.

(2) Correspondence with the Royal Agricultural Society of England 1988–89. The didactic nature of the campaign is revealed in the statement of the Director in a radio interview: 'the aim is to change people's image of the industry caused by misunderstanding and lack of knowledge, to help them see the industry warts and all'. With respect to the AE agencies, the organizer of BFFY 1989 writes: 'I am afraid I have never heard of the WEA'! But the RASE does have a Rural Employment and Training Unit.

(3) For examples of the growing interest in the part to be played by AE in development in the West, see the theme of the UNESCO 1982 conference: 'Towards an Authentic Development: the Role of Adult Education'; the theme of the EBAE Conference in Madrid in 1988; the Council of Europe project on Community Development and Adult Education; Green (1977). See Rogers, A. (1982) AE and development: a Northern Ireland perspective, *AE* 55(1), 28–31; Rogers, A. (1979) Second thoughts on adult education and development, *Indian Journal of Adult Education* 40(7) (July), 1–8; Rogers, A. (1986) Educating adults as a means towards transforming society: some lessons from developmental programmes in the Third World, in ILSCAE (1986); Jarvis, P. (1986) Notions of development and their implication for adult education, *International Review of Education* 32, 85–96; Fordham, P. (1986) West and south: the adult education dialogue, *AE* 59(1) and (2); Kassam, Y. (1986) Adult education, development and international aid: some issues and trends, *Convergence* 19(3), etc. See EBAE (1988) Spain 10, p. 1; for Portugal, see Melo in EBAE (1988); EBAE (1988) papers relating to France; De Sanctis (1988) 1, p. 3; Luna (1988), p. 2; EBAE (1988) Ireland; EBAE (1988) Greece 1, pp. 3–4: for the Greece quotation in full, see below, p. 187.

(4) D. Waterman, The peace discussion, in ILSCAE (1986), pp. 107–9. See the recent work of

the International Council for Adult Education, Toronto, in peace, justice and participatory AE; but even here, Third World countries lead the way—for example, Africa on environmental education, Latin America on education for justice, Asia on participatory research, etc.; e.g. Jayawardana, W. Ananda and Wesumperuna, D. (1987) *Adult Education, Development and Peace*, Sri Lanka: National Association for Total Education.

(5) See Dewey, J. (1900) *School and Society*, Chicago; Morris, H. (1924) *The Village College*, Cambridge; Rogers (1976), pp. 79–80; Lovett (1971); Lovett (1975); Lovett (1980); Jackson (1970); Kirkwood (1980); Lawson (1977); Stewart, B. (1976) A community adult education service, *AE* **49**(2), 69–74; Allen, G., Bastiani, J., Martin, I. and Richards, K. (eds) (1987) *Community Education: an Agenda for Educational Reform*, Open University Press; EBAE (1988) Spain 3, p. 2; McIlroy and Spencer (1988), p. 146; Fletcher (1980); Midwinter, E. (1973) *Patterns of Community Education*, Ward Lock; Fairburn, A.N. (1978) *The Leicestershire Community Colleges and Centres*, University of Nottingham. Jackson (1980), p. 17, speaks of 'informal approaches which link education closely to daily life and social or political activities', calling this community education. Lovett (1980) regards community education and social and political education as the same, quoting with approval various adult education programmes which 'draw no fine distinctions between action and education'; but later he and his colleagues elaborated this by distinguishing between community-development education and community-action education: the former is in but not of the community, the latter is part of the community. Once again, community action is seen as an educational process—Lovett, T., Clarke C. and Kilmurray, A. (1983) *Adult Education and Community Action*, Croom Helm. For a critique of the whole field, see Lawson (1977).

(6) For a summary of the recent literature, see Brookfield (1983), pp. 7–9, 60–125. See also the work and publications of the Community Education Development Centre, Coventry, and the International Community Education Association, including its journal.

(7) University of Manchester paper (1986), cited in McIlroy and Spencer (1988), p. 101, and see ibid., p. 123; Ginzberg, E. (1980) The great training robbery, in Finch, A. and Scrimshaw, P. (eds) *Standards, Schooling and Education*, Hodder and Stoughton; DES (1972); DES (1984); NAB (1984); UGC (1984); Todd, F. (1984) Learning and work: directions for continuing professional and vocational education, *IJLE* 3(2).

(8) Strategy Report (1980), p. 25: 'courses should aim at the *improvement* and development of knowledge, understanding and skill and not merely at its *exercise*'.

(9) See references in Chapter 3, note 6.

(10) Harries-Jenkins (1983); Crombie (1983): 'education is an ineffective means of stimulating socio-economic change'. See Fordham, P. (1976) The political context of adult education, *Studies in Adult Education* **8**(1); Thompson (1980), p. 27, quoting an unpublished paper by Jackson, K., Yarnit,M. and Evans,D.R.; ACACE (1979), para. 6.

(11) See Lowe (1975); Lowe, J. (1971) The role of adult education, in Lowe, J., Grant, N. and Williams, T.D. (eds) *Education and Nation-Building in the Third World*, Edinburgh, ch. 7; Lowe, J. (ed.) (1970) *Adult Education and Nation-Building*, Edinburgh: Edinburgh University Press.

(12) Russell Report; Fordham *et al.* (1979); Jackson (1970) pp. 156–62; Stewart, B. (1976), A community adult education service, *AE* **49**(2); Lovett (1971), p. 2; Illich (1970); Wells, J.H. (1977) Adult education and disadvantage, *AE* **49**(6): 'the patronizing infantilizing and passive role that our society tends to ascribe to the disabled'; Thompson (1980), p. 124; EBAE (1988) Greece 1, p. 3. England and Wales can only report that apart from the DES, adult education received 'finance from at least two other government departments for education programmes for immigrants in inner city areas, and an education element financed by the Department of Health and Social Security for the "Care in the Community" programme': EBAE (1988) England and Wales, p. 1.

(13) Council of Europe (1986b), pp. 9, 10.

(14) Freire (1972), p. 7; Freire, P. (1973) By learning they can teach, *Convergence* 6(1), 79.

(15) Green (1977), pp. 35, 41; Jobert (1988), p. 3. Ettore Gelpi makes the same point: 'Lifelong education could result in the reinforcement of the established order, increased productivity

and subordination, but a different option could enable us to become more and more committed to the struggle against those who oppress mankind in work and in leisure, in social and emotional life': *A Future for Lifelong Education*, Manchester University Press, vol. 1 (1979), p. 1. The language is identical with that of many Development workers.

Bridge

The first part of this book noted that adults continue to learn throughout their lives and examined the relevance of this fact to adult education, seen as the provision of learning opportunities for adults.

It went on to point out that adult education in the West is in a state of turmoil; many of the premises on which it has been built over the last hundred years have been challenged, and many of the structures which have implemented its programmes are being changed out of all recognition. By contrast, Adult Education in Third World countries, although still marginal, is coming to be seen as more important, a tool of government to help solve some of the problems which face these nations. It suggested in closing that the concept of Development as applied in the Third World countries might form the basis of the re-orientation which is being sought for adult education in the West.

Such a claim demands an analysis of Development—what it is, how it works and in what ways it is relevant to the concerns of adult education. To do this requires, as with adult education, looking at many contradictory and complex views. This analysis the second part of this book sets out to provide.

Part II

Development

Chapter 7

Development: Definitions

Development, like adult education, means many things to many people—planners, practitioners and participants. The term can be used for the construction of hydro-electric dams just as much as the provision of a village well, the building of a railway system or the installation of a computerized telephone network, as well as the purchase of a tractor, the holding of a dental camp or craft training workshop or the provision of roadside toilets for an urban slum.

There are many debates about what Development is and what it is not. In this respect, Development has a higher profile than adult education: more books have been written, reports produced and journals published on Development, and their readers drawn from all parts of the world. Changes of view have come about as the drawbacks of successive models have appeared and been evaluated. There is less of a sense of crisis today in Development than in adult education but the pressures for effective forms of Development are increasing.

Because there are so many arguments about the nature of Development, it is necessary to explore the concept down to its bare essentials.

Change and Development

Development is concerned with change; but it is not simply the same as change. Change is going on all the time; it is part of the process of living, whether in societies, communities or individuals. Even traditional societies are not static; they are changing, however slowly.

Some of these changes flow out of and to a large extent perpetuate existing patterns of life. Other changes disrupt this flow—a revolution or famine or war in a nation's history or an accident, illness, redundancy or other personal crisis in an individual's life. The term 'development' as used in general parlance relates not to the interruptions but to the continuities, to those changes which are seen as 'natural' rather than 'unnatural', which arise out of preceding factors; we speak of 'the situation developing. . . .'

Thus one of the basic concepts of Development is continuity. It is concerned with those progressive changes which are rooted in and spring out of the previous situation. The existing state contains within it at least the possibility of the desired changes; the new emerges out of the old. Development is not revolutionary change. It is this idea which lies behind the statement that Development cannot be imported: it must arise from within the community itself as peaceful yet radical change. Development does not mean making everything new but building on natural links.[1]

Yet, when used in a technical sense, Development also means something unnatural, an *intervention* to alter the path of change. Development is a deliberate act, designed to influence society or the local community and so arranged as to lead to certain desired results. Like adult education, which builds on but also intervenes in the natural and continuing process of learning in order to give it direction, purpose and increased impetus, so Development builds on but intervenes in the natural and continuing process of societal change. It is planned, with a goal in mind. 'Development is social change with an inherent and identified thrust or direction; it is not the same as social change because of the existence of this thrust (volition) and the change-agent.'[2]

Development then is a process of planned change.* It has two basic elements:

(a) *Planning*: there is a purpose, an intention behind every act of Development, whether it is done by central authorities or local self-help groups. The intention is to direct and push the process of natural change towards a specified objective. And planning implies the existence of a planning agency.

(b) *Action*: there is an intervention, an activity which it is hoped will achieve this purpose, lead towards this objective. The activity may be a single event leading to a complete result, such as the adoption of some new desired practice (agricultural technique, hygienic practice, etc.), in which case that particular process of Development comes to an end—although there may be consequential Development programmes, for change promotes further change. Or it may be a longer-term process leading to structural change.

Development then is a planned activity aimed at speeding up or directing the process of change which is already going on towards an identified goal. It is not starting off a process; it is not 'kicking a football' from a stationary position, i.e. mobilizing a static society or community into action. Rather it is (to pursue the analogy) nudging the ball as it passes so that it will go into the goal rather than to another part of the field or even out of play.

Some people use the term 'Development' as the goal of the process; thus they speak of some activity as 'leading to development'. The exact nature of this Development-goal is not always spelled out. But if we are to see Development as a process of planned change, then we can perhaps see the Development-goal as not a state but as a process, the process of self-direction of change. In other words, as in adult education the main aim is to end outsider-led education and training and to encourage the learners to take control of their own planned learning processes, so in Development the aim is that outsider-led Development-intervention will come to an end and the participant group will engage in continuing self-directed Development. So that Development is not terminal; one Development-intervention will lead on to further Development in a continuous state of becoming.

* I use Development to distinguish the intervention intended to lead to planned change from the natural development which occurs in all societies.

TYPES OF DEVELOPMENT

A distinction has been drawn between large-scale centrally planned Development schemes and small-scale local grass-roots programmes. There is much to differentiate these two. But in fact they represent the ends of a single continuum, and to some extent the distinction is artificial. Large projects have local implications: a new dam, reservoir and hydro-electric scheme will involve the lives of thousands of people, both those employed directly on the project and those in the communities around who are in one way or another affected in drastic resettlement or more marginally by, for example, having electric light available in their village for the first time. New road schemes and rehousing programmes involve individuals, families and communities. A Spanish report is informative:

> the state has put in hand a far-reaching programme of electrification, industrialisation and . . . land improvement by building dams and setting up an extensive irrigation network. A major national and international road system has also helped to bring this peripheral region out of isolation . . . [a parallel programme was also launched] to dispel a prevailing sense of frustration and even contempt in regard to village resources by encouraging an awareness of the community's own special values, a spirit of participation and enterprise and motivation for learning which can help to develop both individuals and the community.[3]

Development then concerns people, not just things. It is not merely the provision of housing or new fishing nets. There is in all Development, whether large-scale or small-scale, the people who are involved, those whose lives will be changed, those who need to be enabled by changes in knowledge, skills and attitudes to adopt new ways and new equipment, what is usually referred to as the 'target group'.*

Other people have drawn a distinction between those projects and programmes (such as the provision of a well or literacy classes) which are short-lived, the change-agents being withdrawn when the immediate goals have been (theoretically at least) achieved, and those programmes which are continuing (like agricultural or health extension programmes). There is more validity in this distinction, for the relationship between the change-agent and the participant group in a long-term programme is quite different from that in a short-term project, and the goals attempted and achieved—especially in attitudinal change—are wider in the former than in the latter. But here again the distinction is to some extent artificial; for as we have seen, one short-term change usually leads to another. One of the goals of all Development, even the long-term programmes, is to help the participants to take over the process of Development for themselves, to become self-reliant, to take their own decisions and not to rely on the presence of the change-agent/extension worker. Both types of Development programmes have similar overall goals and similar procedures to reach those goals.

---

* The phrase 'target group' has objectionable overtones: it implies that the Development agent is doing something 'to' or 'for' a group of people rather than the people doing it for themselves. I therefore use 'participant group' for those occasions when the people are engaged in part or entirely in their own Development; but I retain 'target group' when I am using the words of Development agents who think in these terms and also when talking about that wider group of people for whom the Development-intervention is intended and from whom the participant group is drawn. The two terms are not totally synonymous.

GOALS IN DEVELOPMENT

Before we look at the goals of Development, we need to ask: who sets these goals? For those who set them will determine the kind of goals set.

For many, Development means national planning (often with the assistance of international aid agencies) to achieve nationally adopted objectives, the harnessing of resources to achieve targets set by the state. The tool is—in this model—central planning; the agencies of state (usually planners) set the goals.

When we look at the local level, however, we see that the goals are set either by the people themselves or by the 'carers' (those who set out voluntarily or statutorily to help the people). There are three main sets of agencies at this level: government or para-statal bodies (local Development officials or state banks or universities working locally, for example); secondly, independent non-governmental organizations dedicated to advance the welfare of the people, usually on a charitable basis (NGOs) but sometimes on a commercial basis (fertilizer or tractor companies, etc.); and thirdly, self-help groups such as local co-operatives or residents' groups.

Insiders and outsiders

A distinction needs to be drawn between those Development workers who live within the local community or within the same sort of community, who may be classified as 'insiders', and those who come in from the outside. Those who live in rural areas and are themselves poor (it is argued) can engage as 'insiders' in the relief of rural poverty; all others are 'outsiders'. In practice, few Development workers are 'insiders'; for since Development is defined as intervention leading to planned change, 'outsiders' usually take the lead in the intervention—although part of the process of Development is aimed at reducing the amount of outsider involvement and increasing the amount of insider involvement.[4]

Many different agencies, then, are engaged in creating the goals for Development. Each group acts in a different way in determining their goals. Some accept national goals set by the state because they believe in them; indeed, a number (even of the NGOs) have been established to promote government Development schemes. Many women's programmes in Third World countries, for example, are based on government welfare programmes, and some are even housed within government departments. Other agencies accept the goals set by the state in order to gain access to the resources which go with these goals—money or staffing or office space or typing assistance or equipment, etc.—even if they are not completely convinced that these are the right goals. But there are groups and agencies—mainly local and non-governmental—which set their own goals, and these may differ markedly from the state's goals. This is particularly true of self-help groups and of some religious and political bodies.

Development as 'technique'

What is regrettable about some of these groups and agencies is the tendency for the *techniques* of the centrally planned Development programme to be transferred to various levels of change-agents without any real understanding of or concern for the purposes behind these techniques. They pursue the activities, taking these to be the goals. Thus they dig wells and plant trees, they run clinics and urge family planning, without seeing these activities as part of a wider programme aimed at the welfare of the people or of the environment in general. They regard the activities as the ends of the Development process rather than as the means: so that once the wells have been dug, the trees planted, the clinics established and the family planning camps been held, the Development process is thought to have been completed.

This is of course not true. The purpose of the Development-intervention is to help to achieve a better life. For all such groups and agencies, it is necessary to ask, 'What are we doing this for? What are the real goals of Development?' The criteria by which the effectiveness of programmes needs to be judged are not the activities—the number of wells or trees or clinics which have been provided—but the measure to which the objectives behind these activities have been achieved: whether the people are in any way better off at the end of the programme. Literacy education, for example, is not just a question of acquiring competencies, for 'the illiterates . . . do not aspire to "literacy" but to becoming more capable, autonomous and therefore freer',[5] and the measure of success or failure must therefore be the increased autonomy and freedom of the participant group. Development seen as technique will be expressed in terms of *provision*; Development aimed at the improvement of life will look for the effective *utilization* of the resources newly made available. It is easier to count trees or clinics or wells than to measure the improvement in the quality of life: but trees or clinics or wells do not always on their own make for a better way of life for the people.

Societal or personal goals?

The question of whether the goals of Development should more properly be directed at the welfare of the individual or of society as a whole is relatively muted in Development. Opinions on this matter have changed from time to time and from place to place. In the West, as we have seen, the climate has for many years favoured the individual, though from the late 1960s, with the increasing concern for disadvantaged groups and for the environment, there has been something of a swing towards programmes aimed at greater benefit to society, even if of lower benefit to the individual. In Third World countries, on the other hand, programmes of Development are based on national social and economic needs rather than the individual needs of the participants. This is often justified on the grounds that the causes of underdevelopment lie not so much in the individual as in society as a whole; the problems cannot be solved without addressing these basic causes.

This dichotomy is, however, not so clear to many people in countries like India. What is of value to the state must necessarily be of value to the individual, it is argued; and what benefits the individual will benefit the whole community. The individual finds his/her wholeness within the circle of the family, which in turn finds its fulfilment in the local community, and that again within the nation (circles within circles, as Gandhi described it). There is in much thinking in the East no distinction between what is of benefit to the individual and what is of value to society.[6]

Development in Third World countries then claims to have found goals which have high levels of benefit for both the individual and society. This is particularly true of those programmes which attach the word 'participatory' to them. It is of the greatest benefit to both individual and society, it is argued, if people participate in the matters which concern them in their everyday lives. But it would seem to Western eyes that most Third World Development programmes in practice aim at goals which either benefit some individuals at the expense of others (income-generating programmes, for instance) or which benefit society in general by making individuals and families conform to nationally set norms (family planning, for example).

Intermediate and ultimate goals

It is useful here to distinguish between different levels and different types of goals.

Intermediate goals (sometimes called 'targets') are objectives which are ends in themselves, bringing with them some sense of satisfaction, but which at the same time are the means to a further end. They are justified largely in terms of their outcomes. *Ultimate goals* are those things which do not need any further justification.

We all possess in our spoken or unspoken value systems intermediate and ultimate 'goods', though we may not be able to define them clearly. Different people will make different judgements between intermediate and ultimate goals. Wealth, health and education, for example, may be seen by some as ends in themselves, by others as means to other things which are seen to be even more important—at a personal level, peace of mind or happiness or the fulfilment of a sense of purpose (divine will or pre-ordained role or the welfare of other human beings or justice, etc.), and at a societal level, communal peace, equality of opportunity and growing enrichment.[7]

What does seem to be clear is that ultimate goals will lead to a greater range of choice: they cannot be normative without denying the self-reliance and self-determination of the participants. Intermediate goals, on the other hand, will more frequently be normative: they will suggest appropriate ways of achieving the ultimate goals.

Development-intervention is normally more concerned with intermediate than ultimate goals. But there is a danger that these intermediate goals become ends in themselves rather than means towards an ultimate goal. For instance, is it right to provide the means of increased production to some members in any local community if that will lead to greater inequalities and to disharmony? And which is more important, the intermediate goal (productivity) or the ultimate goal (social justice)? Surely the ultimate as well as the intermediate goals should in some sense dictate the programme.

Few Development bodies define their ultimate goal, but one or two have. The Sarvodaya Shramadana Movement in Sri Lanka, one of the largest voluntary bodies dedicated to complete rural community Development through a programme of education and training for adults and social action, building its philosophies on Buddhism, is clear that its ultimate goal is 'happiness', and seeks to direct its programmes towards the happiness of those with whom it works. But this clarity of vision is rare—and it is even rarer to find such values carried out in practice.[8]

A wide range of goals

Rather than try to define and pursue ultimate goals, most agencies concentrate on intermediate goals. There is a host of these. They fall into four main categories (which on occasion overlap): economic, social, cultural and political.

- *Economically*—Development programmes may be aimed at increased and more stable national or individual incomes or productivity, at economic growth and modernization, at higher agricultural yields or more efficient industrial and exploitative processes, at resource preservation.
- *Socially*—they may be aimed at communal harmony or justice or welfare or environmental or social enhancement (quality of life).
- *Culturally* (the weakest of the Development programmes)—they may be aimed at preserving and at increasing access to and appreciation of cultural diversity and richness.
- *Politically*—they may be aimed at increased awareness and participation and structural change.

Such goals tend to vary at the different levels of planning and implementation at which the programme operates. At the national level, Development goals are on the whole more concerned with gross national product, economic growth, population control, communal harmony and national integration. At the regional and local community level, there is often a greater concern with sectoral Development, bringing peripheral groups in to play a fuller part in the community, with socialization and participation, with skills for action, and with improvements in both the social and the physical environment. And at the level of the individual and the family, there will be a greater emphasis on income-generating goals, skill training, human resource development, on coping skills and personal empowerment or self-actualization, the fulfilment of individual talents and interests.

Furthermore, Development goals vary in nature. Some are general in character, open-ended, like building confidence or personal growth. Others are narrower, such as saving the lives of babies through oral rehydration therapy (ORT) and nutrition programmes for mothers, or increasing the productivity of farmers through fertilizers or new seed varieties. The effects of the former cannot be quantified (though they can still be evaluated); the results of the latter can be quantified—which is perhaps why many aid and Development agencies prefer the latter type of projects to the former.

Evidently, there is a bewildering array of Development goals, and both national planning and local implementing bodies adopt and drop these goals with a facility which is dictated more by fashion and the demands of the international aid agencies than by principles. Modernization (of attitudes and structures), the development of self-reliance, the meeting of basic human needs, liberation from oppression, overcoming poverty—these are among the many goals established for Development.

There may be multiple goals in any programme. Sometimes these will be arranged in a hierarchy, some being seen as primary goals and others as secondary goals (or valuable by-products, spin-offs of the programme). It may be useful to give an example. In a Kerala village, a central cattle shed was introduced. The main purpose of this was to keep the cattle under control. Secondary intended outcomes included the availability of cattle dung for a biogas plant and the possibility of more controlled breeding. But beyond this, it was hoped that the children who normally looked after the cattle would now be able to go to school. This was not the primary purpose of the programme: for had the agency aimed to get the children into school as its first objective, a different programme would have been pursued. Rather it was considered to be a valuable by-product of the intervention.

A balanced programme

What is clear is that a programme in one aspect, however limited its immediate goals, will in the short or long term involve changes in all the other aspects of Development. All four fields are interrelated: 'a programme of social action . . . will . . . require the launching of activities directed to educational and cultural enhancement; . . . such a strategy should also ensure that economic . . . and socio-cultural aspects be present in all activities.'[9] Development cannot any longer be single-sectoral; the need to have a fully balanced programme involving all the major aspects of economic, social, cultural and political goals is increasingly being recognized.

NOTES TO CHAPTER 7

(1) Arocena (1986), p. 1: 'acceleration of technical changes risks breaking the "natural links" with the technical past . . . the growing marginalization across "non-qualified" population groups constitutes a serious break in the continuity of the social fabric'. Mengin (1988), p. 1, writes that 'the objectives [of development] obviously depend a great deal on the environment, the services available and life in society'.

(2) van Nieuwenhuijze (1982), pp. 101–2.

(3) Council of Europe (1984), pp. 9–10. Lacey, T. R., What is development? in Rogers, A. (1984); see Macpherson, S. (1982) *Social Policy in the Third World*, Wheatsheaf. For roads, see Gascoigne, E. (1986) North Yemen: do rural roads mean rural development? *RRDC Bulletin* (20 September), 11–14.

(4) Chambers (1983), pp. 2–3; Schaffer, B. (1980) Insiders and outsiders, *Development and Change* 11(2).

(5) De Sanctis (1988), p. 4.

(6) The best study of the individual and the community from an Indian perspective is Mehta, V. R. (1983) *Ideology, Modernization and Politics in India*, New Delhi: Manohar.

(7) Colin Wringe, in *Understanding Educational Aims* (Allen and Unwin, 1988), suggests that individual goals of education include happiness, the satisfaction of natural growth needs and interests, and the development of rational autonomy and vocational competencies; and the social goals include law and order (conformity), equality and justice (he refers to gender and race).

(8) Ariyaratne, A. T., Learning in Sarvodaya, in Thomas and Ploman (1985); Ratnapala, N. (ed.) (1978) *The Sarvodaya Movement: Self-Help Rural Development in Sri Lanka*, Connecticut; Coletta, N. J., Ewing, R. T. and Todd, T. (1982) Cultural revitalization, participatory nonformal education and village development in Sri Lanka: the Sarvodaya Shramadana movement, *Comparative Education Review* 26, 271–85; Coletta, N. J. and Todd, T. A. The limits of nonformal education and village development: lessons from the Sarvodaya Shramadana movement, in Bock and Papagiannis (1982).

(9) Melo (1988), p. 3.

Chapter 8

The Purpose of Development

The fact that there are many different goals to Development and many different processes to achieve these goals springs from the way the problem being attacked is defined. For example:

- Some people view the problem as lying in traditionalism—in 'unscientific' approaches such as ancient medical remedies, or in traditional social structures such as caste or group distinctions, or in outmoded activities such as customary ways of preserving fish. In this case the answer lies in the modernization of attitudes or structures or practices.
- Some see the problem as poverty and the lack of resources in relation to the numbers of people using them. In this case, the answer lies in an increase in and/or a more equitable share of the world's resources (aid) or in population limitation or both.
- Some see the problem as one of exploitation and dependency: underdeveloped countries have for long been held in a state of colonialism and subordination, and even after political independence has been won, economic and intellectual colonialism still exists, leading to a lack of initiative and confidence. The need then is to develop self-reliance.[1]

There are three elements making up Development: (a) the definition of the problem; (b) the process; and (c) the goal. Each of these will vary from programme to programme; and the different understandings may be joined in any combination. Examples of all three elements in combination are given in Table 8.1.

Table 8.1 *Some examples of combining the three elements of Development in different ways*

The Problem— seen as:	The Process— proposed:	The Goal— desired:
Dependency	Social action	Liberation
Dependency	De-linking	Self-reliance
Traditional attitudes	Legislation	Modernization
Traditional attitudes	Education	Modernization
Traditional structures	Legislation	Modernization
Traditional farming	Training	Increased yields
Poverty	Training	Income-generation
Poverty	Credit	New economic activities

POSSIBLE TAXONOMIES OF DEVELOPMENT

There have been several attempts to categorize the different models of Development.[2] For our purposes, a distinction based on an understanding of the nature of the problem will be useful. On the one hand, there are those programmes which are based on the concept of *need*; on the other hand there are those which are based on a concept of *exclusion*. We can either see the target groups as being deprived, needy, lacking in resources; or we can see them as kept out, denied access to resources. The first says that there are not enough resources ('the human deficit'); resources need to be increased. The second says that there are enough resources but that some people are excluded from such resources by those who hold control over them. The first says that the problem lies in the developing countries themselves, the second that the problem lies in the whole world and its systems, perhaps more in the rich countries than in the poor. Within these two basic approaches, there are several subdivisions, as shown in Table 8.2.

Table 8.2 *Taxonomy of Development*

Deprivation and needs theories	Exclusion theories
1 Overcoming poverty	1 Dependency and self-reliance
1a Growth and modernization	
1b Social planning	
1c Human Resource Development	2 Liberation
1d Community Organization	
2 Meeting Basic Human Needs	3 Participation

I. Needs-based approaches: overcoming poverty

1a. Growth and modernization

Development programmes have from the start been dominated by the 'overcoming poverty' school of thought, and this view continues to preponderate. Development is to most people inextricably bound up with economic rather than social concepts.

The argument is that poverty is the cause of 'backwardness', and so an increase in economic activity and production is needed. At first, it was thought that Third World countries had 'young' economies and were in the early stages of what the industrialized West had gone through some 150 years ahead of them and that they could get through the subsequent stages at an accelerated rate with the help of financial and technical aid from the West. Later it was felt that the major reason for this poverty was that these economies were stunted, held back by traditional patterns of production and thinking, so that the main strategy to achieve economic growth became modernization—of techniques and equipment, of attitudes and of social structures. By drawing upon the 'more advanced' models of the West, by being encouraged to import what they do not possess (to be achieved by selling natural resources or increased agricultural yields), developing countries can be helped to 'catch up' with their richer world partners.

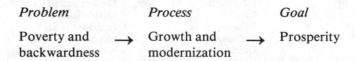

	Problem		*Process*		*Goal*
	Poverty and backwardness	→	Growth and modernization	→	Prosperity

Economic growth models at national level   At the central level, Development under this view means accumulation—more capital and investment, more technical innovations, more modern forms of communication and transport, more produce to be sold in the market and abroad, more power supplies, more water and fertilizers, better farming practices and crop varieties—which will lead to an increased gross national product, increased foreign earnings so as to relieve heavy overseas debts produced by aid schemes and borrowings, and increased consumer goods for all. This process of accumulation leading to greater wealth is seen as an end in itself.

This approach to Development is sectoral, rational and based on modern scientific processes and attitudes: science is the saviour of the poorer nations. Raymond Aron has spoken of 'the application of science to production as the cause and . . . essence of development' and of the adoption of 'scientific rationality' in production as the *sine qua non* of prosperity.[3]

Trickle down   For many years it was believed that this process of economic growth through national planning would start from the centre and lead to a 'trickling down' or 'spreading out' effect, supply creating demand throughout the whole, just as a reservoir leads to water and power supplies reaching many small villages. Programmes were directed towards stimulating the national economy, mainly through the expansion and mechanization of identified areas of industrial and agricultural production.

Bottom-up   When the trickling down did not happen, when it was realized that designating some economic activities as key sectors relegated other activities as marginal to Development, however viable they may have been in their own right, and when the difficulty of reconciling local and regional identities with national Developmental needs was recognized, trickle down was replaced by a 'bottom-up' approach, developing regional economies rather than sectors. This form of Development, building 'islands of modernism in a sea of traditionalism' through integrated Development schemes, is based on demand stimulating production, builds on indigenous knowledge and skills, and allows scope for locally determined goals. Thus there is 'growing awareness of the local and regional area as the best place' for Development. But despite their different approaches, both forms agree that the goal is increased economic growth and the tool is central planning.[4]

Economic growth models at local levels   Most grass-roots Development schemes are based on the same premises as centrally planned programmes—that prosperity is the goal and that the process is one of accumulation, of skill training, of moving from a traditional to a modern form of society. They are more aware that in the process there will be spin-offs, many of them of a cultural and social nature. Thus a rural women's milk-producing co-operative (modern social structures replacing traditional farming patterns) may generate other social and political skills, a carpet factory for tribal women or a jam-making activity in an urban slum may lead to demands for literacy and non-formal education. But the main aim in each case is economic improvement.

1b. Social planning

The problems faced in achieving or controlling (for there were some notable cases of over-production arising from centrally determined plans) this growth led the planners to include two new dimensions. Internationally, they saw Third World countries as tied into a world economy which was working to their disadvantage, so they pursued (somewhat half-heartedly) attempts at *de-linking*. And internally they added *social goals* to their economic goals. A healthy population was necessary for production, a controlled rate of population increase was the basis for planned economic growth, a limit on the exploitation of natural resources was inevitable if the economy was not to decline, a contented and trained work-force was essential in a fiercely competitive world. So economic policy-makers moved towards 'comprehensive Development planning'; health and family planning, environmental and labour issues began to feature in Development programmes, even when these were still primarily directed towards economic growth.

The tool of this form of Development was 'social planning'. Drawing upon the fact that the earlier forms of Development were assessed by statistical criteria, such as life expectation, consumption of protein per capita, the average number of persons per room, school enrolment percentages, the number of houses with electricity or the number of adult education class participants, social planners made these things not so much the instruments of measuring Development achievements as the goals of Development itself. Social planners (it was argued) should

> make the whole planned development social, that is, to direct it in such a way that it should bring about maximum improvement in the conditions in which people live. This is the true sense of 'social planning'. Planning will become social . . . when social variables (i.e. variables expressing the conditions in which people live) will be put in place of the final aims of development plans. They will then serve as criteria for the allocation of resources.
>
> The real economic and financial figures which have to be determined are those which also integrate leisure, quality of life, difficulties and not only 'what viable is but also what livable is' for everyone; we do not want a universal technical model but rather one adapted to the natural conditions of the industrial operation, the available labour force and the needs of the family. The 'economic rationality' thus demanded is the creation of its own development model which integrates all the parameters, including social ones. . . .[5]

The full needs of the workforce had to be met in order to achieve economic growth. And this led social planning into two separate routes, human resource development and community development.

1c. Human Resource Development

From this concern for an active, satisfied and well-trained labour force in order to attain national goals of economic Development, the concept of Human Resource Development (HRD) was born. This is one of the most potent ideas in Development today; much of what is being done is being done in the name of HRD. The biggest potential capital which a nation possesses is its human population, and thus we need to invest in this resource if we are to achieve economic growth. Not all those engaged in HRD would talk in this way, that 'we' need to encourage the Development of other people, but many do, and most HRD agencies tend in practice to work on such assumptions.

Whole programmes (like the Kenya Village Polytechnics) are based on these premises.

HRD then is seen as one of the major approaches to Development. The problem which HRD sets out to alleviate is still 'deprivation', a lack, mainly of skills for the world of work, so that HRD is often spoken of in terms of 'modernizing' skills, knowledge and attitudes. Some people see HRD as an end in itself, releasing human potential, developing individual self-reliance; but most see it as a means to an end, i.e. prosperity.[6]

traditional $\longrightarrow$ HRD $\longrightarrow$ economic growth
skills and attitudes

HRD programmes are usually directed at three main objectives. First, at *securing employment*—initial employment for the unemployed, increased opportunities for the under-employed—through vocational training in craft or industrial skills, apprenticeship schemes and the like. Secondly, at *increasing productivity* of the employed—not just by industrial training schemes, up-dating or more advanced courses, management training, marketing and other such activities but also by inputs such as equipment, intermediate or advanced technology—even the provision of bicycles is seen in some circles as HRD. And thirdly, at achieving *economic self-reliance*—to equip those who work (especially the self-employed entrepreneur) with the necessary knowledge, skills and linkages to enable them to take full advantage of the resources which are available to them. It is in this sense that HRD can be stretched to helping the marginalized rural worker (especially women) to gain access to credit facilities. So that in the end, HRD can cover almost any activity which will help to make for an efficient and contented work-force, tapping and releasing their potential talents and innate initiative and innovativeness.[7]

There are two main problems with HRD. The first is that in much HRD, people are paradoxically often seen only as a resource, a means to achieve an end and not as ends in themselves. Hence people serve the economy rather than the economy serving the people. It is sometimes even urged that, like a tool, people need to be 'honed' in order to be more useful, better designed to do the job they are required to do.[8] In this sense, HRD is dehumanizing, a dressed-up form of one set of people using another set of people for their own ends. It is doubtful if the majority of the urban or rural poor care at all for economic growth, GNP or the like, or even for greater efficiency. They call for enough food, enough resources for their own family needs. A number will, it is true, aim at becoming increasingly productive entrepreneurs, to add to their own wealth above that of their neighbours, and in the process they will unwittingly add to the nation's wealth. But this is unlikely to be the wish of all.

The second problem is one which characterizes much Development activity—HRD has become a slogan, a form of words. Describing a programme as a form of Human Resource Development is seen by many agencies as a sure way of securing accreditation and financial resources. The phrase is fast becoming meaningless: every activity of every government ministry and of every voluntary agency from planting trees or building new forms of housing to erecting vast irrigation dams can now be described as 'Human Resource Development'. And when a phrase comes to mean everything, it ceases to mean anything. HRD is one of the most used—and most abused—terms in Development programmes today; it needs to be carefully defined or dropped altogether.

1d. Community Development

The other strand which sprang out of the social planning philosophies was Community Development. For several years, this became the dominant basis for argument and action: that whole communities should be encouraged to engage in self-reliant economic activities. The concept (as applied to Development) built upon an earlier Community Organization movement in the USA from the 1920s to the 1940s, and it went through various stages. In one of its aspects, Community Development was seen as a programme designed to assist the poor ethnic minorities and the socially disadvantaged, largely through local self-help groups; but during the 1940s, the focus had come to settle on the school as a force for change, a focus for input from all other service and Development agencies. It was only later, under the influence of the social planners, that Community Development came to mean citizen participation in decision-making and problem-solving.

The idea of Community Development was promulgated so successfully that the Ashridge Conference (1947) after the end of the Second World War persuaded the then British Colonial Secretary to urge the remaining British colonies to adopt it as a guiding principle for their own Development. Both inside and outside the British Commonwealth, Ministries of Community Development were set up. India adopted the philosophy on achieving independence, setting up a National Institute of Community Development; the Philippines appointed a Presidential Assistant to carry through the policies, and Indonesia and Thailand established Directorates General. Most have now vanished (the Indian National Institute is now the National Institute for Rural Development, for example), though some still remain (Malawi, for example).

In Third World countries, Community Development sought to turn its back on Western concepts of industrialized and urban communities and instead stressed the values inherent in a balanced rural economy. It aimed at enabling local communities to take control of their own production processes. But as UNESCO indicated in its later definition of Community Development:

> the process by which the efforts of the people themselves are united with those of government authorities to improve economic, social and cultural conditions of communities, to integrate those communities into the life of the nation and enable them to contribute fully to national progress,

the aims of Community Development became more general, especially seeing it as linked with governmental agencies and programmes.[9]

The reasons for the failure of this strand of Development in the Third World are many and complex. On the one hand, governments found the need to direct production nationally, especially in the light of growing internationalism in economic and power structures, so that a loss of local autonomy was seen to be necessary and a clash between central planning and local community self-determination developed. At the same time, local communities, coming increasingly into contact with Western values through more effective media, built their ideals on towns and consumer goods. Those among the rural poor who were able to articulate their needs and make effective changes wanted to leave their communities. The criteria of success increasingly came to be those of income, production and national prosperity, rather than local prosperity. The increase in cash markets, the ideas of international aid agencies, the growing indebtedness of Third

World countries and many other forces undermined this movement. The structural changes espoused by writers such as Batten and Akhteer Hamid Khan were not the diet of the politicians and administrators who were appointed to implement the programmes.

Problems with economic growth models of Development

The Community Development movement reveals many of the problems which have been identified in economic growth models of Development—over-production in some commodities, the selection of some and the marginalization of other viable economic activities, the means of controlling and directing production, the importation of alien practices and materials to meet foreign market demands, the conflict between local and central interests and so on.

The results of economic-growth Development have sometimes been shown to be less than happy. In Kenya, for example, pressure by aid agencies and the national government for farmers to grow maize as a cash crop resulted in the loss of local varieties of seed. Growth and modernization—whether through central economic planning or through social planning, whether through HRD or Community Development—has proved to be in many cases malign to the welfare of the rural poor: 'it is not the lack of growth but its very occurrence that has led to a deterioration in the conditions of the rural poor'. 'Growth has no necessary alleviating let alone eradicating effect on poverty.'

It has been said that 'the economic crisis [brought about by the oil price increases in the early 1970s] ended the existence of the first development model [economic growth] as the ideal, . . . questioning the values it contained'. Nevertheless, most Third World Development programmes at both national and local levels are still aimed at economic growth.[10] Even health and family planning programmes spring ultimately from and drive towards a concept of Development which sees it as alleviating poverty. Women's 'upliftment' (a patronizing term) programmes, Integrated Rural Development programmes, literacy and awareness courses are in practice based on the economic growth and modernization view of Development. Other programmes too are seen to be valuable only insofar as they contribute to wealth generation: they are peripheral to or contributory to economic growth. Their relationship to the ultimate goal of Development can be shown in either of two forms (Figures 8.1a and b).

The economic growth model has recently received revived support. The Brundtland report on sustainable Development reasserted economic growth as the goal of Development—even if it is 'growth which respects limits to environmental resources', for sustainable Development does not see resources as unlimited, as earlier Developmental models did. The increased general concern for the poverty of Third World countries which limits their responses to natural disasters, and the movement towards the emancipation from debts and national economic self-reliance which the United Nations and other bodies are now actively seeking—all of these have thrust economic growth concepts of Development to the forefront once again.[11]

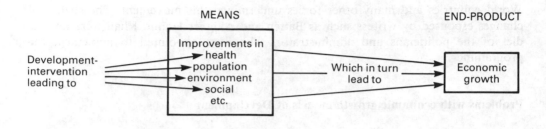

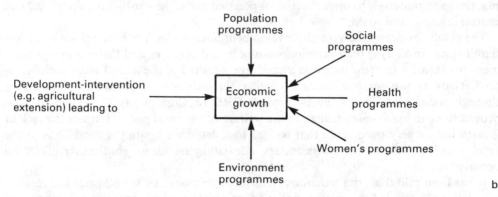

Figure 8.1 Two models of the relationship of Development (seen as social change programmes) and economic growth

Needs-based approaches: quality of life

2. Basic human needs

Since the 1960s, some have been arguing strongly for what they see as a new concept of Development. They urge that economic growth is a subordinate or intermediate goal, not the ultimate or substantive goal; that we need increased wealth not as an end in itself but in order to provide better health, better welfare, a better environment, a fairer way of life for the people. For them, the diagram of Development would be as shown in Figure 8.2. Meeting human needs and improving the quality of life are thus seen as the

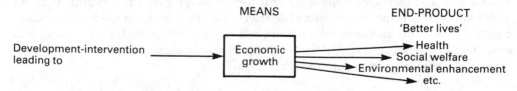

Figure 8.2 A third model of the relationship of Development (seen as meeting basic human needs) and economic growth

main goals of Development rather than building up the economic wealth of the nation. 'The basic questions are neither economic, political nor technical; they are moral'— 'how a population . . . moves away from a pattern perceived in some significant way as "less human" toward alternative patterns perceived as "more human".'[12]

The main tool devised for such Development was Basic Human Needs (BHN). Almost as much has been written about BHN as about Human Resource Development. It too has become something of a slogan to be attached to project proposals without thinking clearly about its meaning. But for many people, it is a serious concept which calls for a radical new approach. People, not economics, come first; and people come last as well. Development schemes, they argue, should be judged and evaluated by their contribution to meeting the basic needs of the people, improving their lot.[13]

What these needs are is a matter of argument. Many lists of BHNs have been drawn up. Goulet suggested three: life sustenance, esteem and freedom; others have used the generic term 'livelihood' to cover them all. On the other hand, the Sarvodaya movement of Sri Lanka listed ten groups of needs relating to the environment, water, clothing, food, housing, health care, communication, fuel, education, and spiritual and cultural needs. Other lists have been made, sometimes set down in an order of priority. Maslow's needs hierarchy (see above, p. 38) for example can be adapted to a societal as well as an individual context: basic economic needs (food) precede housing and defence (shelter and safety) and these in turn precede a sense of national communal harmony (belonging); above this lies the legitimation of the local community or group within the region and nation, and of the nation in the world at large (esteem of others); finally there is the need for the nation and the local community to exploit to the full its own potential (self-actualization). Such a hierarchy has the merit of establishing the position of economic needs as intermediate, and not the highest or chief goal of society.[14]

One widely agreed list centres on five clusters of needs:[15]

1. Personal consumer goods—food, clothing and shelter . . . the minima required to sustain life. . . .
2. General access to minimum physical and social services—good water supply, sanitation, preventive and curative medicine, energy for light, cooking, heating or cooling . . . it is arguable that education itself is a minimum social service.
3. Productive employment of individuals, families or communal units, yielding high enough output and fairly distributed rewards so that they may both contribute to and benefit from the supply of goods and services.
4. Physical, human and technological infra-structure and capacity necessary to produce goods and services.
5. Opportunity to take part in decisions about social and economic policies and about the ways these policies are carried out.

There is, however, no general consensus of these needs. Some people's 'basic' needs are regarded by others to be relative. And they are often seen as going beyond 'necessities' to 'rights'—to free speech, access to education, communications, consumer goods and credit facilities, for instance, the right of people to keep enough of what they produce or earn to enable them to accumulate capital, the right to participate in decision-making and to monitor the implementation of these decisions at local community and national level.

The BHN concept of Development then establishes a wide range of goals instead of simply economic growth and the modernization of industrial processes and social structures. It sounds good and commands immediate acceptance.

deprivation   →   meeting BHN   →   improved quality of life

Problems with BHN

There are problems with the BHN approach.

(a) First, few programmes have in fact been based on BHN despite the rhetoric. The main reason for this seems to be the practice of 'aid-giving' by which the rich give to the poor and expect in return economic results. Most programmes can be dressed up in the language of 'basic needs', but the underlying assumptions often remain economic, and this will affect the way in which these programmes are run, the attitudes the participant group will learn from the change-agents, the outcomes of the intervention, and the point at which the programme is seen to have achieved its goals. Indeed, this 'welfare economics' approach to Development 'does not appear to come to grips with the problem of welfare in any effective manner'.

(b) A second problem lies in the word 'need'. For needs are inevitably and essentially outsider-defined. Beyond the absolute minimum needs to sustain life itself, they represent value judgements made against standards which are drawn from outside the community concerned. Indeed, a thing cannot become a need except as judged against externally set concepts of what is the required norm. So that Development built on BHN comes to be an outsider-defined process. Local lists of wants often differ markedly from lists of 'basic needs' drawn up by aid agencies (see below, pp. 150–3).

(c) Thirdly, the words 'basic human needs' often come to mean 'minimum physical needs'—the lowest level of subsistence and services needed to ensure that the people can work efficiently. There is, for instance, no mention in the list above of spiritual or cultural needs, although it is recognized that 'secure and decent livelihoods . . . are not sufficient on their own'. These unspoken emphases can lead to two equally unspoken and unintended consequences:

(i) that meeting BHN becomes a process which necessarily one person must do to and for another person, i.e. that *I* must meet *your* (basic human) needs. Apart from the patronizing implications of this statement, meeting BHN seems to do little to promote 'self-reliance'; like all needs-meeting programmes, it can, unless careful steps are taken, create dependency;

(ii) that it is sometimes felt that once Development has met these basic needs, there is no further call for Development. Meeting identified needs can be taken as the end of the process; Development thus becomes a terminal concept. But Development by definition is never-ending, a continued pattern of directing change towards particular goals which the people increasingly set and undertake for themselves. It is difficult to see how people can come to meet their own needs, set their own goals, control their own Development from a programme of BHN.[16]

II. Exclusion-based approaches

It was to overcome these problems that some added to the list of BHN the concept of 'liberation'. But this marks a major change of perception; for those who are the subject of Development are no longer viewed as 'deprived', in need of some form of outside assistance, but as oppressed, excluded from the sources of power. The problem has been totally redefined. Development is no longer a tool of governments and the existing social elites, used to help the less fortunate, 'the result of the political will of the power structure, to initiate desired change' (as HRD and BHN are), but an instrument of the people themselves, a way of changing society fundamentally, 'a means of disturbing the status quo'. Instead of reinforcing or merely modifying contemporary social structures (as the needs-based programmes seek to do), Development now contains a formal challenge to existing structures.[17]

There are three main kinds of 'exclusion' views. The differences between them as revealed in the language they use are real. One speaks in terms of dependency and self-reliance; a second speaks of oppression and liberation; while the third speaks of marginalization and participation.

1. Dependency or appropriate self-reliance

The argument goes like this. Most Third World countries have experienced colonialism, often for very long periods. During this time, they have been treated as dependent economies and dependent peoples, often as workers and slaves; and they were taught by their masters that the things which made for Development lay in the attitudes, structures and practices which the 'more developed' countries possessed. It was of course in the interests of their masters that only limited advance should be made; but Western values were held up to them as the ideal to which they should strive. When these countries won or were given independence, their leaders (most of whom had been educated in the West) continued to accept this picture as 'reality'. They saw their own countries as dependent on the more industrialized countries and visualized progress as importing from the West economic theories, structures and attitudes. Western educational systems and curricula and Western practices (such as shares and the stock market, banking systems, etc., but with rather more hesitation about trade unions and industrial relations) became models to build on. Nothing much changed after independence; and it was in the interest of the West to see that nothing changed.[18]

This neo-colonialism, under which modernization meant 'Westernizing', provoked its own reaction. The problem which Development now sought to solve was 'dependency' and the goal of Development became national self-reliance: building up what is appropriate within the country itself, accepting as valuable and using traditional rather than alien knowledge and structures and practices. Post-independence Tanzania, led by Nyerere, and revolutionary Cuba both built their Development programmes on the 'difference between being the agent of one's own development as defined in one's own terms and being a mere beneficiary of development as defined by someone else'; 'development is not a cluster of benefits "given" to people in need but rather a process by which a populace acquires a greater mastery over its own destiny'. Western models taken as the norm for 'One World' are to be replaced by 'a prospect of a pluri-cultural world'.[19]

dependency $\rightarrow$ indigenization $\rightarrow$ self-reliance

It follows from this that the process of Development cannot come from the West any longer. While one may be 'given' independence, one cannot be 'given' self-reliance: it has to be built up by action on the part of the participant peoples themselves. The dependency model is seen to be a new approach to Development, reinterpreting all concepts, including 'modernization' (which no longer means asking others to build in one country what can be seen in the West but rather building for oneself what is appropriate to one's own country, its past and current traditions). The goal is to become self-reliant and the process is action by the Third World countries for themselves—using as *they* feel appropriate the help and resources of those Western societies whom they helped to make prosperous. The West may assist by building a New International Order, but in the end, the Third World must create its own futures—with help where it can get it.[20]

2. Oppression or liberation

It is argued, though, that such action by Third World countries—and in this sense truly 'developing' countries—will be (and is being) resisted by the more industrialized countries, just as the building of self-reliance by the poor in all countries, Western and Third World, will be (and is being) resisted by the powerful and rich within those countries. So there has sprung up a further set of views which sees the problem as being not simply dependency but 'oppression', which sees the process as being one of assisting the oppressed to take action for themselves, and which sees the goal as being liberation.

oppression   →   social action   →   liberation

We must not over-emphasize the newness of this model. For just as the BHN approach has grown out of HRD, so the concept of liberation to some extent grew out of BHN. Many of those who advocate BHN see the goal of Development in terms of freedom—from hunger, from want, from poverty, from ignorance. They too want the people to be liberated. But whereas the BHN approach sees the problem as arising from vast impersonal forces, the advocates of liberation Development have personalized those forces. The people, they say, are oppressed by other people—by multinational companies, capitalists, entrepreneurs, the educated elites, political cliques—individuals, groups and classes who are exploiting others. The language is that of power—of domination and subordination, for instance. The target groups are no longer viewed as poor and ignorant, unable to help themselves as in BHN, but as oppressed, deprived of power.

The term 'oppressed' in Development contexts has a technical meaning which embraces but goes wider than physical oppression visible in countries like South Africa. While it includes repression and exploitation, it has also come to mean 'denied access to resources'. There are enough resources in this world for everyone, it is argued; but some peoples, some countries, are denied proper access to those resources by other peoples, other countries. The poor are kept poor by the rich; the newly freed colonial countries are kept in a colonial state by new (largely economic) ties; slum dwellers are denied proper housing by those who own the land. These are the 'dispossessed', denied their birthright by the few.[21]

Much of this oppression is unconscious on the part of both the oppressor and the oppressed. Indeed, many of the oppressors would deny that they were involved in any such oppression. But oppression is inherent in the structure of society today. Men oppress women in the sense the word is used here: even those men who seek to help women to achieve a more just relationship cannot help being (as men) part of the problem. One example of this is the so-called literacy problem. In countries like India and Bangladesh, where literates form a minority of the population, there is much talk by that educated minority of the 'illiterate masses' as being 'outside society: they must be brought in'. But how can 70 per cent of the population be excluded from the society in which they live? How can they be 'brought in' to a society of educated persons who in some cases form less than 30 per cent of the total population? What is implied is that the 30 per cent are the 'true' society and that the 70 per cent are an 'inferior' society; that the illiterate many must learn to behave like the literate few before they can be trusted with transfer from the outer to the inner circle, they must learn the language of their masters before they can be granted membership of the 'true' society.

Oppression then is pushing other people to one side, keeping groups of people out. There are many ways this is done—by structures leading to the exploitation of the poor by the wealthy as well as by the non-recognition of the abilities and power of the oppressed (whether majority or minority), by the acceptance by the oppressed of the abilities, power and value systems of the elites. It is not only a question of systems (as with the dependency model of Development) but also of attitudes, beliefs and values as held by both oppressed and oppressors and the imposition of one set of values on other peoples.

Underdevelopment seen as oppression is caused by the oppressors, not by the oppressed. And thus the oppressor as well as the oppressed find themselves bound, in need of liberation:

> This is the great . . . task of the oppressed: to liberate themselves and their oppressors as well. The oppressors who oppress, exploit and rape by virtue of their power, cannot find in this power the strength to liberate either the oppressed or themselves. Only power that springs from the weakness of the oppressed will be sufficiently strong to free both.

Development then becomes a process of liberating the oppressed by a process of conscientization—that is, helping the oppressed (and the oppressor, if possible) to become aware of what is going on and to act upon this situation in a way which will change it radically. It is a process of changing values as much as changing structures.[22]

The liberation view of Development suffers from a number of problems similar to those of BHN. For one thing, it may come to be seen as a terminating rather than a continuing process. Once the programme has achieved its goal (liberation), Development may be seen to come to a stop; whereas true Development, seen as planning and controlling change, never ceases. Furthermore, the process of liberation appears to depend upon outsider help to begin the process of conscientization. Such judgements misunderstand the basic assumptions on which these ideas of oppression and liberation are built; but they have been enough to suggest to other practitioners a somewhat different approach.

3. Empowerment for participation

There has of late been an increasing stress on 'participation' as the goal of Development—participation in the community's and the nation's decision-taking and planning, and in choosing, criticizing and controlling those who carry out the programmes. This view sees the people's oppression as deliberate exclusion from power by others who control social and political structures and tools of communication. Participation in the local community's and the country's economic, social, cultural and political activities is the intended goal of Development, to be achieved through a process of empowerment, 'people gaining an understanding of and control over social, economic and/or political forces in order to improve their standing in society'.[23]

marginalization → empowerment → participation

This is the real revolution in Development thinking. For instead of thinking of the people in negative terms—as poor and backward (the growth and modernization views of Development), or as deprived, ignorant and needy (the BHN school of thought), or as oppressed and exploited (dependency views), or as blind and powerless (the liberationists), we can now view them in positive terms, as marginalized potential participants.

Development then is the process of empowerment, of helping peoples of regions or communities or sectors to identify and maximize their own potential to contribute to society by participating more fully in all its activities. The poorest region, the most illiterate groups, the itinerants, the aged, the poorest of the poor, the slum dwellers, are already part of the society in which they live and not outsiders needing to be brought in. They already contribute something to society, to the richness and diversity of its culture, for example, or to its economic well-being or to its stock of indigenous knowledge and tradition or to its means of communications. They are 'blood donors', not 'blood suckers'. All parts of society go to make up the whole. But equally all parts of society could contribute more and participate more in order to make society richer, more rounded, more whole.[24]

The use of the word 'empowerment' is not meant to imply that the people do not possess power already. Development-as-empowerment seeks to help all peoples, individually or in groups, to see themselves for what they are and the contribution they are already making. For the main instrument of exclusion is the range of attitudes which the oppressors have induced the excluded to adopt towards themselves. (See below p. 177.) Oppression involves the concept of alienation, by which the oppressors make the oppressed feel foreign. The aim of Development is to help all people to enhance their own contribution by identifying, developing and harnessing their potential. In this way, peripheral groups can be legitimated to society as a whole, the invisible can be seen, the voiceless can be heard to speak for themselves; those who feel negatively about themselves can begin to see their positive contribution to the welfare of themselves and others. And this becomes a continuous process: for if individuals or groups develop the ability and the confidence to see and to use more fully their own power, the process of Development becomes self-generating.

Development in this model does not stress *need* (which must be met by others); rather it lays emphasis on the richness more than the poverty of the poor, the potential for action rather than the helplessness of the powerless. Development comes to highlight the positive rather than the negative, participation 'in' something desirable rather than liberation 'from' something undesirable. It is a process of helping the people to join in helping others to develop—of directing and controlling the processes of change which they are themselves helping to bring about.

Such a view is less directly economic in emphasis:

> Any action which gives [the people] more control of their own affairs is an action for development, even if it does not offer them better health or more bread. Any action that reduces their say in determining their own affairs or running their own lives is not development and retards them even if the action brings them a little better health and a little more bread.
>
> Development means both the elimination of oppression, exploitation, enslavement and humiliation, and the promotion of our independence and human dignity. Therefore in considering the development of our nation and in preparing development plans our main emphasis at all times should be the development of people and not of things. If development is to benefit the people, the people must participate in considering, planning and implementing their development plans.
>
> (Declaration of Tanzania ANU Party Guidelines)

COMMENTARY

Such a summary of so many different views runs the danger of over-simplification of what is a complex reality. In practice, it is possible to view the Development world as consisting of one major view (economic growth) and many newer fragmented views. But all these may be fined down to two basic approaches: one which sees the participants as deprived and the goal of Development as satisfying needs; and the other which sees the participants as potential partners prevented from joining in partly by others and partly by the negative view of themselves and their own potential which has been imposed on them by others, and the goal of Development as freedom to participate.

Two general points need to be made here:

(a) First, that more models of Development will inevitably arise and take their place alongside these approaches. Already there is discussion of 'transformation' as the goal of Development.[25] Old views never die away completely; they live alongside the new. Policy-making in Development as in adult education is incrementalist in character.

(b) Secondly, that the economic 'growth and modernization' model is in fact still dominant; it provides the basis of most current programmes. The rest are still minority views or academic slogans.

Why so many views?

The reasons there are so many different approaches are complex. In part it is because the viewpoint of the participant groups (farmers and the urban poor, for example) is different from that of the Development agencies. But more particularly it would seem to spring from a number of contradictions inherent in Development itself and the consequent unease which practitioners feel with any one approach;[26] for example:

- the tension between respect for the autonomy of the participant group and commitment to change through intervention
- the tension between respect for indigenous knowledge and practices (e.g. in traditional medicine or farming practices) and commitment to change through new knowledge and new practices

- the fear of a uniform culture and a desire for plurality set against commitment to change through the adoption of common standards
- the tension between Development seen as intervention and Development seen as a self-controlled voluntary process

And with all this unease comes the search for newer and better formulations of Development, more truly representing the ideals and values of the change-agents.[27]

Development and the West

But whichever approach we adopt, Development is not just of relevance to Third World countries while the richer countries can look on and offer aid out of their generosity. Western industrialized societies are changing rapidly and there is a need here as well as in the Third World to control and direct that process of change towards desirable ends. There are in every country underdeveloped and marginalized regions, sectors of the population who have basic needs, people who are voiceless and powerless and whose potential to contribute to the welfare of the whole has never been freed and tapped— those 'victims' (as a recent report on the 'genuine crisis in the global capitalist financial system' put it):

> workers, peasants, small producers and the rural and urban unemployed [who] make up the majority of people in even the most developed nations. . . . They are organising to seek their own emancipation . . . we identify with the aspirations of these people to control their own destinies by creating alternative self-reliant paths. . . .
>
> (GATT–Fly 1985)

Concepts of Development worked out in the Third World are then of direct relevance to those who live in more industrialized and richer societies. One of the many things we have to learn from the so-called underdeveloped parts of the world is that we can and should strive to direct change towards meaningful goals and that we have a choice in those goals—between wealth generation or meeting the basic human needs of all the people or of freeing all sectors to play their full part in society as a whole. The choice is ours: but we who live in the West should not see Development as applying only to 'them'; it applies to us also.[28]

NOTES TO CHAPTER 8

(1) See Kitching, G. (1982) *Development and Underdevelopment in Historical Perspective*, Methuen; Frank, A. G. (1969) *Capitalism and Underdevelopment in Latin America*, New York; Cole, J. (1987) *Development and Underdevelopment: a Profile of the Third World*, Methuen. See also La Belle, T. J. (1976) *Nonformal Education and Social Change in Latin America*, California; La Belle, T. J. (1984) Goals and strategies in nonformal education in Latin America, *Comparative Education Review* **20**(3); and for a review of these, Rogers, E. M. (1976) Communication and development: the passing of the dominant paradigm, *Communication Research* 3, 121–48; Horowitz, I. (1966) *The Worlds of Development*, Oxford.

(2) See, for example, Havens, E. (1972) Methodological issues in the study of development, *Sociologia Ruralis* **12**(3–4), 252–72, which distinguishes between those approaches which see the world as in a basic state of harmony temporarily disrupted and capable of restora-

tion ('equilibrium' models) and those which see society as in a constant state of change and struggle ('conflict' models). He subdivides these into the following: (1) Equilibrium: (a) the behavioural (in which people need to change their practices); (b) the psycho-dynamic (in which people need to change their attitudes, to adopt modern approaches); and (c) the diffusionist (mainly economic growth); and (2) Conflict: (a) structuralist (non-Marxist); and (b) Marxist.

(3) Quoted in Mengin (1988), p. 1. See Wignaraja (1976), p. 3. For growth, see Rostow, W. W. (1952) *The Process of Economic Growth*, Oxford: Oxford University Press; Rostow, W. W. (1960) *The Stages of Economic Growth: a Non-Communist Manifesto*, Cambridge; Baran, P. A. (1962) *The Political Economy of Growth*, London; Rostow, W. W. (1971) *Politics and the Stages of Economic Growth*, Oxford: Oxford University Press; Mishan, E. J. (1967) *The Costs of Economic Growth*, London: Staples; Mishan, E. J. (1977) *The Economic Growth Debate*, Allen and Unwin; Weaver, J. H. and Jamieson, K. P. (1978) *Economic Development: Competing Parables*, Washington. For modernization, see Russell, C. S. and Nicholson, N. K. (1981) *Public Choice and Rural Development*, Washington; Inkeles, A. and Holsinger, D. B. (1974) *Education and Individual Modernity in Developing Countries*, Leider; Lerner, D. (1958) *The Passing of the Traditional Society*, New York; Eisenstadt, S. N. (1966) *Modernization: Protest and Change*, New Jersey: Prentice Hall.

(4) Stohr, W. B. and Taylor, D. R. F. (1981) *Development from Above or Below?*, John Wiley; Grant (1973); Council of Europe (1986b), p. 5. See Mengin (1988), p. 2: 'farmers [are looking] at the problems of development within their geographical region . . . not only in respect of . . . agricultural activity. A certain number of socio-economic categories can only seek salvation in a collective development plan'. In this illuminating paper, she draws a distinction between two models of economic growth development: (a) sectoral stimulation through scientific processes (later changed to scientific attitudes or 'rationality') using inputs and based on externally set goals; and (b) regional stimulation through what she calls 'economic rationality' (i.e. social attitudes) using indigenous resources and based on internally set goals in an integrated pattern. But the aim in each case is the same—economic growth. At a different level, the World Bank demonstrates the same attitudes: 'Rural Development is a type of social change in which new ideas are introduced into a social system in order to produce higher per capita production methods and improved social organisation', Education Sector Policy Paper (1974), p. x.

(5) Seers (1969), pp. 2–6; UNRISD (1979); Mengin (1988), p. 1. See Adelman, I. and Morris, C. T. (1973) *Economic Growth and Social Equity in Developing Countries*, California; Oakley, P. and Winder, D. (1981) *The Concept and Practice of Rural Social Development: Trends in Latin America and India*, Manchester: University of Manchester; Pitt, D. C. (1976) *The Social Dynamics of Development*, Pergamon; Bennis et al. (1964); Lippitt, R., Watson, J. and Westley, R. (1958) *Dynamics of Planned Change*, New York.

(6) Seers (1969), p. 2: 'the realization of the potential of the human personality'.

(7) Harbison, F. H. and Myers, C. A. (1964) *Education, Manpower and Economic Growth*, New York; Harbison, F. H. (1965) The development of human resources, in Jackson, E. E. and Blackwell, B. (eds) *Economic Development in Africa*, Collins; Nadler, L. (1979) *Developing Human Resources*, Texas; Nadler, L. (ed.) (1984) *Handbook of Human Resource Development*, New York; Nadler, L. and Wiggs, G. D. (1986) *Managing Human Resource Development*, San Francisco: Jossey Bass; Frank, H. E. (1974) *Human Resource Development: the European Approach*, Houston; du Bois, E. E. (1984) Human resource development: expanding role, in Klevins, C. (ed.) *Materials and Methods in Adult and Continuing Education*, California.

(8) An article in *The Hindu*, 5 November 1987, spoke of 'honing the rural workers' skills through competent training programmes . . . giving a big push to productivity'.

(9) Green (1977), p. 3. For the Community Development movement, see Batten (1959, 1967); Biddle, W. W. and Biddle, L. J. (1965) *The Community Development Process: the Rediscovery of Local Initiative*, New York; Ross, M. G. and Lappin, B. W. (1967) *Community Organization: Theory, Principles and Practice*, New York; Sperger, I. A. (1972) *Community Organization: Studies in Constraint*, London; Long, H. B., Anderson, R. C.

and Blubaugh, J. A. (eds) (1973) *Approaches to Community Development*, Iowa; Minzey, J. D. and le Tarte, C. E. (1972) *Community Education: from Program to Process*, Michigan; Midgeley, J. *et al.* (1986) *Community Participation, Social Development and the State*, Methuen; Kuitenbrower, J. (1973) *Continuity and Discontinuity in Community Development Theory*, The Hague: ISS; Sinclair, M. E. and Lillis, K. (1980) *School and Community in the Third World*, Croom Helm; Brager, G. A. and Specht, H. (1973) *Community Organizing*, New York; Greifer, J. (1974) *Community Action for Social Change: a Casebook of Current Projects*, New York; Grosser, C. F. (1976) *New Directions in Community Organization: from Enabling to Advocacy*, New York; Cox, F. M. (1974) *Strategies for Community Organization: a Book of Readings*, Illinois. For social action, see Alinksy, S. D. (1946) *Reveille for Radicals*, New York (reprinted 1969). See Council of Europe (1986b), p. 26, for Community Development still in Turkey. The movement is beginning to revive in Third World countries in the form of community schools and colleges—a rather different form of development from that originally proposed.

(10)   van Nieuwenhuijze (1982), p. 90; Ghose, K. A. and Griffin, K. (1983) Rural poverty and development alternatives in south and south-east Asia, *National Labour Institute Bulletin*, **5–6**, 183; Mengin (1988), p. 4. See Meadows, D. H., Meadows, D. L., Randers, J. and Behrens, W. S. (1972) *The Limits to Growth*, New York; Goulet and Hudson (1971); Szentes (1976).

(11)   Brundtland (1987); see Ramphal, Sri S. (1987), The environment and sustainable development, *RSA Journal* **135** (November), 879–90: 'The hope lies in economic growth . . . some may be shocked by the thought of turning on its head the environmental doctrines of the 1970s . . . the Commission is calling for nothing less than a new era of economic growth'.

(12)   Goulet (1975), pp. vii–x: Goulet sees the key to development as lying in changed power relationships; Nerfin (1977); Nyerere, J. (1974) *Man and Development*, London: Oxford University Press.

(13)   Goulet (1975), ch. 3; Donald, G. (1971) International development strategies for the Second UN Development Dialogue, *Development Digest* **9**(2) (April), 18–28; see Wignaraja (1976); Erb and Kallab (1975); Green, R. H. (1976) Adult education, basic human needs and integrated development planning, *Convergence* **9**(4), 45–59; Streeten, P. and Burki, S. J. (1978) Basic needs: some issues, *World Development* **6**(3); Streeten, P. (1977) The distinctive features of a basic needs approach to development, *International Development Review* **19**(3); Ponsioen, J. (1979) The basic needs strategy: a commission to the modern sector, *International Development Review* **21**(4); Allen, D. W. and Anzalone, S. (1981) Basic needs: a new approach to development—but new approach to education?, *International Development Review* **27**(3); Simmons, S. and Phillips, T. (1977) *Education for Basic Human Needs*, World Bank; World Bank, Education sector working paper (1980); Noor, A. (1981) *Education and Basic Human Needs*, World Bank.

(14)   Bradshaw, J. (1977) The concept of social need, in Fitzgerald, M. *et al. Welfare in Action*, Routledge and Kegan Paul; Halmos, P. (1987), Concept of social problem, in *Social Work, Community Work and Society*, Open University Unit for course DE20; Sarvodaya Development Education Institute (1981) *Ten Basic Human Needs and Their Satisfaction*, Sri Lanka: SDEI; UNRISD (1979); Todaro, M. (1977) *Economic Development in the Third World*, Longman, p. 63. Lawson (1979) draws a distinction between educational and other needs; an educational need is a 'deficiency [which] can be remedied by the help of a learning [he means educational] process.

(15)   Bown, L. in Rogers, A. (1984), pp. 30–1, based on Green (1977), pp. 17–23.

(16)   Chambers (1983), p. 146; Green (1977), p. 16; van Nieuwenhuijze (1982), p. 90.

(17)   Muyeed, A. (1982) Some reflections on education for rural development, *International Journal of Development Education* **28**(2), 299.

(18)   Perlman, J. (1976) *The Myth of Marginality*, California; Cohen, B. J. (1973) *The Question of Imperialism: the Political Economy of Dominance and Dependence*, New York; Frank, A. G., The development of underdevelopment, in Wilber (1973), pp. 94–103; Szentes (1976); Goulet (1975); note 1 above. For a case study, see Leys, C. (1975) *Underdevelopment in Kenya: the Political Economy of Neo-Colonialism*, Heinemann.

(19) Parmar (1975); Goulet (1975), p. 155; Goulet and Hudson (1971), p. 19; van Nieuwenhuijze (1982), p. 90; Nyerere, J. (1969) Education for self-reliance, *Convergence* **3**(1), 3–27; Cardoso, F. H. and Faletto, E. (1979) *Dependency and Development in Latin America*, California.

(20) Goulet, D. (1974) Development and the New Economic Order, *International Development Review* **16**(2), 10–16; Inkeles, A. and Smith, D. H. (1974) *Becoming Modern: Individual Change in Six Developing Countries*, Cambridge, Mass.

(21) See works on hegemony by A. Gramsci as surveyed by Ireland, T. (1987) *Antonio Gramsci and Adult Education: Reflections on the Brazilian Experience*, University of Manchester; and Musgrave, F. (1979) Curriculum, culture and ideology, in Taylor, P. H. (ed.) *New Directions in Curriculum Studies*, Falmer Press. See Brookfield, H. (1975) *Interdependent Development*, Pittsburg; Lipton, M. (1977) *Why the Poor Remain Poor*, London: Temple Smith; Gutiérrez, G. (1973) *Theology of Liberation*, New York; Nyerere, J. (1976) Liberated man, the purpose of development, *Convergence* **9**(4), 9–16; Kurien, C. T. (1978) *Poverty, Planning and Social Transformation*, Delhi.

(22) Freire, P. (1973) *Education for Critical Consciousness*, New York (repr. as *Education: the Practice of Freedom*, London: Writers and Readers Guild, 1974); Freire (1972).

(23) Owens, E. and Shaw, R. (1979) *Development Reconsidered*, Mass.; Kindervatter (1979), p. 13.

(24) Oakley (1984); on participation, see pp. 142, 226 below.

(25) M. Anisur Rahman (1991) Towards an alternative development paradigm, *IFDA Dossier* 81 (April–June), 17–29.

(26) Mengin (1988), pp. 3–4, sees one dominant concept/model of development and the appearance of a galaxy of alternative models which 'theorize in some way . . . the dissimilarities, even the antagonisms, of the varying situations and possibilities of progress of those concerned . . . the concept of development as understood by the different socio-economic categories is profoundly affected by the position they occupy in the economic and even the social structure of the region. . . .'

(27) Bendavid, A. and Bendavid, L. (1974) Developed and underdeveloped, a radical view of constructive relationships, *International Development Review* **16**(1), 9–14, denied that there can be any universal definition of Development which is more properly to be defined by each country and peoples; the West is arrogant in thinking it can define Development for others. Such an approach would bring to an end all Development—and that in itself would be to side with the existing forces working for inequality.

(28) Nerfin (1977); Rogers, A. (1984).

Chapter 9

Processes of Development

The two contrasting views of underdevelopment, that based on deprivation and needs and that based on exclusion and oppression, lead inevitably to two different kinds of Development-intervention, two opposing processes—the 'input' process and the 'social action' process.

THE INPUT PROCESS

The intervention which springs from models of Development based on deprivation or needs is one of supplying a required input:

$$\text{deprivation/needs} \quad \rightarrow \quad \text{input} \quad \rightarrow \quad \text{growth/quality of life}$$

An analogy is a plant; it cannot grow until an outsider (for the plant cannot do it for itself) provides water. Countries, regions and sectors of the population are seen to be lacking in particular resources. For growth to occur, they need to receive what they do not possess—capital, technology, skills, knowledge, infrastructure. This 'aid' must come in from outside, for the target population does not by definition have what they need. And the result of this input will be growth, accumulation, a better life.

Most existing Development programmes are built on this premise. The use of words like 'provide' and 'impart' in connection with these programmes makes this clear: 'The objective of this programme is to impart skills (or knowledge or literacy etc.) to . . .'; or 'The aim is to provide capital (or power supply or new technology) to . . .'

Difficulties with the input process

Input Development has secured considerable achievements in terms of economic growth. Nevertheless, over the last few years serious problems inherent in this process have been identified:[1]

1. It has become clear that the input process leads to and is based on *dependency*. 'Target groups' are seen to be unable to do anything to help themselves; they rely on other people to help them.

    I am reminded of a visit I paid in south India to a group of villagers who had been the 'recipients' of an awareness-raising programme. I asked the participants what they intended to do next.

    'We don't know', they replied; 'he [the change-agent] must tell us'.

    'What does this village need?' I asked.

    That was an easier question to deal with after a twenty-four-week course.

    'We need our own village bakery', was the response; and they spoke at length of their need.

    'What are you going to do to get one?'

    'We can't do anything: someone must give us one.'

    Such attitudes are common in input-dominated models of Development. The people come to accept the viewpoint of the Development agent—that because they do not possess what they need, someone from outside must give it to them. Such a view imposes both the nature of the problem and the solutions on the people, sometimes against their will (dams are built, land for forestry appropriated, in the name of the people); it creates and confirms a sense of helplessness and dependency.

2. The input approach implies that Development can only take place so long as there are richer and more powerful people and nations to help the poorer and 'weaker sections' (the terms used are usually negative). Thus Development depends on and perpetuates the existing *imbalance* in the world. More than one Western leader has been heard to declare that they can only assist Third World countries by remaining richer and stronger than these countries. There is a basic contradiction: in order to help developing countries 'catch up', developed countries need to maintain the gap. The gap itself is an essential feature of aid—a fact which encourages some Western countries to justify their seeking to profit from aid.[2]

    If this is true of nations, it is also true inside countries and regions. Inputs or aid (whether money, technology or knowledge) have often increased, not diminished, internal inequalities. The inputs go to a few, and these consolidate their position, arguing that in so doing they in their turn can help those who are deprived and needy. This kind of Development produces attitudes and patterns of behaviour which enable a hierarchical society to achieve Developmental goals while leaving the vested interests of the dominant groups untouched or even enhanced—though there are those who doubt if such results can truly be called Development.

3. Input-Development seems to see resources as being *infinite*. The richer and stronger sections can continue to create new resources (new money, new skills, new technology, new knowledge, etc.) and pass these on in the form of aid to those in need. But we now see more clearly, through the 'interdependent world' debate of the 1970s and 1980s, that resources are not infinite, that what is needed is a more equitable distribution of these resources. We may not have finished locating and exploiting new forms of resources, but in the end the resources of this planet are not infinite.

4. Such Development, by which A (a richer, stronger, wiser person or country) does something for B (a poorer, weaker, ignorant person or country), assumes that only the receivers of aid need to change, not the givers. Input-Development can lead to the recipients of aid being treated as virtual beggars. Even the BHN approach can

dehumanize and patronize the poor; it views their needs from the viewpoint of the West. What they want (their aspirations and visions) and what they know (their experiences and culture) are frequently discounted. Many people have argued that the strings which are often attached to aid destroy self-respect and self-reliance on the part of the recipients. Examples of the use of tariffs, trade embargoes and other forms of pre-conditions to aid abound in all parts of the world. The World Bank, in giving cash to the city authorities in Bombay for urgently needed housing, 'required' the city to repeal one of its legislative enactments; President Reagan threatened to cut one-third of American aid to Bangladesh unless it agreed to drop abortion from its family planning programme, while the US Congress cut aid to India by 15m dollars to 'penalize' India for voting against it at the United Nations and for its trade ties with Nicaragua.

This neo-colonialism amounts to a rejection of indigenous ways of thought, indigenous knowledge and indigenous practice, and replaces them with alien ways of thought, knowledge and practices. The answers which the planners have devised—*their* equipment, knowledge and ways—are better than those of the localities and adequate to solve the problems which they themselves have identified.

There are fashions in this. At times, input-Development agencies relax and say: 'We must trust these guys, treat them as responsible adults', and the number of strings attached is reduced for a time. But after a few cases of what look like corruption and wastage, stricter controls are imposed. 'After all, we are responsible for the proper stewardship of these resources to those behind us who provide them', they argue. And so the roundabout continues as long as aid continues.

There was in the early 1970s in India (in the south at least) a 'moratorium movement': 'Let us', it was argued, 'refuse all aid for a period, say five years. Let us see if we can stand on our own feet, make and implement our own decisions, live within our own resources for at least a short time.' The movement died away after the next major cyclone; aid continued to be requested and given. The dependency so created and the patronizing attitudes seemed relatively small sacrifices compared with the literally life-giving aid.[3]

5. Fifthly in this litany of problems inherent in the input model of Development is the fact that problems tend to be seen as *technical* in nature rather than human; and they are capable of relatively simple solutions. Human needs can be met with technical inputs: the shortage of water will be solved by a new well or irrigation channel without looking at the social implications; community health can be controlled by a purification plant and immunization; poverty and unemployment can be alleviated by skills training in some appropriate craft.

Since input-Development sees problems and their solution as purely technical, large areas of human activity are not seen as lying within the scope of Development. While income-generating programmes for women, for instance, are deemed to be a necessary part of Development, programmes for women's political involvement are not; while social welfare is Development, cultural activities are not. The HRD and the BHN approaches have widened the scope of many programmes, it is true; but too often these approaches also think that the process of meeting needs is to provide inputs of a technical nature—new housing, money to buy consumer goods, technical training for new economic activities, clinics for health care, etc.

And the results of these inputs will, it has been assumed, flow automatically. New techniques or equipment are thought to be all that is needed; if properly presented they will be adopted and lead to their own rewards. Money will be used to create more money; clean water supplies will be properly used and maintained; inputs will lead to improvements.

Because problems are thought to be capable of solution by material inputs, and because it is assumed that the results will automatically flow from the input, the Development process comes to an end not when the objective has been achieved but when the input has been made. The yield of rice, for example, will (it is thought) inevitably be increased by applications of agrochemicals; fishing catches will be increased by larger or more efficient nets; health will improve with new tubewells. Once the farmer has learned to use the right amount of fertilizer, he is thought to have no further needs; once the fisherman has received his new net, the programme of Development is ended. The digging of tubewells, not the improvement of health, becomes the goal.

Input-Development programmes then come to be evaluated solely by objective-achievement rather than by their outcomes. The results of these interventions on the lives of individuals, on the local economy or on the social structure of the community are rarely assessed. Such impacts are felt to be beyond the scope of Development seen as input. Only the achievement of the specified objective of the input programme is of importance; this is the criterion of success or failure. Input programmes will by judged by the numbers of latrines erected, trees planted, or cattle or human beings vaccinated rather than by any improvement in the quality of life, for latrines, trees and vaccinations can be counted and their provision will, it is assumed, inevitably mean that life has been improved.

But time and again it has become apparent that the intended results of the programme do not flow automatically from the inputs, that Development has not sprung from inputs alone. New boats were not used to enlarge fishing grounds and catches; new nutritional practices were not followed, though all the inputs were there. One of the clearest instances of this is the provision of toilet facilities in urban slums: ignored by those who live around or used on the outside rather than the inside for purposes of defecation, they have done nothing for hygiene or health or the quality of life. More than technical inputs alone is needed if Development changes are to take place. Gradually 'inputters' are coming to see that target groups need to be encouraged to *adopt* and *utilize* their inputs for effective Development.

THE SOCIAL ACTION PROCESS

With such a list of problems attached to input, it is perhaps strange that most Development programmes at both central planning and grass-roots level are still based on this model. In part this is because it is easier to give aid than to solve problems, easier to make quantitative than qualitative evaluations. But it is not strange that a new process has been urged, springing from the alternative view that the target groups are not so much deprived as excluded and that *action* by the participant group rather than inputs from others is needed to achieve Development. This model may be represented thus:

excluded $\rightarrow$ social action $\rightarrow$ liberation/participation

This view rejects the idea that people are like plants, unable to move in search of resources. Instead it asserts that they are able to take action, to forage for themselves. The people, they point out, have collectively been meeting their own needs for centuries, using traditional strategies and not relying on outside help; outsider aid and central planning are relatively new features. If problems today are bigger—drought in Africa, starvation in Asia, unemployment everywhere—we need to understand why they are bigger and help those who are involved to take action against the causes of the problems as much as against the problems themselves.

This is an 'insider', not an 'outsider', concept of Development. The intervention comes in the form of helping the people in their own social groupings to identify their own problems and to set their own goals. Instead of being seen as needy, passive recipients of aid, the participant populations are seen as already possessing much which will enable them to decide and to act for themselves. But they are stopped in this process by other interests. What then is needed is collective action by the people through which they build up their awareness, their confidence and their competencies to free themselves and to gain access to resources.

Examples abound of this kind of Development from all parts of the world. In Rajasthan, in the face of long-persisting drought, villagers are being enabled to rebuild for themselves the traditional land resource systems which were previously employed to combat such natural disasters. In Mauritius, herds of highly productive Friesian cows specially imported (some of them cross-bred with the native Creole cow) are being replaced (after local research) by the more traditional single Creole cow managed by the communal cow-keeper. Elsewhere, participant groups, after a review of their own needs and aspirations, have been helped to establish appropriate social forms (co-operatives in many cases) and economic activities, ways of controlling their own affairs, drawing on their own experience.[4]

The goal then is the liberation and full participation of the oppressed and marginalized target group in the Development of society as a whole. And the process as well as the goal is liberation, self-reliance: one cannot learn about freedom without experiencing it in the learning process itself, one cannot learn about participation without participating.

Advantages of the social action model

What are described here are two quite different models of the Development process (Table 9.1). It is not possible to dress up one model in the clothes of the other (though several agencies attempt to describe input programmes as participatory when they are not). Social-action Development will have processes and results quite different from those of input models:

1. It will not result in dependency but in self-reliance, freedom of action and thinking, decision-making and execution; local groups will decide for themselves what they want to do and develop the confidence and appropriate competencies to do it. The criteria of successful Development will be whether participant groups take action for themselves.
2. It works towards the reduction of imbalances and inequalities both between countries and inside countries rather than preserving them. Rich as well as poor, givers

Table 9.1   *Comparison of the main features of input-Development and social action-Development models*

	Input-Development	Social action-Development
Based on view:	That target group is deprived, needy and helpless	That participant group is potentially rich and powerful but oppressed
Process:	Outsider-led inputs	Insider-led action programmes
Results:	Dependency Maintains structural gap Neo-colonialism	Increased self-reliance, liberation Reduced structural gap Greater equality
Assumptions:	Resources are infinite Only aid-receiver needs to change Problems and inputs are technical Take-up will be automatic Areas of life excluded from Development Development is terminal The indigenous is not valuable	Resources are finite Both participant group and change-agent need to change Problems and action needed are social Take-up depends on attitude change No areas of life excluded from Development Development is continuous Development is based on the indigenous
Evaluation:	By objective-achievement	By outcomes

and teachers as well as receivers and taught will change. Those who deny the people access to resources will be called on to surrender at least part of their power if Development is to take place.

3.   It views resources as limited and tries to ensure that all people at global and local level have equal access to them.

4.   It is indigenous Development. It builds on existing processes of change, the existing knowledge of the people, because the people are doing it for themselves. They control both the objectives and the process, what they want to do and how and when they want to do it. It recognizes the validity of the participants, does not treat them as ignorant or unmotivated or incapable but as human beings with their own different but valid viewpoints, experiences, knowledge systems and goals. It is not dehumanizing nor patronizing; it is not neo-colonialism. It opens doors to the people to take from the more developed what they feel they need in order to obtain a more secure, comfortable and productive way of life.

5.   Problems are not seen as purely technical but as human, social, cultural, political and psychological. Denial of access to resources is seen to arise from attitudes and social constructs. The low status of women, for example, springs not so much from economic deprivation (for we need to ask *why* women are kept in poverty) as from attitudes and behaviour within a man-dominated world. Similarly, unemployment is not merely a question of lack of work, to be met by capital injection and training schemes while leaving those who are at work untouched; rather the problem is seen to be political and social, including attitudes towards work, unemployment and the unemployed: all will need to change. Again, the 'problem of illiteracy' is not so much the fact that so many people are 'still illiterate' (spoken in hushed tones as if

illiteracy were a disease which 'must be eradicated'); rather the problem is caused by those of us who can read and write having built a society in which the assumption that everyone ought to be literate is unquestioned, and thus a stigma attaches to anyone who cannot read and write; we manage to make those who cannot do so feel a failure, guilty, inferior. A participatory view of Development urges that it is the rich, the powerful, the Development agency who have to change as much as the participant/target group.

And because problems are seen to be human, psychological and social, no areas of life are excluded from Development. Participant groups choose for themselves what is important to them—whether that lies in the economic, social, cultural or political dimension. And they take action across the board, not just in the areas of technical knowledge and skills.

6. Social-action Development is assessed and evaluated not only in terms of objective-achievement but also by outcomes, long-term and uncertain though these may be. Development is a never-ending process. In collective action, the people practise ways to control the process of change and acquire the attitudes and skills to continue to control it and to meet the new challenges created by the continuing outcomes.

The social action model will, it is argued, lead to the solution to the problems which characterize the input model. What is needed is not to treat the people as passive recipients of other people's generosity but to help them become active participants, not just in their own Development but in the Development of the whole of society.

Problems of social action

But what if after the social action, the people are still poor? Can we reject completely the input model, asserting that all that is needed is action by the people? To argue that social action will always lead to access to resources (knowledge, technology, capital, etc.) and thus to a redistribution of those resources sounds a little too much like slogan-making to ring true. Those who have seen the life of a woman, deserted by her husband, transformed by a small grant (input) which enabled her to buy chickens and start her own egg-producing business or who have seen the increase in business and extra freedom obtained by a rural rope-maker through the acquisition of a bicycle will not feel that input must inevitably result in dependency. It is true that in each of these cases more was involved in the way of motivation and confidence; but motivation and confidence alone will rarely overcome poverty. Given these other factors, inputs can lead to self-reliance. And those who have seen the starvation victims in Africa will doubt if these people really can obtain through their own social action access to the world's food resources.

Nevertheless, it is increasingly agreed both by needs-based and oppression-based agencies that Development built on input, if it is to avoid creating dependency, needs to be accompanied by, if not replaced by, social action. But this is still lacking in many programmes today. Many agencies still seem to believe that the world's problems (national, local and individual) can be solved by a minor adjustment of resources, by the rich giving to some of the poor a little of their wealth in the form of aid. Whereas a world that is to become a little more stable and harmonious will need more radical readjustments—a better balance between human demands and the finite resources available, and a more equitable distribution of these resources so as to build a more just and peaceful world and national and local communities—in short a programme of social action.

NOTES TO CHAPTER 9

(1)   Jolly, R. (1971) Manpower education, in Seers, D. and Joy, L. (eds) *Development in a Divided World*, Penguin.

(2)   For example, the EEC has a directive about patenting seed varieties: it is significant that there is virtually no plant-breeding in Third World countries. The UN World Intellectual Property Agency has had a mixed effect on Development.

(3)   Church of South India Synod Report 1976; see Illich, I. (1970) Planned poverty: the end result of technical assistance, in Illich, I. (ed.) *Celebrations of Awareness*, New York, pp. 157–74.

(4)   See Oakley (1984); Cahn, E.S. and Passett, B.A. (eds) (1971) *Citizen Participation: Effecting Community Change*, New York; Cohen and Uphoff (1977); Bryant, C. and White, L.G. (1982) *Managing Development in the Third World*, Colorado, pp. 14–15.

Chapter 10

Routes to Change

For Development to be effective, for planned change to occur, the participant groups must *act*. Farmers must not only receive inputs of high-yield varieties and fertilizer, they must also sow and fertilize; communities need to utilize and maintain wells and canals, fisherfolk to use the boats and nets provided, families to adopt appropriate hygiene practices.

The Development process then consists of helping participant groups to take such action. A model of this process has emerged from recent discussions and may be represented as shown in Figure 10.1.[1] Starting with their *existing state* or *activity*, the participant groups will first need to *become aware* of the necessity for change, then (through a programme of education and training) to develop those *skills*, *knowledge* and *understanding* which are necessary for them to take action, and then to *act* in such a way as to bring about the *desired change*. These stages are not all distinct, they frequently overlap, but they are all necessary to a fully effective Development programme.[2]

Those who base their approach to Development on a 'deprivation-and-input' model, whether to achieve growth and modernization or to meet basic human needs, will express this route in different terms from those who believe in the 'exclusion-and-social action' model. The former will use phrases like 'to *impart* awareness', 'to *give* skills, knowledge, etc.' so as to express the necessary inputs; they stress the role of the Development change-agent. The latter will speak of '*helping* the participants to become more aware, *assisting* them to develop their skills, knowledge and understanding, *encouraging* them to act, etc.', in order to stress the active role of the participant group.

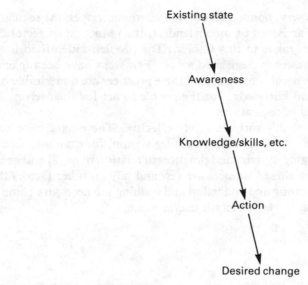

Figure 10.1 Steps essential to effective Development

PARTIAL ROUTES

All the alternative routes to Development that have been and are being used are adaptations of this basic route.

The bureaucratic route

This route omits the awareness and the knowledge/skills stages; it proceeds straight from the existing state to action (Figure 10.2). This is the route of legislation, of direction.

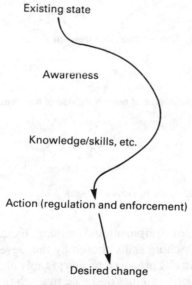

Figure 10.2 The bureaucratic route to Development

Attempts at the abolition of dowry, bonded labour and youth marriages, the regulation of land-holding sizes and the activities of moneylenders, the reduction of sectoral or communal tensions, have been made in this fashion. The problem, identified by the central planning authorities, has been 'legislated away'. Few steps have been taken to arouse awareness and obtain general consensus that these practices are undesirable or to develop the necessary skills and knowledge for the people to act for themselves. The action taken is the enforcement of regulations.

Legislation and regulation of this sort are rarely effective. There have been some exceptions: equal opportunities and fair employment legislation, for example, have on occasion played a part in changing opinion and practices in relation to racial and gender equality in some countries. But these instances are few and rely on other factors than legislation alone. Awareness-raising and education and training are necessary components for effective social change, not bureaucratic decree alone.

The technocratic route

A second route includes some limited elements of education and training but omits the awareness stage, proceeding straight from the existing state to inputs of a technical nature (Figure 10.3).

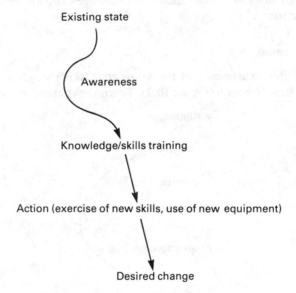

Figure 10.3 The technocratic route to Development

Inputs consist of new kinds of equipment and training. Examples include: most income-generating programmes; teaching skills chosen by the Development agency (outsider); literacy courses using a centrally prepared primer; family planning campaigns; nutrition and agricultural extension programmes designed to teach the participants skills or technical knowledge. The inputs, decided upon by the change-agents and imposed on the target groups, are of a narrow technical nature and are the same, presented in the same order and using the same methods of communication, irrespective of the different groups participating in the programme. Those who follow this route believe that knowledge, once presented and grasped, will be acted upon—a fallacy which smoking campaigns in the West and family planning campaigns in many Third World countries clearly demonstrate. It is strange how after so many years of relatively fruitless experience, many Development programmes still work on the principle that all that is needed is to 'give knowledge to the ignorant': 'as long as the people are illiterate and ignorant they will remain helpless . . . knowledge is power, and the people must acquire knowledge to move ahead'. If the people do not 'move ahead', they argue, it must be that they do not yet *know* enough, and thus another 'injection' of knowledge is given, as if ignorance were a disease. We never seem to learn that it is not so much lack of knowledge as negative attitudes towards the new practices which is the root cause of the lack of Developmental success.[3]

Development based on technical inputs without the other elements of the process will, therefore, be a failure. Development is not synonymous with technical assistance but with a changed way of life.

The direct action route

A third route starts with arousing awareness but omits the education and training stage and proceeds immediately to action (Figure 10.4). This is the route of revolution, of action groups, demonstrations and riots or (less violently) of government campaigns, residents' and tenants' associations, amenity societies, environmental pressure groups and so on.

Existing state

Awareness

Knowledge/skills, etc.

Direct action

Desired change

Figure 10.4 The direct action route to Development

There is much that is appealing about this route. It seems to offer quick solutions and appeals to those in a hurry. And such programmes may eventually lead to a demand for educational and training programmes to enable the activists to carry out their plan of campaign or to consolidate their newly won position.

But revolutions rarely seem to result in stable solutions; their outcomes are volatile. They tend to produce their own divisions, new inequalities, new forms of oppression. Such programmes are built on partial and flawed perceptions rather than on a basis of understanding. By their very nature they disrupt and even deny the process of Development; the desired change does not emerge out of the existing state. The result of direct action is purposed change but it is rarely 'Development'.

THE FULL ROUTE TO DEVELOPMENT

It may be possible to achieve some measure of planned change while leaving out one or more steps in the path, but permanent Development calls for all stages—developing critical awareness; developing a solid basis of knowledge, skills and understanding; engaging in a programme of social action.

Four points need to be made here:

- that education and training of adults (ETA) lies at the heart of this route to Development and cannot be omitted
- that attitude formation and change must form a major part of this ETA process
- that decision-making is involved in this Development path
- that the sequence of the steps will vary in a dynamic process

Education and training of adults (ETA)

Education and training of adults (ETA) lies at the heart of every Development programme. Without ETA, all interventions will be ineffective. The formal system of education, the schools and colleges, cannot be relied on for this purpose; a series of activities designed to help adult participants to increase their knowledge, skills and understanding and to develop attitudes is needed to bring about the desired Developmental change.

But this stage is frequently omitted. New equipment is provided without developing understanding of the appropriate use of this equipment. It has been reported that 'almost half the 300,000 bio-gas plants installed in India . . . are routinely out of action . . .' because little attention was paid to educating the villagers in looking after the plants once they were installed.[4] Or if the process of ETA is included, it is short-changed: narrow technical training without wider understanding is all that is offered. There will always be a temptation to take short cuts, the problems are so pressing; so that it is understandable that some programmes leave out a full treatment of this essential step. But most do this because of flawed assumptions—of which the assumption that knowledge transfer and skill development will of their own result in changed patterns of behaviour is the most common.

Attitude formation and change

It is clear that transfer of knowledge and skills alone does not alter behaviour. Families fail to adopt family restraint methods, not because they do not *know* enough but for other reasons. Farmers do not farm efficiently, unemployed workers do not engage in income-generating programmes, adults do not learn literacy, slum dwellers do not use publicly provided toilets, not because they do not know enough but because they decide not to act in the desired way. What lies at the heart of this failure is a question of *attitudes*. It is quite possible for awareness to exist or to be aroused, for knowledge to be grasped, skills to be acquired, understanding to be developed, but for the participants still not to take action. Indeed, awareness and understanding heightened by the Development process itself can on occasion help to increase the sense of the forces ranged against the desired change and of the relative powerlessness of the participant group; such learning may diminish the will or the confidence to take action.

It is thus essential that every Development programme contains within it provision for the promotion of positive attitudes among the participant group, especially the development of *confidence* and the focusing of *motivation*. Without these, no programme will succeed.

Decision-making

In many programmes, the action is often imposed on the participant group by outsiders: a carpet factory, for example, making luxury items for the foreign market opened with foreign assistance in a tribal area without full discussion with the villagers about whether this is what the people want, or whether this is the right product to meet local needs. But a properly devised programme ought to help the people to develop the ability to determine their own Development path.

Decision-making by the participant group is a necessary step in the Development route. It is here that the development of confidence and motivation emerges; without a sense of power and without a strong desire to act on the part of the people, there will be no decision. All the elements in this process are indissolubly tied together.

There are serious implications in including decision-making within the Development process. The possibility of some alteration in the objectives of the programme must be accepted. What may come out of participant-controlled Development may be something other than the 'desired change' as set by the agency when the people choose their own goals.

We must be clear here. Development workers cannot become mere rubber stamps, simply facilitators for the programmes of the participant groups. They have a larger function than this. Nevertheless, they need increasingly to be willing to allow for dramatic changes in the goals as the process continues.[5]

Sequences

But the inclusion of decision-making (creating a five-fold path to Development—

- existing state
- awareness enhancement
- ETA (including attitude formation and change)
- decision-making
- programme of action)

means that the sequence of the steps becomes complicated. Development is a dynamic situation, not a pre-set and inflexible series of programmed learning. It involves human intervention in the lives of others, the interaction between a change-agent and a group of participants; and many things can (and often do) happen in the course of such interactions.

Awareness-raising of the issue to be addressed or opportunity to be realized comes first in almost all Development programmes. It certainly precedes the ETA component, for to be effective adult learning, which is voluntary in nature, needs to be based on the learners' sense of awareness. But beyond this initial requirement, the pattern will vary. Some programmes will build on awareness to determine a course of action and then engage in ETA in order to execute that course of action. In this case, the route to the desired change is as shown in Figure 10.5.

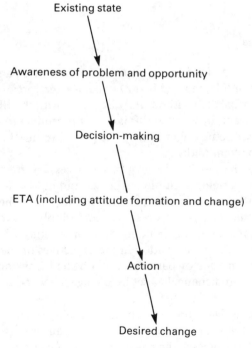

Existing state

Awareness of problem and opportunity

Decision-making

ETA (including attitude formation and change)

Action

Desired change

Figure 10.5 Early decision-making in the Development route

The first task . . . is to create an understanding that change is possible and knowledge of alternatives [i.e. awareness] leading to desire for change. The second is to enable individuals and communities to identify what types of change they wish to achieve and how to set out to attain them [i.e. decision-making]. The third, not the first, is training in particular skills and the provision of particular pieces of knowledge. . . .[6]

But other programmes move from awareness-raising to ETA and after that to decision-making. For these, the chain is shown in Figure 10.6. A more thorough exploration of all the possibilities will be undertaken before a decision is reached by the participant group as to the way forward.

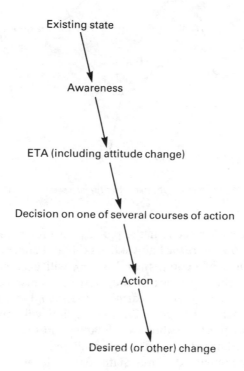

Existing state

Awareness

ETA (including attitude change)

Decision on one of several courses of action

Action

Desired (or other) change

Figure 10.6 Late decision-making in the Development route

A dynamic change process

More often, however, the process is confused. As awareness rises and insights develop, so the demand for new knowledge, new skills and new understandings will often grow; and as knowledge, skills and understandings grow, so the picture of the possible range of actions and of the goal will change. New knowledge, skills and understandings in their turn often lead to changed attitudes; and as the activities are carried out, so awareness develops further and the knowledge and skills requirements alter (Figure 10.7).

Which stage of the process contains decision-making will vary according to the ideology of the agent. Some will seek to involve the participants in decision-making at the earliest possible stage, others will seek to delay it. This choice is part of the planning responsibility of the Development agency.

There are advantages and disadvantages in each of these procedures.

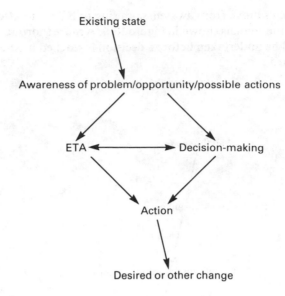

Figure 10.7 Possible interactions in a dynamic change process

(a) If decision-making comes early, if the participant group decides on a course of action and sets out to acquire the knowledge, skills and understandings necessary to carry out that course of action, their learning will become more relevant and meaningful as they relate it to the task they have set themselves. Motivation will be high as they see the purpose of the learning process and the material and feel that they are moving closer to their goal. But the decision will have been made without knowing the full range of possibilities available; and the programme of learning will on the whole be limited to what is seen as directly relevant to carrying out the decision. Everything outside the immediate goal-achievement will be ignored, and learning will tend to cease when the participants feel they possess sufficient knowledge, skills and understanding to carry out their plan of action.

Thus an income-generating programme for a small cluster of tribal villages which decided as a first step to establish a women's milk-producing co-operative[7] adopted the following route: Existing state—Awareness raising of need—Decision-making (to set up a co-operative)—Development of necessary skills/knowledge/understandings/attitudes (subjects needed to run co-operative)—Action (setting up the co-operative)—Intended change (relief of poverty and women's participation). This is a route which many Development projects take, especially those run by charitable bodies. Sometimes the decision is a joint one of the change-agent and the participant group; occasionally it is taken by the participant group alone. But more frequently it is made by the change-agent alone.

It is important to note that much of the ETA needed was implemented in the course of engaging in the action programme. The early decision set the curriculum for the learning programme—animal husbandry, milking procedures, credit, marketing, dealing with the local carrier and officials, co-operative administration and joint decision-making, record-keeping, etc. Since the decision was a joint one and not an imposed decision, the initial motivation to learn was high. But the choice was made without a full and realistic consideration by the target group of other possible alternatives such as basket making, weaving, etc., and whether a co-operative form of management was the most suitable in this case. Secondly, the range of subjects chosen for learning left out much—other craft skills, for example, or political structures, social and environmental concerns, personal and family health and welfare, etc. and other matters not seen to be directly relevant to a milk-producing co-operative. It is of course not necessary for these other matters to be omitted; many programmes make efforts to relate them to the programme of learning about a particular form of action. But because in this case they were not seen as immediately essential to the task in hand, setting up a milk-producing co-operative, motivation to learn these other subjects was very low, and in practice they were left out.

(b) If, on the other hand, the ETA stage comes before decision-making, the participants will be able to decide their course of action on the basis of a clearer perception of the range of choices and a more realistic appraisal of what is possible. But since the learning comes first, the choice of the learning matter will lie with the Development agency, and the participants may not see the relevance of much of what they are learning to their goals; their motivation during the learning stage will in general be lower.

Many Development projects follow this second route, delaying the decision-making until later in the programme. Thus a programme with fishing villages in Tamil Nadu worked for some time with local groups, surveying felt needs before a joint decision was made to improve marketing and supply outlets using motorized cycles and ice boxes. The route was: Existing state—Awareness-raising of need—Development of a wide range of knowledge/skills/understanding and attitude change, including an exploration of different possibilities—Decision-making (to change marketing procedures)—Action (acquisition of new forms of transport, developing co-operative forms of selling, etc.)—Intended change (increased income for fisherfolk).

In this case, the curriculum of the ETA stage needed to be wider and more exploratory. Instead of being limited to a particular range of knowledge and to specific skills, it posed and sought to answer many more questions. But there was a danger that the decision would be postponed until the process of exploration was completed, that it might never be taken at all. And the relevance of some of what was learned was not clear to some of the participants, thus leading to loss of interest.

Early decision-making then helps motivation and a sense of relevance but limits perspective; delayed decision-making helps increase the range of choice but reduces motivation.

Ideally the two processes should go together, but experience indicates that this is not easy in practice; for attitude formation and change and the other components of ETA call for a lengthy process, whereas decision-making often occupies a much shorter time. In reality it is hard to avoid a situation where the change-agent and the group have to make up their minds whether to choose a course of action at an early stage in the Development process or defer it until later. The choice will need to be made in every case in the light of the circumstances and the objectives of the programme; it is not possible to follow a set rule. And flexibility is necessary; any decision arrived at early should as long as possible be kept under review, with a willingness on the part of both the agent and the participant group to change it as the situation develops.

The change-agent and the process of Development

In most programmes then there comes a choice, whether to introduce participant (insider) decision-making at an early stage or at a later stage. And this means that action-Development calls for a high level of commitment and abilities on the part of the change-agent—attitudes and skills of sensitivity, of innovativeness, of listening and responding rather than teaching by the book, of thinking on one's feet. Some will argue that a mass Development programme does not have at its disposal many such change-agents and that we need to settle for less. The answer to this must be two-fold:

- that all these steps—awareness-raising, attitude change and confidence building, ETA, participation in decision-making, and action—are *essential* for effective Development; they are not just desirable options, some of which may be left out
- that Development agencies should spend a great deal more time, care and resources on selecting and training and supporting the change-agents

We shall need to look at this topic in more detail later.

THEORY AND PRACTICE

It will perhaps be argued that so far the models outlined are theoretical rather than practical. I do not believe them to be merely matters of theory; they are constantly in use, consciously or subconsciously informing Development programmes in both Third World countries and the West. The bureaucratic route is regularly used by governments for all kinds of issues—untouchability, casteism and religious disharmony, for example, in India; and racial, colour and gender prejudice in industrialized countries. Direct action is often followed in, for example, nuclear and environmental protests—Greenham Common in the UK and the Chipko movement in India. The technocratic route is perhaps the most frequently used—primer literacy, for example, or training programmes for unemployed youth or technical assistance programmes.

But these are less than fully effective; they run into problems because they omit one or more elements from the process. Two examples may give some indication of this.

Case-study: fishing villages

The Bay of Bengal Project, an FAO programme aimed at coastal communities in south-east Asia, provided some fishing villages of Tamil Nadu with a new type of boat. The needs were thoroughly surveyed; the new boat was designed and tested as carefully as possible to suit the fishing environment. The fisherfolk were shown how to use the new equipment.[8]

The model was thus one of outsider input, not of action by the participants; the route was technocratic. It was assumed that the knowledge and the equipment once given would automatically be utilized, that the fishermen would use the new boats' greater capacity and greater seaworthiness to exploit resources further afield. But the fisherfolk did not go any further from the shore. They used the larger nets and storage to exploit existing resources more thoroughly (too well) and to take catches from those less fortunate than themselves.

For this project to be fully effective, several missing elements needed to be provided: an awareness programme with the fisherfolk designed to highlight the problems facing these communities because of changes which were already occurring, leading to a sense of urgency on the part of the fisherfolk themselves and to a perception of the range of possible solutions from which they could choose; a programme of attitudinal formation and change involving confidence building, leading to decision-making by the fishing communities themselves; and a programme of education and training wider than the technical know-how provided.

Not that these extra elements in themselves (to be fair) will guarantee success. A parallel programme in which the fishing communities identified, with the assistance of the agency, other needs and settled upon a motorized cycle to take the catch to market was equally ineffective, this time because of local rivalries within the communities and because of the failure of those who leased these new machines to maintain them. Awareness-raising and local decision-making were in this case added to the process; but there seems to have been inadequate education and training. The path to Development is a difficult one and calls for a long time devoted to working through each of the steps with the participants; there are no short-cuts.[9]

Case-study: water supply

In arid areas, Development is frequently seen as the provision of wells or irrigation channels together with training in the use and maintenance of the system. Programmes thus concentrate on inputs of technical resources (money and technicians) and technical knowledge and skills (building and maintaining wells and canals).

This is obviously an important step forward; but the experience of schemes such as Ukai and Nirmada in India, Mahaveli in Sri Lanka, Mwea in Kenya, where huge hydro-electric power stations are being built, large areas of valley or forest land flooded, whole populations displaced and the irrigation water taken many miles away, leaving villages close to the dams still without water, has shown that there are many problems in these programmes. Even if the village is connected to the irrigation system, often the water does not run in these new channels for months at a time.

For the provision or withholding of water is not simply a technical matter but a political question concerning power. The decision as to which villages should be provided with wells and channels and which not is taken at an official level, remote from the people, and it is rarely related to need. Politicians, administrators and engineers are involved; and the power of the local leaders is crucial to the decision that is made. Discussions among the farmers themselves (as at Ukai in 1987) are not just on matters relating to irrigation farming and dry land crops but include such topics as 'Why does this landholder obtain water and others do not?' 'What is the proper role of an engineer?' 'Where do decisions lie and how are they taken?' 'Why are the local MPs behaving in this way?' The issues are seen by the people to be social, psychological, cultural and political, not just technical.[10]

A programme leading to effective change in water supply in these circumstances demands more than technical input and training. It calls for awareness-raising of the social situation, for a programme of learning leading to new skills (how to deal with the local power-brokers, for example) and new understandings (of influence and bribery, of how other communities cope, etc.), and for action to develop in the people confidence to tackle the problem instead of a feeling that there is little they can do about it all. Without these elements, nothing will have changed—except the existence of empty irrigation channels as a constant reminder of the people's oppression.

NOTES TO CHAPTER 10

(1)   The model arose from the community development programmes, see Chapter 8, note 9.

(2)   For an example of the route used in evaluation of a programme, see Council of Europe (1986b), p. 8: local problem/arousing public awareness/identifying needs/ETA/identifying resources/defining strategy/undertaking tasks.

(3)   See for example Mamdani, M. (1972) *The Myth of Population Control*, New York; Ehrlich, P. (1971) *The Population Bomb*, Pan.

(4)   *Ceres: FAO Review on Agriculture and Development* **18**(1) (1987). On the role of education in Development, see the important series of reports on the UNESCO Project 1977–81 *Integrated Rural Development and the Role of Education* in Cuba, Kenya, Bangladesh, Guinea, Sudan, etc.: ED 81/WS/7,14; 82/WS/55.

(5)   Berger, P.L. (1977) *Pyramids of Sacrifice: Political Ethics and Social Change*, Penguin.

(6)   Green (1977), p. 21.

(7)   Amari Mandli, Tarpada near Fort Songadh, papers of Indian Tribal Women's Trust.

(8)   Bay of Bengal Programme (FAO) in association with Tamil Nadu Government Department of Fisheries (Extension), BOBP REP, 25 (1986).

(9)   Natpracha, P. and Pietersz, V.L.C. (1986) *Attempts to Stimulate Development Activities in Fishing Communities of Adirampattinam*, BOBP REP 25.

(10) See, for example, Chaturvedi, Y.S. (1987), Central India: Pani Panchayat, *RRDC Bulletin* (University of Reading) **21**, 26–28.

Chapter 11

The Five-fold Path

In order to see the way in which education and training lies at the heart of Development, we need to examine each of the steps in this process in more detail.

Development as experience

We should, however, first note that the Development process is best seen as an experience in which the target group participates. Development is not just the building of a dam or roads *for* the people; it is a process in which the building of the dam or roads is seen as part of the experience of change which involves the people and affects their way of life. It calls from the people a range of decisions and actions in order to make the Development change effective. If the Development change is seen as an experience in the lives of the target group, then the Development process must become an experience for them as well.

EXISTING STATE/ACTIVITY

Development starts where the people are. It is into their existing state and activities that the desired changes need to be introduced, that the Development interventions occur. This includes their cultural life, their values and beliefs, as well as their material condition. Nutrition programmes come into the lives of families as they are being lived today; thus these programmes need to be based on existing food practices, preferences and food availabilities rather than on some theoretical material expounded without reference to what exists in each particular case, on what is on the shelves or the market stalls rather than on what is in the textbook. In the same way, agricultural extension comes into existing patterns of farming, literacy comes into the current way of life of the learners, and so on.

This 'existing state' is not static. Those we work with are already involved in a process of change. It may appear to be slow change in many so-called traditional societies according to Western eyes, but changes are occurring and will be recognized by the participants themselves. Such changes cannot be ignored by the Development planner. Any assessment of 'baseline data' should reveal the communities to be on the move, not static.

Surveys

Sometimes agencies take a great deal of care to survey the existing state of the target groups and try to build their interventions on the results of these surveys. More often, however, agencies rely on their own preconceptions of what life is like within a region or community. They assume that they already know the existing state and that there is no need for further investigation; or that a special survey is irrelevant to their already tested programme. They often assume that what is true for one local community will be true of other similar communities—that once they have surveyed the economic or health situation in one fishing village, tribal group, or region, their findings will remain true for all other communities or regions of a similar social or geographical nature.

This is understandable. For one thing, accepting generalized surveys or common assumptions saves time: to do a survey each time one extends a programme to another set of villages can be seen to be wasteful of time. Accepting such generalized surveys is often thought to be necessary when constructing a mass programme—in family planning, for example, or literacy or community health. For those programmes which use large numbers of locally based workers (extension officers or animators) and provide them with basic training, the apparent necessity of accepting at face value existing surveys of the state of the target group is almost irresistible.

But it must be resisted. In order to achieve the utilization of the Development intervention, it is necessary for the programme to build on the existing state of the specific community concerned. This cannot be ignored: we are not working in a vacuum but in a situation where change is already going on. In each fishing village, each agricultural community, each tribal group, caste colony, or urban slum, each region, the way the intervention will be received will depend not just on how it is presented but on what is already there at the time of presentation. The programme will be ineffective unless it is related to the *particular* rather than to the *generalized* existing state of the target group.

All local communities, target groups and regions vary in at least three respects:

1. They are not all at the same stage of change, because the *past experience* of each local community has been different. What groups know and feel will in each case vary.
2. Their *resources* will vary—and their perception of the resources available to them will vary also. Some will see, for example, a river or forest land as a resource; others will see these as an obstacle to the desired change.[1]
3. Their *aspirations* will vary. Each target group will want different things. These aspirations are often ignored. Agencies assume that all farmers and all fisherfolk, all nomads and all unemployed, all mothers with very young children—even all women—want the same things. This of course is not true. The aspirations of the participant group cannot be ignored without running the risk of creating frustration and thus hostility towards the goals we are trying to promote. Local aspirations

must form the basis of our programme; to change these aspirations so that they come to incorporate the goals of the change-agent is itself a form of Development.[2]

Each programme then begins with the unique rather than the generalized existing state of the community or region or population sector which forms the target group, including their past experience, their perceptions of resources available and their aspirations. True Development will build on what exists, not start as though nothing has happened to this town or village or group before the arrival of the agency or as though all existing states are the same.

Some survey of the existing state of each community will then be necessary before the commencement of any programme. This survey, to be valid, needs to be done with the participant group, not by the Development agency alone. For the question must be asked: whose existing state is it? The view of this existing state depends on how and by whom the problem which the Development intervention is designed to solve is defined. The outsider's perception of the nature of the problem will often be very different from that of the target group. The existing state is not absolute: it is a set of perceptions about reality, and those of the outsider agency may not always be superior to those of the insider group.

AWARENESS ENHANCEMENT

The second step is to help the participants to enhance their awareness, to assist them to develop their perceptions and to increase their concern for some change in their social or economic, cultural or political circumstances.

The process

This process of awareness-raising does not consist of a series of lectures about social problems: this is more likely to put the participant group to sleep than to make them more awake! Large-scale projects often seek to secure the co-operation of local resident groups who may be affected by their schemes by arranging lectures, exhibitions, slide shows and demonstrations; family planning programmes often contain lengthy sessions (beautifully illustrated) 'to make the target group more aware'. These are almost always complete failures in increasing awareness.

Awareness enhancement is not merely informing the public. Nor is it the same as having a series of discussions, though this is often a good way of sharing perceptions. Some discussions may lead to increased awareness but often they do not. Again it is not a matter of the Development worker telling the participant group the way things are as he/she sees them. Many agencies believe that they know better than the local group what their real problems are and set out to help the participants to see themselves in the same light. But this is not true awareness-raising.

It is dangerous to talk of awareness in terms of 'waking up'; this implies that we see the participant group as asleep until we (like the handsome prince) wake them up with the gentle kiss of our awareness programme! But the participant groups are already awake, aware of many things. They may not be aware of what we want them to be aware of, but they 'see' things which are important to them.

An awareness programme then needs to be designed to listen to the participant group, while discussing with them the concerns of the programme. We must never dismiss their insights as wrong or unimportant. The purpose of awareness programmes is surely to *share* perceptions, not to impose one set of standards on another person or group.

Changing awareness

Awareness is the way we look at the world, the questions we ask about it. There are two main ways in which our programmes may help to change this perception:

Overcoming selectivity

We all have gaps in our awareness. There are some things each of us cannot see because of our past experience or because of our personality. Many of us are rarely aware of ourselves, and most of us have only a partial awareness of our social, physical and cultural environment. Some are more aware of people than of things; for others it is the reverse. We all have a highly selective awareness.

An example will demonstrate this. A group of university students were shown photographs of streets in their town with the buildings *above* the shopfronts blocked out. The students were able to name the streets and identify the places. Then they were shown photographs with the shopfronts blocked out and the rooflines above left in. The students could not in most cases identify where these streets were, even though they knew the area well. They were aware of what was important to them—the shopfronts— but although they had walked along those streets many times, they had rarely lifted their eyes above the shop signs.[3]

We all (participants and change-agents alike) are aware of only a small part of what is around us. We need to realize just what we are aware of and what we are leaving out of our picture. An awareness programme should help both participants and change-agent to fill in some of these gaps.

Sharing different perceptions

Just as important is the significance which each person gives to the various elements which make up this social and natural environment. Some people are aware of and value things which are unseen or less highly valued by others, largely (but not entirely) on the basis of whether the perceived feature is relevant and useful to the perceiver.

Community mapping   A programme of 'community mapping' will help to illustrate this. Different people are asked to direct a stranger to a certain place in their town or village. Some will refer to road junctions as indicators: 'go as far as the third turning on the left . . .'. Others tend to use prominent buildings—a shop or post-office, for example; or a colour ('the green building . . .') or a feature ('the large tree . . .' or 'the hole in the road . . .'). When these 'signposts' are collected together, those landmarks which feature most frequently can be recognized as important elements in the life of the community; their change or removal would alter significantly the 'shape' of that town or village in the minds of many of the inhabitants. These are major features in their awareness.[4]

The same process may be done for the social environment: who in the community is to be consulted? who takes decisions which will affect the rest? who causes trouble? whom is it necessary to please? who can be ignored? who will provide help and advice?—all these are features of the social 'map'. Those persons who feature most frequently are clearly the more important creators or influencers of community opinion—and they may not always be the most obvious persons at first sight.

An awareness programme of this kind will help the members of the participant group to learn how they see themselves and their changing physical and social environment and how others see different things or attach different values to what they see. It will provide an opportunity for the participants to change these views in association with others if they so wish. It will in effect take the participants out of their immediate context, help them to look at themselves as it were from afar (as Coady said, 'A fish doesn't know he lives in water until he is taken out of it'). What it should not do is to create states of awareness in which the participant groups come to accept the frames of reference of the outsiders, come to look on themselves as poor and needy and dependent, for example.[5]

Continuing reinterpretation

Our awareness programme then is designed to help the participant group first to fill in some of the gaps in their picture of reality—to get them talking about things they do not talk about much, either because they do not like to (the taboo subjects) or because they never think about them (the invisible subjects); and secondly, to reassess the value they place on the various elements within this reality.

Such a programme will never end; we can never say of any participant group, 'Now they are aware'. Awareness is a continuing process, a constant reinterpretation of reality in the light of fresh perceptions, fresh experiences, fresh insights, a constant monitoring of our reactions to our physical and social environment which is itself also changing.

Critical awareness

Awareness is, however, more than just being alive to what is about us, being sensitive, receptive. It implies being 'critical' of it: not just criticizing but asking questions about it, probing deeper and seeking answers to our questions, looking for the ways in which this social and natural environment is changing and can be changed. Awareness is an active, not a passive process.

A Development awareness programme then will not be something which a change-agent can *give* to a target group. It is a process of sharing different ways of seeing ourselves and our world, and in the course of doing this, challenging the assumptions on which these perceptions are based.

The 'CIA test'   One device which has been found to be very helpful in developing such critical awareness is what may be called the 'CIA test'—helping participants individually or in groups to identify those parts of their everyday lives which they can 'control', those parts which they can 'influence' and those parts which they need to 'accept'. The aim is to help them to enlarge the areas of control, to find new channels of influence, and to turn to their own advantage or seek ways round those constraining features which they are forced to accept.

Learning awareness

A Development agency must not imagine that it can engage in an awareness programme with a participant group without itself changing, becoming more aware. The change-agents will learn much while helping the participants to explore and to look at their own world in a different way. They will meet other views, be challenged as to whether their own opinions make more sense of reality than other approaches. Every Development worker who has engaged on an equality with others in an awareness programme has learned much about his/her own world and about him/herself.

Being aware of oneself and of one's environment calls for skills—of looking and listening, of perceiving and of asking questions. Such skills can be developed with practice: the more they are used, the more we will be able to use them, just as the less they are used, the more they will atrophy. The awareness stage in the Development process must call for the participants to practise these skills, actively asking questions and searching for answers, not just listening to talks (however well illustrated) or engaging in discussions. Awareness needs to be learned.

Some examples will help. Awareness of family planning cannot be increased merely by the change-agent dividing up an apple between all members of a family. While the visiting expert knows the facts theoretically, the parents of a large family know experientially much better than the visiting expert what it *feels* like not to have enough of something to meet all the demands. Nor will it be achieved by asking the group to consider national needs above the needs of their immediate family. Awareness in family planning is not increased by talking at the participants. It is achieved by sharing insights—listening to their views and opinions, helping them to explore more thoroughly some of the implications of the practices they follow, to identify what is stopping them from doing what they want to do or what the change-agent wants them to do. Similarly, an awareness programme for villagers on social forestry will not be effective by reference to global strategies and global needs ('to think globally, act locally'), however well presented; what is needed is a joint detailed exploration of local needs and local resources and local strategies.

Preoccupations and awareness

Programmes of awareness enhancement, however, need to go further than simply changing perceptions and viewpoints. As R.K. Narayan, the celebrated Indian author, has put it, 'a man in a village will be preoccupied with the rains, the monsoon, his neighbours and the cattle, though he will be aware of the important things from outside that affect his life, like chemical fertilizers'. The distinction between preoccupation and awareness is vital. Our awareness enhancement programme is a matter of making a preoccupation or a concern out of what is at present an awareness. And that calls for active processes of learning. A programme for fisherfolk presenting different techniques of catching fish and different ways to process them and to market the product will not be effective simply by a series of discussions and demonstrations. It will require the fisherfolk to analyse for themselves the way they are doing a particular activity, the reasons for and results of doing it in this way—and to experiment with new ways of following old occupations.

The process then calls for changes in the way we look at the world—an ongoing sensitivity and curiosity in relation to what is around us, attaching new values to different parts of our world picture. Creating such sensitivity will take a long time. Some agents imagine that awareness can be 'given' to the participants in a one-day meeting. But it is a process which will go on all the time the Development intervention is taking place. Planners often urge that they do not have the time to engage in such a lengthy process; the task is too urgent. This is an understandable point springing from commitment; but the programme will be a waste of time if it does not take all the time needed to increase the awareness of the participants. The awareness stage is a major component, not a short introductory step preceding the 'real' Development. At least half of Development is achieved once awareness is increased.

EDUCATION AND TRAINING (ETA)

Some Development programmes consist almost entirely of training. Agricultural extension, for example, comprises mostly the passing on of 'new' knowledge, the demonstration of new skills. Literacy and numeracy programmes in practice similarly consist of developing new knowledge and skills. Income-generating Development often includes little other than new techniques, new equipment, new processes and the 'imparting' of knowledge and skills to the participants. At times it seems there is not much more to Development than the transfer of (technical) knowledge and the creation of new (technical) skills.[6] There are programmes which comprise more than this; but many consist of a series of lectures and demonstrations—for example, on nutrition or family planning methods, on hygiene and medical welfare, on production techniques, processing and marketing, on management—as if this were all that was needed.

The acquisition of new knowledge and skills, and especially of new understandings, is an essential element in the Development process. So it is not surprising that many books have been written about it, that courses on communication in Development abound. Indeed, its outlines are so well known, especially in the form of extension (agricultural and other forms), that it is odd that other programmes omit this step altogether or treat it in a superficial manner. The introduction of tractors some years ago into south India was accompanied with the minimum of training, entirely technical in nature; the introduction of intermediate or 'appropriate' technology often has even less. Large-scale infra-structure Development, sometimes involving the transplantation of whole communities, frequently is completed without a programme of education and training for those involved. But developing the range of knowledge, widening horizons and increasing perceptions, enhancing further the competencies of the participant group and enlarging their sense of perspective are all essential if Development is to be solidly based and permanent.

More than simple training is needed. We have noted above (p. 12) three main kinds of learning—instrumental, communicative and emancipatory. All three are necessary in Development as well as in adult education. Instrumental learning (which is what training is, i.e. managing the world) is not enough on its own; our participant groups need to learn in the fields of social relationships (communicative learning) and in self-knowledge (emancipatory learning) if they are to become free.

The practice of ETA

A number of points may usefully be made:

1. We ought not to treat the participant group as if they were completely ignorant about the topic concerned; even illiterates know something about literacy. We should not ignore, let alone despise, what the people already know and what they do. We need to explore what they know, to confirm what is acceptable, and to provide new knowledge and new skills where needed. Such new learning will only be effective if it is related to the existing knowledge and skills of the participants, not treated in a compartment by itself. New farming practices need to be related to existing practices, not imposed upon the earlier ones without making efforts to integrate the two. New nutrition and environmental health practices need to be related to existing community practices. Much extension work seems to be based on the assumption that we are telling the participants something they have never thought about before. The Development change-agent has much to learn from the participants' indigenous knowledge, whether in farming or fishing, in medicine or environmental matters, in the exploitation of resources or the making of products. One of the most striking cases of this was with the Mbeere tribe in Africa where exotic varieties of trees introduced for Developmental reasons nearly drove out the more useful and more durable native varieties until just in time the local residents put the Development workers 'right'.[7]

2. New knowledge and skills are best learned if the learners acquire them for themselves rather than if the change-agent 'gives' them to the learners. Exploration of the environment, identifying and seeking a solution to a problem, discovering by trial and error, experimenting, practising—these experiential forms of learning result in more permanent learning than listening to talks and watching demonstrations. In some areas this is obvious: tailoring and typing, for example, are learned through doing rather than by watching. But the same is true of hygiene and plant cultivation, both of which in much current practice rely more on the target groups looking and listening than deciding and doing for themselves. Participant groups need to act for themselves, not just to listen to and watch 'experts'.

3. The development of understanding is a distinct part of this process of ETA and needs careful attention in itself. Some people assume that new knowledge and skills will lead inevitably to new understandings, but experience of many Development and educational programmes shows that this is not true. Again, some change-agents act on the assumption that understanding is of a higher order, beyond the grasp of the 'simple' villagers or slum dwellers who form the target groups of their programmes. Thus elementary skills are taught mechanically by rote, not with under-

standing. Much literacy teaching is handled on this basis, forming letters and identifying words without wider understanding. So too is the teaching of income-generating skills: to learn how to make jam or mats or cloth or jewels or high-quality carpets, or how to keep bees or to cultivate and utilize seaweed, for example, is sometimes thought to call for only a limited range of knowledge and skills and is not seen to require understanding. But for such learning to be long-lasting and usable in other contexts, a wider perspective based on understanding is essential.

4. Work with adult learners indicates that it is best not to compartmentalize the ETA stage in the Development process. It is desirable for the participants to engage in the planned end-activity (the goal of Development)—suitably broken down into manageable steps and practised under supervision—*during* the Development intervention instead of waiting until the end of the programme. The learning in Developmental education and training is for immediate rather than future application. The participants will learn the new knowledge, skills and understanding in the course of doing the required activity rather than separate from the task. And the learning will be experiential and practical rather than theoretical. Education and training will then infuse the whole Development process. There is a danger in this, that the learning will be restricted to what is necessary for the Development activity alone. To counteract this, our programmes should seek to go wider—to open doors, widen horizons, develop new perspectives, increase the range of choices.

Attitude formation and change

The enhancement of knowledge, skills and understanding does not of itself lead to action. Participant groups may know all about something, they may know how to go about it and be competent to do it, they may even understand what is involved—and yet still not do it.

It has often been said that the biggest obstacle to Development changes is traditional culture—those sets of beliefs and emotions which go to make up attitudes (personal dispositions) and which, reinforced by the values and customs of the social context (the culture or subculture), control all behaviour. To understand and (if necessary) modify these attitudes and values is the most necessary, most difficult (and therefore most neglected) part of the Development process—one to which there is much lip service but relatively little action.[8]

We must not assume that all the attitudes of the participant group are opposed to the kinds of behaviour we hope our programme will lead to. Sometimes the participants will already be predisposed towards the goals; in this case, the change-agent needs to reinforce this willingness. But in other situations, this will not be so. And there is no point in proceeding further until these negative attitudes have been modified.

It is possible to argue that attitudinal changes need to be made before a programme of education and training is begun, that the participants will only learn the new knowledge and skills and develop the new understandings when they have come to form positive attitudes towards that learning. On the other hand, it may be only during or after the process of education and training that the barriers to learning are clearly seen to lie in attitudes rather than in the lack of knowledge and skills. Positive attitudes are generated in the course of engaging in the Development activity itself.

The range of attitudes

It is at this point that the idea of 'concept distance' and 'cultural otherness' in adult learning are particularly important. As we have seen above (p. 16), adults build up for themselves a map of reality, a world picture, in which they locate new information and new practices as they receive them. Every learner places the material with which they are confronted at a specific location within their own sense of reality. The distance between where they place this new material and where they place themselves is usually expressed in terms of space (it is of 'remote interest' or a matter of 'close concern', etc.) or in terms of social relationships (it is 'alien', etc.). If the Developmental material (literacy or new farming practices or new habits of hygiene, for example) is placed far from themselves, these practices are regarded as 'culturally other', and thus learning them will be more difficult; on the other hand, if they are placed close to themselves within their picture of reality, learning will be facilitated.

This process has been identified in Development programmes for a long time, and attempts have been made to bring the new material 'closer' to the learners. Care is taken to make sure that agricultural extension is taught in relation to existing farming practices; literacy primers and post-literacy materials are compiled using terms drawn from everyday life, so that the learners will place the new material close to themselves on their 'maps'. But this does not overcome the problem, for it tackles it from the wrong end. The problem is not how the Development agent sees the new material but how the participants see the new material. Some studies have shown that literacy learners, even when taught on the basis of material drawn from within their life experience, still regard literacy as an activity not relevant to themselves. In a UNICEF experimental project in Mahbubnagar near Hyderabad, for example, women saw literacy as 'belonging' to young, male, ambitious persons who were hoping to acquire a white-collar job in the town rather than for themselves, even though every effort had been made to use literacy materials which were apparently relevant to the lives of these women. Such attitudes have been noted in other programmes; for example, von Freyhold found that the people he dealt with in Tanzania held the view that 'education is important mainly for those who want a job in town, not for those who have buried such ambitions'.[9] The 'distance' between literacy and the learners, and the 'cultural otherness' of the desired learning were too great to facilitate learning.

What then is needed is to explore with the participants *their* perception of the material being learned and to help them to reduce any large gap which may exist. The formation of new attitudes towards the Development materials will be required to reduce this distance and to promote learning. This is not a process which once undertaken can then be left; it will be a continuous reassessment with the participant groups of how they regard themselves as well as how they regard the subject matter of the Development programme—and how these views change during the programme.

Confidence and motivation

This sense of congruity between participants and the material being learned will help to determine the level of confidence and motivation of the participants. It is important for the change-agents to realize that they cannot 'give' these attitudes to the participants, that they cannot 'instil' confidence or 'motivate the people', as is so often said. They can encourage, help, reinforce—but the participants themselves will build their own confidence and develop their willingness to engage in the activity and to change their way of life and they will do this on the basis of the perceived relevance of the new material and their experience in handling it.

Other attitudes will be needed for a full Development programme. Concern for the goals and commitment to the task, openness to new ideas, a willingness to innovate and experiment, a sense of questioning and curiosity, an entrepreneurial spirit willing to seize the opportunities presented—all these will form part of an attitudinal formation programme. And there will also be a question of values—the balance between self-interest and social responsibility, for example. These too will need to be the subject of exploration.

Because it is possible to build up knowledge and skills without changing attitudes, it must be seen as a distinct part of the ETA process, separate from the giving of new knowledge and the development of new skills. For attitudes are on the whole only weakly influenced by new knowledge and skills; they are rather more strongly influenced by new understandings. They are certainly much more closely connected to increased awareness. And in their turn, attitudes affect behaviour much more strongly than they affect any of the other elements in the Development process. It is for these reasons that although attitude change is properly seen as an educational task and thus as part of a full programme of ETA in Development, a separate stage specifically devoted to the promotion of attitude change is often needed.

Attitude change takes time, often a lot of time. It took many years, for example, to persuade girls in some countries to receive vaccination in their arms. And attitude change needs to be constantly reinforced. It is rarely a once-for-all conversion but rather a tentative and growing experimentation with new possibilities.

The process of attitude change

Enhanced awareness does not always lead to new attitudes, and new knowledge, skills and understanding do not always lead to new attitudes. But attitudes are most effectively influenced by two mechanisms: by *experience* (and therefore by experiential learning—especially those activities which rely upon the exercise of the new desired attitudes, role play, decision-making, simulation, for example); and secondly by close identity with a *group* which shares the new desired attitude.

The necessity to incorporate both strategies into the process of attitude formation and change is most clearly seen in those programmes designed to lead to new community or personal health practices—clean food handling, sanitary behaviour, smoking or diets, simple medical treatments and the like; but it also applies to agricultural and income-generating programmes, to literacy and basic education.

DECISION-MAKING

'Missionary Development'

At one end of the continuum of Development programmes lie those which are based on prior and centrally determined objectives; decisions have already been taken. In these cases, the wishes of the target groups are assumed or ignored and the people are required to participate in the agency's programme. Development becomes a process of persuasion. This is the case with most health and family planning and much agricultural extension—all those programmes with nationally or externally set goals. These 'missionary' programmes will still need to utilize the steps we have identified—enhancing awareness, increasing knowledge, skills and understanding, and especially reinforcing positive rather than negative attitudes. The problem is to make the desired attitudes and the desired Development behaviour fully internalized and thus permanent.

Participatory Development

At the other end of this continuum are those programmes which have open-ended goals, in which the participant groups are encouraged to control their own Development, to plan their own future. Unlike the 'missionary' programmes which may stifle initiative for the sake of some agreed desirable goal, these programmes encourage diversity of views, a choice from a range of possible actions, decision by the participants rather than by the Development agents.

The validity of Development which does not contain an element of participant decision-making in regard to the objectives is not in question. There is little scope for choice in some health programmes—for example, AIDS or vaccinations. Oral rehydration therapy (ORT) seeks to persuade mothers and other carers of very young children to feed infants with diarrhoea with a life-saving mixture of water, sugar and salt in prescribed quantities. The goals of a management training course for those who are already running their own co-operatives are already largely set. But most programmes have more scope for participant decision-making than they currently employ: the use of fertilizers or herbicides or pesticides or new techniques in agricultural production is not a simple matter of adhering to a textbook model but of choice from a range of possible alternatives. It is better to encourage and enable the participants to make these choices for themselves than for the Development agent to make them for them.

There is one decision which every participant will have to make for him/herself—whether or not to carry out what they have seen and experienced and learned, whether to make the desired Development changes or to stay as they are. Mothers and carers will in the end decide for themselves how they will treat their infants when sick; women will choose for themselves what to give their families for meals and whether to use hygienic methods of food care or not; farmers will decide for themselves on a day-to-day basis what they and their labourers will do in the fields; fishermen will choose whether to adopt new practices and equipment or not.

It is, therefore, all the more desirable that such decisions should be made, if only in role play or simulations, in the course of the Development process itself. The participants need to practise under controlled conditions the behaviour which the change-agent expects them to follow at the end of the programme, and that behaviour will include decision-making. In too many cases, the change-agents deny to the participants the right to take decisions; like a doctor, they give out prescriptions. They restrict the amount of choice and experimentation, mainly out of fear that 'they will get it wrong'. But it is surely better that the participants 'get it wrong' (if they are going to) in the context of a programme where it can be put right than in the field when the agency has left.

Participant decision-making, then, like attitude formation and change and education and training, is an important part of the Development process: it cannot be left out without endangering the ultimate success of the whole programme. The encouragement of the participants, individually and collectively, to make and re-make decisions needs to be provided during the Development process and not left to a post-Development stage or omitted.

ACTION

The fifth step is the collective execution of some course of action, activities which when engaged in under supervision will demonstrate the desired change, help to change attitudes and motivate the participants to learn new knowledge and skills and to develop new understandings, and bring about the planned change which is the objective of the programme. Literacy learners will begin the activity of reading and writing, neo-literates will produce their own community newsheet. Farmers will plant and fertilize, process and market their crops under the eye of the extension worker. Co-operative members will, with the help of their guide, draw up their rules, arrange loans, organize activities and sell their products.

Some programmes intended to bring about changed behaviour provide no activity inside the programmes themselves—nutrition courses in which the women being taught never handle any food, let alone prepare a meal, but simply listen to talks and demonstrations; a programme designed to encourage a group of women to begin poultry farming and egg production, with no chickens to be seen except on the visual aids of the instructor. Participants are asked to do nothing except listen to the lecturer and look at pictures, and yet at the end of this experience they are expected to *act* on what they have heard. Surely the programme should give the participants an opportunity to try out the desired behaviour first in the context of a supportive group before they go away to do it in their own homes and villages.

Development projects and programmes are intended not just to add to the people's store of knowledge but to persuade them to *behave* differently, to take action in some way or other—to produce different things or more of the same, to process what they produce in different ways, to practise hygiene, to exercise a new skill which will make their lives easier, to utilize resources (whether it is irrigation water or credit facilities) in more effective ways, to participate more fully in the deliberations of the local community. Without a programme of action, without in short an *experience* of Development, there can be no social change, no Development.

Action in this sense is both the goal of the Development process and a part of the process itself. Talk by the change-agent alone will not result in Development; only an action programme which involves all the participants will lead to the desired and purposed change that is Development.

CONCLUSION

There are then five elements in the path to Development. All five need to be present in some form or other. The *existing state* has to be built upon; *awareness* enhanced; a process of *education and training* (including the building up of positive attitudes, especially confidence and motivation) engaged in; *decisions* taken; and a set of *activities* engaged in within the Development programme itself.

Such an analysis must not be taken as a prescription for Developmental success, to be followed rigidly and unthinkingly. Nor are these steps necessarily arranged in a strictly linear progression, with awareness first and then the others in succession. Development is a dynamic process, an encounter between change-agent and participants. Sometimes awareness enhancement will lead to the participants immediately calling for a course of action, to be followed by education and training; at other times, action will be delayed and even resisted for a variety of reasons. Sometimes one path of action, pursued for a time with its consequent acquisition of knowledge, skills and understanding, will need to be abandoned and another activity taken up. There is never only one route to the desired Development change. New knowledge may lead to new awareness or open up new options, new possible decisions, and these in their turn will call for more new knowledge. The process of Development is not a finite one, though some of its constituent parts may be terminal in nature: it is rather, like education itself, lifelong and continuing. The parallels between the learning cycle and the Developmental cycle are very close, as illustrated in Figure 11.1.

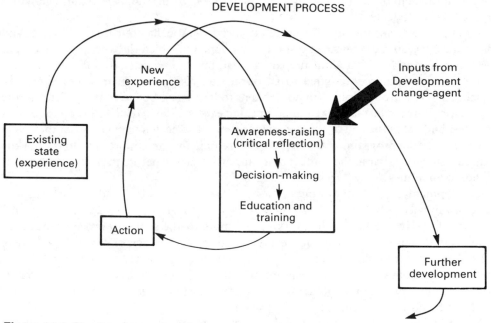

Figure 11.1 The Development cycle

NOTES TO CHAPTER 11

(1) Esman, M. J. (1978) *Landlessness and Near-Landlessness in Developing Countries*, Cornell.

(2) Chambers (1983), ch. 6, uses Isaiah Berlin's categories to distinguish between the fox (the exploiter of many resources) and the hedgehog (the exploiter of one main resource). See also Hill, P. (1977) *Population, Prosperity and Poverty: Rural Kano*, Cambridge: Cambridge University Press; Hirschman (1970).

(3) Experiment conducted in Glasgow in connection with Heritage Education Group (Civic Trust, UK) during European Architectural Heritage Year, 1975.

(4) Devised and used by the author: the results are as yet unpublished.

(5) Smith, J. and Harris, G. (1982) Ideologies of need and the organization of social work departments, *British Journal of Social Work* 12(1) (I am grateful to John Lewis for this reference); Laidlaw, A. F. (1971) *The Man from Margaree: Writings and Speeches of M. M. Coady*, Toronto, p. 57.

(6) On the role of education in Development, see Moulton, J. M. (1977) *Animation Rurale: Education for Rural Development*, Centre for International Education; Hanson, J. W. (1966) *Education and the Development of Nations*, New York; Fagerlind, I. and Saha, L. J. (1983) *Education and National Development: a Comparative Perspective*, Oxford; Wedell, G. (ed.) (1972) *Adult Education and National Development*, Commonwealth Foundation; Rao, S. V. (1986) *Education and Rural Development*, Sage; Ahmed, M. and Coombs, P. H. (eds) (1975) *Education for Rural Development*, New York; Garrett, R. (1983) *Education and Development*, Bristol: University of Bristol; Thompson, A. (1981) *Education and Development in Africa*, Macmillan; Aziz, S. (1978) *Rural Development: Learning from China*, Macmillan. The ACP-EEC Joint Assembly working documents, *Towards 2000: People-Centred Development*, edited by C. Jackson (August–September 1986), speak of 'the importance of training in the development process': in these papers, education is seen as school-based, training as skill enhancement.

(7) See Brokensha, D., Warren, D. M. and Werner, O. (eds) (1980) *Indigenous Knowledge Systems and Development*, USA; Chambers, R. (ed.) (1979) Rural development: whose knowledge counts? *IDS Bulletin* (special edn) 10(2) (January); Hewage, L. G. Global learning: east–west perspectives with a future orientation, in Thomas and Ploman (1985).

(8) See for example UNRISD (1979) and other reports of the UN Research Institute for Social Development (Geneva); Szentes (1976); Ryan (1971) and references cited in these works; Pearce, A. (1980) *Seeds of Plenty, Seeds of Want: Social and Economic Implications of the Green Revolution*, Oxford.

(9) *The Mahbubnagar Experiment: Nonformal Education for Rural Women*, Council for Social Development, Delhi, 1976; von Freyhold, M. (1979) Some observations on adult education in Tanzania, in Hinzen, H. and Hundsdorfer, V. H. *Education for Liberation and Development: the Tanzanian Experience*, UNESCO Institute for Education, p. 165.

Chapter 12

Target Groups: Needs, Wants, Aspirations and Intentions

Since the early 1970s community-based Development has to a large extent been replaced by programmes aimed at target groups* chosen because of their special resources (farmers, fisherfolk, etc.), their potential (mothers with young children, rural women, unemployed youth, etc.) or their perceived need (illiterates, urban slum dwellers, etc.). Some target groups are general (for example, school drop-outs or backward classes, inhabitants of drought-prone areas or low-income groups) while others are more specific (a local community or district, or those with a particular handicap like the blind or the hearing-impaired, etc.). Some practitioners regret this selection of some persons out of the community to become 'beneficiaries', since they feel that it weakens the ability of the community to combine to solve its own problems but it nevertheless is the focus of Development today.

We should notice three things about these target groups. First, they are defined and chosen by outsiders. They are rarely volunteers; the initiative does not come from themselves. Whether this is a good thing or not can be argued endlessly, but it has implications for Development and especially for the education and training programmes. Many of the participants will be reluctant participants, many of the learners will be reluctant learners. Target groups selected for Development will to some extent have been pressurized to 'come in'. The very phrase 'target group' carries the implication that Development is something done to and for other people rather than the people doing it themselves.

Secondly, these target groups are seen as detached from their local communities. Some people in a particular village or slum (for example, the poorest of the poor or those aged between 15 and 35) are chosen, others are left. The results of this separation may be to negate the effect of the programme. One example will suffice. In an oral rehydration therapy programme in Andhra Pradesh (India),[1] an evaluation found that the women who had engaged in the programme (the mothers with very young children) in a group of villages knew what to do; nevertheless the mortality figures showed that in many cases

---

* I have retained the term 'target group' rather than 'participant group' in many instances in this chapter as it examines the approaches of Development agencies which use this term regularly.

they were not practising ORT when their infants became sick. Part of the problem was identified as lying in the limited nature of the 'target group': by concentrating on mothers with infants, it excluded the older women (who usually gave advice and made family decisions) and the young girls (who often had the care of the children while the mothers were working in the fields). Thus the 'target group' of mothers, who were apparently both informed and convinced, had not only to resist the pressure of older and more respected members of their community and families, but also to pass on their newly acquired insights and skills to their baby-minders. The 'target group' was too narrowly drawn and too isolated from the rest of the community in this case to be fully effective.

Thirdly, the target group is seen as a category of people with generalized needs, not as individuals with personal needs. Many programmes of Development are built upon the assumption that all farmers, all illiterates, all mothers with young children are the same (despite some consciousness of cultural and class differences). So programmes are devised centrally for general categories of people and are implemented locally by change-agents who have had no part in their preparation.

NEEDS

The problem is how to adapt centrally determined and provided programmes to groups which are each different in their background and in their response to the programme. This issue has been widely recognized, and it is frequently urged that Development should be based not upon predetermined and imposed decisions but on the specific needs of the area or population sector concerned.

A great deal has been written about needs, and differing lists of needs have been compiled. Some are based on the planner's preconceptions, some on internationally accepted definitions (like Basic Human Needs), some on academic conceptualizations (like Maslow's [learning] needs) without any local survey. Identified needs have been arranged in hierarchies, some having higher priority than others. They have been categorized into individual needs in opposition to the needs of society; or set along a 'hot–cool' continuum, the strongly emotive (such as freedom) being at the 'hot' (political) end and the less emotive (such as infrastructure, e.g. roads, wells) being at the 'cool' (technical) end. Or they have been arranged in a matrix of who loses or gains (Figure 12.1).

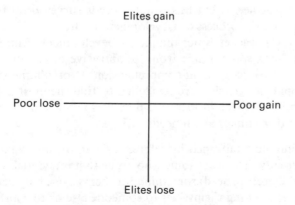

Figure 12.1 'Losers and gainers' needs matrix

But, however combined together and arranged, needs are seen to lie at the heart of most Development packages, even at the macro-level (thus 'energy needs' are used to justify new power stations). And they are identified by the planners in one way or another, often by a needs survey.[2]

Needs surveys

Agencies often take great care to survey the existing state of the target groups and try to build their interventions on the results of these surveys. There has sprung up a whole industry of 'needs surveys'. Students in university courses, especially at postgraduate level, go to the villages to conduct a needs survey as part of their programme of work. Courses are run on survey techniques. These 'base-line' surveys form the foundation for all kinds of Development programmes. Literacy primers, for instance, are written for farmers or for women on the basis of such surveys; and programmes for economic advancement are devised after surveying local communities.

There are several different kinds of needs surveys:

(a) 'Satellite' observation' (perhaps even 'the eye of God' approach), where the expert, sitting at a distance from the community or region, draws up a needs list from an overall superior position: this is the way most central planning authorities and academics do it.
(b) The 'space invaders' approach, where field inspections are made by groups of experts, wearing what are in effect alien clothes and using an alien language, but no real communication is held with the target group.
(c) The 'explorers' approach, where the visiting experts meet local residents (or more usually, *some* of the local residents: the 'take-me-to-your-leaders' needs survey) and listen politely to the ('uninformed') comments of local spokespersons before going away to write up their report.
(d) More rarely there is the 'surveyor-in-residence' approach, where the visiting expert(s) spends time in the local community, listening and talking with them, sharing insights, before the list of needs is drawn up.

There is of course another approach, by which the experts and the participant group jointly write the list of needs; but this is not a needs survey *prior* to determining the Development goals but the process of Development itself.

Such a range of approaches is not unique to Development. Anthropologists distinguish research methods which range from 'unobtrusive observation' (the 'fly on the wall') at one extreme to 'participant comprehension' ('total immersion') at the other. They, like Development agencies, are struggling to find the most appropriate ways of creating a relationship between insiders and outsiders in the making of such surveys.

We need to note three things about needs surveys.

1. A need can only be established by reference to an outside standard; it cannot be validated internally. There are some who argue that individuals can determine that they lack (and therefore need) something for themselves, but such a judgement can only be made by relating themselves to someone else or to some earlier time. One cannot know one 'needs' what one has never had or known about. The very word

'lack' in connection with a need indicates that the missing item is present in other places or that it has been present at other times—that the locality once had it but no longer has it. One village lacks the clean drinking water or irrigation or range of economic activity or electricity supply which other villages possess; rural areas lack the opportunities which town dwellers possess; a decayed market town lacks the trade it once possessed—these things become 'needs'.[3]

2. A concept of 'needs' involves judgements; they can never be absolute. The BHN (basic human needs) approach was an attempt to give a set of absolutes to 'needs', and in relation to the minimum needs essential to survival (water, food, etc.), they have been successful. But the use of ideas like 'ought' implied in a statement such as 'The target group needs adequate education' (i.e. they 'ought' to have it), and 'appropriate' and 'adequate' reveal that the determination of needs is made by a series of value judgements. This is why one person's list of needs will inevitably differ from another's; and why a list of needs will always be changing as new values and new standards are set. A radio, for example, was once seen as a luxury; now it is a need for all rural communities. And needs will vary from place to place: in many local communities, a telephone is seen as a need, in others it will be a luxury. Needs then are value-loaded and relative: they vary from context to context and change over time.

3. Because of this, outsider-led surveys frequently get it wrong. There is a real danger of misjudgement, of imposing externally perceived needs on local communities. One example will demonstrate this. In the mid-1970s, a survey of fishing communities on the southern beaches of Madras conducted by students and other 'experts' established housing as a high priority. A series of tower blocks was built nearby under the government's Low-Income Groups Programme, and the fisherfolk were encouraged to leave their canvas and timber shacks for the greater shelter of concrete tenements. Some of those who saw these communities daily felt that this was not a major felt need for these people; and a series of discussions with the women in the daytime and with the men in the evening (conducted on the steps of San Thomé Cathedral by the notable Madras adult educator, Sister Catherine McCleavy) led to different conclusions: 'Housing?' they said, 'What's wrong with our housing? When they blow down, we can put them up again.' What was worrying these people was that some aid agency (they thought it was the World Bank) had given motor boats to fishing communities further up the coast and these fishermen were working the traditional Madras fishing grounds, were cutting their nets, 'and above all, they are smuggling'. The major concerns of these communities at that time were local rivalries—which later led to open conflict on the beaches.[4]

'Space technology' surveys by outsiders with their concentration on 'needs' will then often fail to identify the real preoccupations of the target group; and the result will be a programme which misses the mark and which is imposed on reluctant participants who will all the time be thinking of something else—their own concerns.

WANTS, ASPIRATIONS AND INTENTIONS

In response to these failures to identify needs correctly, Development planners have taken two different lines of approach. Some have urged that the people should be made aware of the needs identified by surveyors, that the outsider-determined needs should become insider-felt needs. Unless the target group, they argue, come to see the need for themselves, they will not willingly participate in the Development process. This is clear from many programmes: the abolition of dowry and family planning in many societies are not felt needs, and the programmes in these areas are therefore to a large extent ineffective.

Others, however, suggest that that the programmes should be confined to, or at least commence with, the needs already felt or perceived by the target group, that what the people want should be the criteria for the Developmental objectives.

Wants

The target group has many wants. A number of these will be more strongly felt than others, and the people will use the term 'needs' for these—that is, they are 'felt' or 'perceived needs'. Perceived needs and wants then should be distinguished. Wants are wider than perceived or felt needs. Some of the wants which the target group identifies will fall into the category of needs as identified by outsiders, but others will not. In many cases the villagers' sense of wants will be influenced by concepts drawn from the outside world: there is no wall around rural areas to keep them untarnished by outsider views of needs. But there will be many things in the expressed wants of target groups which are not regarded by outsiders as 'needs'.

'Wants' and 'needs' then overlap (Figure 12.2). So that the wants of the target group may be divided into two categories: 'need-wants' and 'non-need wants'. The 'need-wants' are shared by both insiders and outsiders. But insiders will not normally distinguish between those things which they want which fall into the outsiders' category of 'needs' and those things which they want which do not fall into the outsiders' category of 'needs'. It is only the outsiders who will make that distinction.

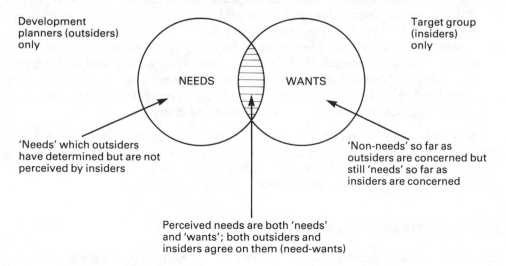

Figure 12.2 The relationship between needs, perceived (felt) needs and wants

An example will help to make this clearer. In a list of village 'wants' recently compiled by a group in one south Indian village under the guidance of a literacy animator were the following items:

improved road facilities
keep village streets clean
* sanitation
* latrine facility for women
* school facilities
hospital transport facilities
loans for housing construction
* supply of water
co-operative activities in the village

The animator (who by virtue of her training had been exposed to outside Development agency thinking) agreed that the items marked * were 'needs' (and since the villagers had listed them, they were 'perceived' or 'felt' needs); the others she listed as 'wants', of a lower order of priority. The value judgement attached to the definition of some of these items as 'needs' is that of the outsider. And the order of priority too varied: to the outsider, the importance attached to each item may be different from that of the villagers because it is based on different criteria.[5]

Wants and awareness

Wants arise from the existing awareness of the target group. The objectives of the awareness-enhancing stage of the Development process will then include helping the participant group both to distinguish between their 'non-need wants' and their 'need-wants', and to become aware of other 'needs' which they have not yet recognized: in other words to enlarge their sense of want by considering the standards and priorities which the outsider holds.

But wants, often sharply focused, do not always address the issue fully. A want is usually expressed in terms of a concrete *solution* to what the Development agency sees as a generalized need. Thus a village may want a well where the agency speaks in terms of a need for water; or it may want a bakery to meet a need for a cheaper and more effective food supply under local control. Most target groups will continue to use the language of needs for these wants, just as children often plead that they 'need' an ice-cream when what they need is any cool or sweet refreshment. A want then will be only one of many ways of meeting a need. But its very existence may prevent the target group from seeing the need clearly. The awareness stage of the Development process can help the participants to see behind their wants to the needs and to identify a range of possible ways to meet those needs.

Aspirations

Beyond needs and wants, there lie aspirations. These are different from wants. The Development agency may have identified as a *need* a clean water supply; the villagers may *want* a nearer source of water than one three kilometres away; they may *hope* for a well or tap of their own, not subject to the control of some landlord or other. Aspirations are built on a greater understanding of the situation and on some more or less realistic assessment of probabilities. On the whole aspirations relate to the provision of solutions by outsiders rather than by themselves. They will cover only a small portion of the wants identified: most of the wants will be judged to be unobtainable (Figure 12.3).[6]

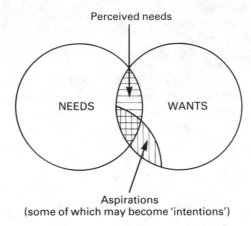

Figure 12.3 The relationship between needs, wants and aspirations

Intentions

Finally, aspirations too need to be distinguished from intentions. Intentions relate to those aspiration-wants which the participant group intends to do something about: to repair a road or to plant trees, for example. Intentions are the fruit of decision-making and reflect the confidence of the local people to take action. Both aspirations and intentions will usually exist before the Development process begins. We must not underrate our participant groups, their sense of their own situation and their aspirations and (in some cases) their intentions to change their situation themselves (see Figure 12.4).

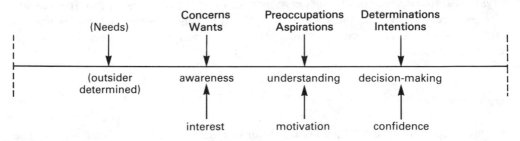

Figure 12.4 The needs–wants continuum

Wants, aspirations and intentions in Development

These variations in the perceptions of the participant groups are important for Development (see Table 12.1). Groups which can be found with *intentions* already established, especially intentions which relate to the Development goals, are the groups most ripe for Development programmes. The task of increasing motivation will be substantially easier. Groups with realistic *aspirations* will be relatively more quickly motivated to take action than those with *wants* only. For the first two sets of groups already possess insider-set objectives and positive attitudes towards the desired goals.

Table 12.1 *An example of the relationship between needs/wants/aspirations/intentions*

Needs (outsider identified)	Wants (insider identified)	Aspirations (hope to get from others)	Intentions (plan to do for selves)
Hygienic practices	*Need-wants*		
Nutritious diets			
Clean water supply	Well/pump/piped water supply	Water tap in/at/ near house	
Literacy			
Higher crop yields	Fertilizers, seeds	Credit to buy seeds,	
Income-generating activities	More money	etc.	
Better marketing			
	Non-need wants Village bakery Repair village street		Repair village street
	Electric light TV Village co-op	Electric light* TV*	Establish village co-op
	New houses		
		*Note: local politician has promised these.	

Groups with strongly felt wants will however on the whole still respond to the initiatives of the Development agency more readily than those whose sense of wants is weak or non-existent. Such groups as the last are many, however; there are those who, when asked what they need or what they would like, are unable to identify anything, often because they are unable to see the possibilities for change or improvement in their environment. Just as we must not underestimate our target groups, so equally we must not overestimate them and attribute to all of them from the start the desire and will to participate.

Many communities when consulted about their needs ask for unrealistic things which they are unable to carry through. Others reply that they don't know what is available—and respond positively and indiscriminately to every suggestion made by the agency. The reason for such responses is probably that the agency is looking for awareness among the community of those things which the agency has already determined as needs. It is important that the agency try to see what the target group sees, be willing to promote what they want to happen. The agency needs to develop its own awareness of the target group.

The nature of the awareness-enhancement stage in the Development process will, therefore, vary greatly according to the aspirations and intentions of the participant group. If mothers are already concerned about infant diarrhoea, it will be easier and quicker to move to a sense of aspiration and then to intention than if they are not aware of the problem. This is one way in which all groups differ from each other, even groups of mothers of very young children. Some will be very conscious of the issue; others will be less concerned. Even amongst those who are aware, some will be searching for an answer while others will feel that they can do nothing about it. Each will perceive the problem and react to it in different ways. The reasons for these variations lie in the personality construct and past experiences of each person in the group. And their articulation will depend upon the strength of the group and the role of the group leader. Change-agents need to take account of these differences, for they will affect the receptivity of the participants to the Development messages. To give each group exactly the same programme, ignoring these differences, will be damaging to the desired process.

GOALS AND WANTS

It has been argued that it is not right for the change-agent to impose health (or fertilizers or new boats) on people when they want something else: even if it is, as one agency put it, a case of 'I give you bread when you are asking for a stone'! Rather, it is argued, the Development process should start with this sense of wants, however vague, however remote, and proceed as follows:

- to accept and indeed encourage the existing want
- to enhance the awareness until the want becomes an aspiration, building up in the process confidence
- to bring the participants to an intention through a process of decision-making, thus strengthening their motivation
- to engage with the participant group in *their* chosen activity, not that of the change-agent

After all, it is pointed out, the purpose of Development is that the people should be better off *in their own terms*. Achieving what they want, being self-determining and self-reliant must be part of the goals of Development: anything else smacks of neo-colonialism or copyism.*

The danger of neo-colonialism is most apparent when the Development goals are based on Western models and are attached to aid (for example, fluoridized water or high-level technology), as has been the case with international agencies such as the World Bank, WHO or FAO, with their imported concepts (most GNP standards, for instance, are set by international comparisons). But neo-colonialism also exists inside any country when the Development goals are set by minority interests, whether governmental or voluntary, and when programmes are designed to persuade the people to accept these goals.[7]

---

* Copyism is not of course the same as imitation, which is a useful tool of learning.

This issue is similar to the debate among adult educators about whether education is a form of manipulation. Clearly there is some truth in this. But does it mean the abandonment of all externally determined needs in favour of locally determined wants, even when these seem to be irrelevant to the real needs of the community? Surely not: for this would be to deny Development itself, a process of intervention to achieve a predetermined goal. Nothing would remain other than facilitation—and facilitation (because it lacks goals of its own) is not the same as Development. In any case, many Development goals are not matters of option; they are issues of life and death, literally.

One answer to this is 'entryism': to start with those wants and intentions of the participant group which are relatively clearly defined and to proceed through the satisfaction of these to the goals of the change-agent. 'Starting with the priorities and strategies of the rural poor themselves', the programme chosen by the participants becomes the entry point to a longer path which may lead to the Development goal. Development then will not stop when the goals of the participant group have been achieved; this achievement can be used to lead on to further goals.[8]

Case study

So much for theory: does it work? One example is suggestive. In a project run in 1972–73 by Alan Duncan of the University of Sydney in the outskirts of that city, a group of Aboriginal residents were approached with the intention of establishing an adult school in their midst. 'A school?' they responded, 'We don't want a school. What we want is a telephone box.' Instead of ridiculing this suggestion, asserting that this was just a status symbol or that it would be vandalized in no time at all, arguing that they had no one outside the community to ring up—in other words, doing the work bureaucracy usually does (and in this case did) so well—Duncan and his colleagues agreed to co-operate.[9]

The process went something like this. 'Who provides telephone boxes?' asked Duncan and his fellow change-agents. 'We don't know: you tell us.' 'No', came the reply, 'you find out.' And find out they did. 'Now', offered the helpers, 'we'll help you by writing the first letter, but after that you are on your own.' And so the letter of application for a telephone booth was written and dispatched.

Then came the most crucial part in the role of Duncan and his fellow workers. At their next meeting, they were greeted with statements like 'It's all over, it's finished; they've said "no"' (giving of course all the usual quite reasonable reasons: a telephone box was not, after all, a 'need'). To which the reply came from the encouragers (they were by now friends): 'No, it isn't all over; it's only just begun.'

And together they worked for a telephone box in that community, constantly spurring the group to make their own decisions, to act for themselves, not to become reliant on the outsiders. And before they had achieved *their* goal, Duncan had achieved his: for the participants came to say that what they needed, if they were to achieve anything, was some educational experience and training as a tool to further Development.

The process may rarely be as dramatic—or as long drawn out—as that of Alan Duncan in Sydney; but it is always the same. A simple and at the time irrelevant question about pests in an agricultural extension programme can lead to effective learning not only on crop protection but also on yields, on marketing, and particularly on how to find out. A problem of a sick child can lead to new insights in nutrition: why give a lecture on proteins and fats when the mother's mind is on her sick child? Why not 'use' the concern of the mother as a legitimate stepping stone to Development (in this case, nutrition)?

Two-way learning

The word 'use' in the preceding sentence has inverted commas because I feel guilty about employing this term about people; and I quickly added (to calm my own conscience) 'legitimate'. But of course this begs the question. Is starting with the participants' wants and moving through them, by what may seem sleight of hand, to our own goals, a valid process? Is it not using often very vulnerable people for our own ends?

I do not think so, for two main reasons. First, the change-agent is a person, equal to the participants, not superior but equally not inferior. He/she will have their own concerns, their own insights; and part of the Development process is to help the participants to treat others as equals, to share experiences and viewpoints. An imposed goal (needs) will come from a sense of superiority of the change-agent over the participants; a subsumed goal (i.e. the wants of the participant group alone) will come from a sense of the inferiority of the change-agent to the participants. A sequence of goals or a single negotiated goal will come from a sense of equality, from mutual respect and understanding—and of course from great patience.

We must assert this middle position as strongly as we can. The change-agent is not God (or even Moses), to impose a set of commandments on others. But equally, neither is the change-agent merely a rubber stamp with no ideas of his/her own. The change-agent meets the participants on a level of equality, with a sharing of opinions and skills. Development, like adult education, is an encounter between equals—'teaching and learning on equal terms'.[10]

Secondly, and consequentially, the goals the change-agent has to offer will be offered as one alternative among others (including the option to do nothing).

We could give many examples. Agricultural extension, instead of being a set of unilateral instructions, would start with what the farmers want to do and then explore whether there are alternative (some better, some worse) ways of doing it, out of which the farmers will come to exercise genuine choice. Health Development would begin with real-life problems (wants) in the village or slum, some seemingly remote from the set curriculum of the programme—for example, the state of the village road about which there may be much concern, or irregular attendance at school or at work—and lead through these to the main Development programme. In many cases literacy wants come second to other wants and intentions which can be made the starting point for the programme; in Peru, for instance, programmes devised for the development of market centres led to a demand for literacy.

In each case, the wants, aspirations and intentions of the participants will become the gateway into the Developmental field. This will be truer Development than outsider-discovered and imposed solutions to outsider-identified problems. It is true that such 'bottom-up' Development will take much longer than a traditional 'top-down' process; but none of that time will be wasted.

Many international funding agencies are of necessity looking for time-bound results related to predetermined objectives, and the reality of these demands needs to be taken seriously. But the challenge must equally be seen clearly. Must all the change be on the part of the target groups and none on the part of the aid agencies? When they call for open-mindedness and new learning on the part of their target groups, can they not themselves be open-minded and learn from the participants? It is not just a matter of 'teaching' on equal terms but also of 'learning' on equal terms.

An approach to Development based on what the people want to do is more positive than an approach based on needs. To start with needs is to view the local community and target group in negative terms; to start with what they intend to do is to start with positive attitudes towards the participants. Moving from needs to intentions is to move from an input model of development to an empowerment model of development (Table 12.2).

Table 12.2   *Models of development: characteristic words used*

Input model		Self-action model	
Negative view of target group		Positive view of community	
Deficiencies	*Needs*	Resources	*Wants*
Despise what they do	$\left\{\begin{array}{l}\textit{Traditional}\\ \textit{Modernize}\end{array}\right.$	Value what they do	*Indigenous*
People are passive	$\left\{\begin{array}{l}\textit{Beneficiaries}\\ \textit{Target group}\end{array}\right.$	People are active	*Participants*
Development agent is supplier	*Donor*	Development agent is catalyst	$\left\{\begin{array}{l}\textit{Helper}\\ \textit{Sharer}\\ \textit{Facilitator}\end{array}\right.$
Process is inputs	$\left\{\begin{array}{l}\textit{Impart}\\ \textit{Aid}\\ \textit{Give}\end{array}\right.$	Process is self-help	$\left\{\begin{array}{l}\textit{Action}\\ \textit{Empowerment}\\ \textit{Decision-making}\end{array}\right.$
Result is dependency		Result is independence	

NOTES TO CHAPTER 12

(1)   ICDS programme in south Andhra Pradesh visited by the author and the staff of the Home Science Department of S V University Tirupati between 1976 and 1980.

(2)   See for example Chambers (1983), pp. 162–4; Heyer, J. (1981) Rural development programmes and impoverishment: some experiences in tropical Africa, in Johnson, G. and Maunders, A. (eds) *Rural Change: the Challenge for Agricultural Economists*, International Conference of Agricultural Economists, pp. 215–25; Morehouse, W. (1981) Defying gravity: technology and social justice, *Development Forum* 9(7) (September).

(3)   Chambers (1983), ch. 3; Lawson (1979), pp. 36–9.

(4)   This programme was one in which the author and the University of Madras Department of Adult and Continuing Education were involved between 1976 and 1979.

(5)   Programme in Tamil Nadu worked on by the author and the University of Madras Department of Adult and Continuing Education 1987–88.

(6)   Studies of rural aspirations include Hirschman (1970); *Peasant Perceptions: Famine*, Bangladesh Rural Advancement Committee, 1979; Hill, P. (1972) *Rural Hausa: a Village and a Setting*, Cambridge: Cambridge University Press.

(7)   Barratt-Brown, M. (1974) *The Economics of Imperialism*, Penguin; Wilber (1973).

(8)   Chambers (1983), p. 140; Fernandes, W. (ed.) (1980) *Development with People:*

Experiments with Participation and Nonformal Education, New Delhi: Indian Social Institute, p. 29.

(9)   Personal visit by author to project in 1973 while visiting the University of Sydney.

(10)   Phrase from Rogers, J. (1969) *Teaching on Equal Terms*, London: BBC.

Chapter 13

Change-Agents in Development

Programmes which take as their starting point the expressed aspirations of the participant group (rather than needs which agencies have put into their mouths or assumed
they possess) and use these to work towards the Development goals call for special
aptitudes on the part of the change-agents. Aspiration-led Development calls for
innovativeness rather than stereotyping of change-agents.

An example will serve to illustrate this. During a literacy class for farmers late one
night, I watched an instructor teaching the learners from a primer how to write simple
words relating to crops and farming techniques suddenly face an unexpected question:
'How much fertilizer do I put on my rice?' The instructor could not answer, either
because he did not know the answer or because he was not expecting such a query and
was not accustomed to having the flow of the set lesson broken. Certainly he did not use
that question to advance his literacy lesson. To him, it was an unwelcome interruption,
seen perhaps as an attempt by a reluctant learner to get away from the learning task.

But it was a matter of considerable concern to the farmers present. When the
instructor failed to provide an adequate response, some of the other learner-farmers
spoke up; then others joined in, and for more than a quarter-of-an-hour there was
creative hubbub in the class. The supervisor of this Farmers' Functional Literacy Programme who was also present joined in and the mêlée increased; it was some time
before the class settled down again to its literacy exercises. There was more animation
during this brief period than at any other time that night.

Such episodes are common in all forms of programmes, the unexpected interruption
which reveals that the concerns of the participants are some distance from the objectives
of the programme. And such events may be seen by the change-agent/instructor either
as a hindrance or as an opportunity which can lead towards the Development goals.

To view such an incident positively rather than negatively requires responsiveness,
rapid decision-making and quick thinking on one's feet which, it is argued, most
change-agents do not possess, whether they are part-time locally-based animators or
full-time professionally trained extension workers. Their training has not encouraged
them to acquire these skills. In every country, it is possible to find innovative change-
agents; but the problem remains, how to recruit enough persons to make for a mass

movement, and how to develop in these change-agents attitudes of openmindedness and entrepreneurial energy which will enable them on the one hand to identify and harness those factors and incidents which will help on the programme, and on the other hand identify and attempt to nullify those factors which serve as barriers to learning and to Development.

A recent study of literacy instructors in south India and other surveys of animators have suggested three main factors as being relevant here: the process of selecting the change-agents; the training offered to them; and the support systems provided for them during the programmes.[1]

SELECTING THE CHANGE-AGENTS

Throughout the literature on Development, it has become axiomatic that apart from some full-time extension workers and short-term project workers, change-agents (however they are called) should be chosen from the same or a similar local community within which they will serve. There are several reasons for this. First, as insiders, they will speak the same language (linguistic and cultural) and thus communicate better than outsiders with the target groups. One of the causes of the failure of the family planning programme in India is that the change-agents come in from outside like angels from heaven, virginal and chaste, dressed in strange clothes, talking differently from the mere mortals they are exhorting to a better way of life, young purists instructing mature matrons how to behave. The gap is so wide and the barriers between change-agents and target group so high that the learning results are minimal. More effective, it is argued, will be the use of change-agents who live in the community, who have been trained, and who work under supervision in the village or slum concerned. They will serve more effectively as a social model, being listened to with more respect and imitated. It is on this basis that the World Bank's Training and Visit system of agricultural extension with its contact farmers has been based; much literacy and mother-and-child care is taught using local animators.

Secondly, it is cheaper to train local change-agents and send them back to work part-time in their own locality than it is to train special bands of full-time change-agents who then itinerate among the communities or target groups. Contact can be maintained for longer periods with groups by using local animators working under supervision than by the use of outside extension workers.

Thirdly, and perhaps most importantly, the Development work will continue. It will not be seen as conditional on the presence or absence of the worker; it will not be short-term intervention, ceasing when the goals have been reached. The choice and training of local change-agents, so it is argued, is a form of Human Resource Development, strengthening in the long term the resources of the local community.

Some problems have, however, been identified. Reviews have suggested that this 'role diffusion' model has not been entirely successful in agriculture or some other fields. Selecting and training some persons can set them apart from the rest of the local community, and access to and control of developmental resources can cause conflict in the community. Thus one project in Ghana specified that the choice of (fulltime) animators was limited to a similar community two days' walking distance from the community being served.[2] Nevertheless, the selection of 'insider' animators is seen to be a prerequisite of success in Development.

Two points appear to be important in this process: commitment and educational level.

Commitment

The extension of Development programmes to a mass population using change-agents drawn from the local community has (sometimes? often?) resulted in what may be called 'The Reluctant Change-Agent'. Every mass programme has experienced the uncommitted change-agent who undertakes the work more out of self-interest (usually money) and leaves during the programme if another door opens. In some literacy programmes, the drop-out rate of animators is as high as 50 per cent. Some agencies choose older married women as change-agents rather than younger people, even though they will often have had less formal schooling; for they argue that these older women are more permanently resident, more committed, more mature in their approach to the participant group than the more mobile and more ambitious younger women. This (like its opposite) is an over-simplification: there is no general correlation between age and level of commitment (though there is a clear correlation between age and mobility, for more of the younger people are mobile). But it does remind us that commitment to the Development goals has been shown to be vastly more important than any other factor, including formal qualifications.

Educational level

Too much attention is frequently paid to formal education in the choice of local animators/change-agents. It is often argued that a graduate is to be preferred to a college student, who in turn is to be chosen rather than a person with a (secondary) school leaving certificate, who in turn is seen to be better than a school drop-out.

But such an attitude is too simplistic. The survey of literacy animators mentioned above indicated that there were proportionately more drop-outs among the better educated animators than among those with less formal education and fewer qualifications. Concentration on educational experience means that the choice of change-agent is unnecessarily limited. We were frequently told in the course of the survey that there was only one possible animator in the village who possessed the required educational qualifications (and the survey confirmed this) but there were often other persons, less well qualified, who would have made more effective change-agents.[3]

For working with adults in Development programmes is quite different from formal education with children or college students. It calls for approaches which are not found in formal education—listening to the learners, for example, instead of talking. Formal education is often a positive disadvantage for a Development worker.

Two instances may be given of this. The Mahbubnagar Experiment tested several modes of delivery in a health programme. One of its findings was that nurses given training in appropriate methods of working with adults were more effective as change-agents than schoolteachers given some health components. This is not because expertise in health matters is more important than educational approaches; rather it is that the formal methods of instruction of schoolteachers by which they keep their distance from the learners and treat them like ignorant children prevent the adult target groups from learning. A similar feature is seen in the village programmes offered by Indian universities. Those run by Adult and Continuing Education Departments are frequently conducted on formal lines—lectures, input sessions by experts, training programmes which include lectures on not lecturing to adults! They often see adult education as the extension of schooling to villagers and slum dwellers. Those programmes offered by university persons trained in social work rather than in formal education are almost always more effective in their approaches to adult participants, while the programmes offered by the Extension Departments (in Agriculture and Home Science, etc.), which see their work in the villages and slums as being quite different from formal education, calling for special attitudes and skills, are the best parts (sometimes the only effective parts) of a university's contribution to Development education and training.[4]

In the selection of change-agents, then, formal educational qualifications should count less than a willingness to learn and a desire to help. We must not of course go to the other extreme; Development work is a difficult task, calling for considerable skills and commitment. To ask someone with virtually no educational achievements to engage in it without a full programme of training is rather like asking a beginner on the piano to play a Beethoven sonata in public. And again it requires the attention of someone who is already regularly engaged in the desired activity. We cannot ask persons who *can* read but read very little regularly, to help others to learn to read. A basic level of competency and experience is required for all Development programmes. But equally the level of commitment to the programme goals is important.

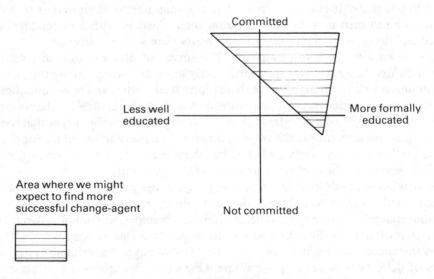

Figure 13.1 Selecting a change-agent: commitment–education matrix

Commitment and education combined

We do not of course need to see these two criteria as opposites; rather they form a matrix (Figure 13.1). The position of the prospective change-agent on the 'committed–not committed' continuum is more important than their position on the 'educational' continuum, which is the normal (and sometimes the only) basis for the selection of change-agents. Indeed, too much learning may be a handicap, not an asset, for an animator. Agencies are beginning to see the need to change their criteria for the selection of change-agents.[5]

HELPING THE CHANGE-AGENTS

Once chosen, a programme of help will be needed—pre-service and in-service training and guidance and the creation of support systems. Each of the change-agents will need different approaches in their training and support. The less formally educated may have less 'unlearning' to do than those who have received more formal education, but at the same time they may well need more confidence building, while those who are more formally educated but who may be rather less enthusiastic about the programme may well need more in the way of motivation building.

Pre-service training

There are large variations in pre-service training programmes for grass-roots level change-agents. Some consist of one-day orientation sessions (in at least one case given one month after the beginning of the programme!); some are residential courses of three weeks or even longer. For full-time extension workers/officers, there are now certificate, degree and postgraduate courses of two, three and even four years' duration.

There is little in the way of common understanding or common standards in the training of change-agents. Each agency engages in its own training; they rarely seem to learn from others. Reports on training and training manuals abound. Useful as these are for disseminating ideas and sharing experiences, they have their dangers as well, for they may promote an unthinking application of the proposed training strategies. And there seems to be relatively little learning from past mistakes. The Bay of Bengal Programme, for example, evaluated its experimental training programme for co-operative managers and published an enlightened report; but it did not attempt to run a second pilot programme to try to overcome the faults the evaluation detected.[6]

In-service

There is increasing awareness of the need for continuing training for change-agents whether they are formally or informally trained; these workers cannot learn all that they require for their demanding task during their pre-service training. In-service programmes vary even more than initial training. Much additional training takes place when change-agents and animators meet their supervisors to discuss administrative aspects of the programme. But other in-service events of a more formal nature are held in short residential or non-residential meetings dealing with specialist aspects of the programme (credit and banking facilities, marketing, animal husbandry, population or health camps, etc.). Such sessions are usually arranged by or in association with outsider bodies—government departments or resource centres or academic institutions. Some workers get very little in-service training, others receive a good deal.

Support systems

If they are to be innovative and responsive, change-agents need constant support systems, advice and encouragement networks, perhaps even more than in-service training programmes.

Supervisors and project officers of the Development programmes are normally full-time workers on temporary rather than permanent contracts. Most of them have been chosen for their educational attainments rather than experience—because they possess a certificate or diploma or even a degree in Agriculture or Development Studies or Adult Education or some other appropriate subject. Their own practical training for Development is patchy: some have been extensively trained, others have received little or nothing. Relatively few have themselves been change-agents.

Many supervisors do not see their role as much more than monitoring the change-agents—checking to see if the task is being done according to the rules and guidelines of the agency; theirs is a control function. The training and experience they possess are, in general, inadequate for them to adopt any other role; and the social relationships normally involved prevent them in many cases from becoming a friend and assistant to the change-agents under their care. Change-agents who need constant support to encourage them to be sensitive, responsive and innovative in helping participant groups to achieve their own Development goals are unlikely to get the support they need from supervisors, even less from academic trainers, whose influence on Development training programmes is more often than not baneful.

The recent survey of animators in south India, already referred to, suggested a number of strategies for ongoing support: networks of change-agents, especially in those cases where there was more than one Development workers in a village; the use of more experienced animators to assist less experienced animators; the development of self-training groups; and the involvement of experienced change-agents in the running of training programmes and in the planning and implementation of new Development programmes. Instead of using change-agents for a short time to achieve the set goals and then discarding them, some agencies are seeing them as long-term partners in a joint enterprise.[7]

TRAINING THE TRAINERS

In order to achieve the constant support which the change-agents need, there is a need for more training for supervisors and project officers—training appropriate to their proper role of resource persons working alongside their Development workers and instructors. Those concerned with programmes of 'staff development' have identified two main models: a 'developmental' (bottom-up and problem-solving) model and a 'deficit' (top-down, input-based) model. The former is more concerned with the needs of the person, the latter with the needs of the organization he or she serves. Much the same is true of the training of supervisors. They may be moulded to fit the needs of the programme and the agency, or they may be made innovative and free to exercise judgement in the fulfilment of their role of helper of the change-agents.[8]

Such training, if it is really to help the change-agents, needs to be pragmatic and practical rather than textbook and academic. Supervisors exist to serve rather than to control and instruct the change-agents. In this capacity they need to have had some experience of Development, to be good practitioners rather than good theoreticians. Theory in Development, as in adult education, grows out of practice more than practice out of theory. Supervisors and project officers thus need to be trained practically in Development. And this in turn creates demand for new patterns of training the trainers for Development: training is best conducted by those who are themselves experienced in the problems of being a supervisor and of being a change-agent rather than by experts in the theory of Development.

Unfortunately, this bottom-up approach to training is in many cases a long way off. What usually exists is a top-down model, in which academics tell the supervisors what they should know and these in turn pass it down to the change-agents. The trainers set the format, the timing and the content of the training rather than helping the change-agents to plan their own training.

Training is Development

Most training programmes in Development (even those which call for participatory methods) seem to be designed to limit initiative, to discourage decision-making by the trainees, and to encourage conformity to an ideal. They set out to create a model extension worker or change-agent, to foster the adoption of approved methods of animation (demonstration, role play or simulation, etc.); they try to 'give all the answers'. Rarely do training programmes set out to encourage the change-agents to innovate, to solve problems, to identify for themselves resources which can help them.

But the demand for innovative change-agents on a mass scale is bringing about changes in the content and methods of these initial and in-service training programmes. These latter training programmes may be analysed in terms of our Development model.

(a) They start with the *existing state*, the intentions and aspirations of the change-agents, with what they want to learn rather than with topics chosen by the supervisors, trainers and agencies.

(b) The articulation of these concerns by the change-agents will serve to heighten their *awareness* as they reflect critically on their role as change-agent, the resources available to them, and their own needs and aspirations.

(c) Such programmes seek to develop the *knowledge, skills* and *understandings* necessary for an effective change-agent—not just a limited range of communication skills and extension techniques, but a deeper understanding of the process of changing society, including identifying barriers and resources in their environment.

They pay attention to *attitude formation* as well as knowledge change—attitudes that the change-agents hold towards themselves, towards the task, and towards the participant groups.

(d)   They practise *decision-making* by the trainees, building confidence in the change-agents to plan their own learning.

(e)   And they build in a programme of *active learning* (instead of merely listening and watching) during the training programme—activities which will help the trainees to become more effective change-agents.

In other words, these programmes in all their phases—pre-service, in-service and continuing support—have become a Development programme for the change-agents themselves; they experience for themselves the process of Development. And the trainers in their turn have come to act as change-agents in this Development process.

Such trainers have come to realize that they themselves should use during training the same methods they wish the change-agents to use in the field. Research has shown that when change-agents are uncertain of themselves (and that will happen frequently if they engage in participant-led Development), they will tend to use the methods by which they were themselves taught. So that if during their training the change-agents receive lectures, they too will lecture to the target group; if the training programme helps them to identify and to solve problems, they will use these methods when they are engaged in the Development programme. It is strange in the light of so much recent practical experience that many of the training courses for change-agents continue to be formal; even such a participatory organization as Sarvodaya in Sri Lanka uses formal blackboard lectures and notes to try to encourage its workers to use non-formal methods in the field, although more active non-formal methods are available.

Knowledge inputs in Development and training

A word then needs to be added on the use of 'experts' in training programmes and in Development programmes. Knowledge inputs are often seen as necessary; but equally they are often not only ineffective but de-motivating.

There are many reasons for this. First, the frequent use of visiting experts who give lectures or conduct sessions breaks the continuity of learning; the programme becomes fragmented. There are gaps or overlaps or inconsistencies between the various elements of the programme which are never resolved in the minds of the trainees or participant group. Unless there is some overall director who provides continuity, the relationship of the separate parts to the goals is often not perceived.

Secondly, the presence of a visiting expert raises a number of questions in the minds of the trainees or participant group members. The expert knows so much and tells so much: are the listeners expected to know everything that the expert tells them? If not, which bits are they expected to know and which bits can they ignore? Sometimes in response to these questions (which, out of deference, are rarely articulated), the trainer will say that the learners can 'choose for themselves'. But making a selection from the wide range of knowledge presented by visiting experts is a complicated task, calling for special skills and wide experience. The expert and/or the trainer needs to provide help in this selection, and this help is rarely given; the expert gives his/her talk or demonstration and then departs from the scene.

Lectures by experts have all the faults of aid. By their very nature, they are 'input' sessions and therefore dependency-making. The attitudes of the experts are essentially those of 'I know, you don't know'. There is nothing in the lectures to encourage the listeners to find out for themselves, to become problem-solvers. They are in fact encouraged to believe that they are not capable of this, that they must rely on the expert, that they are dependent, not independent persons. This 'hidden curriculum' may contradict what is said during the lecture.

Visiting experts, then, both in training and in Development programmes, need to be used sparingly. They should be a resource for the people, brought in when the participant group requests their presence, not at some time or in some sequence set by the planners or at the convenience of the lecturer. They should be invited to deal with subjects requested by the participants, not with topics chosen by themselves or by the trainer/change-agent. In other words, the experts need to be responsive, dealing with the expressed needs of other people. The participants, not the visiting expert, should control the process. This will mean briefing the visiting experts, orienting them into a situation to which they will not be accustomed, helping them to develop new attitudes, assisting them in fact to become change-agents. This process of orientation is itself a form of Development; the experts themselves will thus have come to experience the Development process for themselves.

To be effective as Development workers, then, the change-agents need to become the participants in a Development process themselves; and the supervisors, academics and 'experts' who train them also need to experience Development as they in their turn learn how to train. For education and training *is* a form of Development—and those who experience it will make the best Development workers.

NOTES TO CHAPTER 13

(1) The material in this chapter is based on several years of participating in the training of animators and extension workers and other teachers of adults in different development programmes in India and in the UK and in conferences and other courses for trainers. The survey mentioned here and above (Chapter 12, note 5) was funded by Rotary International and was conducted in Tamil Nadu 1987–88; for report see Rogers, A. (1989) *Partners in Literacy*, Education for Development; Elias, M. *et al.* (1988) How do you feel? *Adult Education and Development* 31, 93–107, Bonn: DVV. For a general survey, see London, M. (1988) *Change-Agents: New Roles and Innovatory Strategies for Human Resource Professionals*, San Francisco: Jossey Bass.

(2) Piet Dijkstra, personal communication concerning programme in Ghana.

(3) See note 1 to this chapter; Upadhyay, B. V. (1986) *A Case Study on the Characteristics of Adult Education Instructors and their Performance*, Shramik Vidyapith, Surat; Misra, A. and Kabthiyal, K. C. (1988) A study of attitudes of instructors towards adult education, *Indian Journal of Adult Education* 49(2) (April–June), 35–39.

(4) For Mahbubnagar, see note 9 to Chapter 11. *The University System and Extension as the Third Dimension*, Report of Universities Grants Commission, Delhi, January 1986.

(5) Department of Adult Education, Government of India, *Training of Adult Education Functionaries: a Handbook*, Department of Adult Education, Delhi, 1978.

(6) Dutta, S. C. and Fischer, H. J. (eds) (1972) *Training of Adult Educators*, Bombay; Bay of Bengal Programme: Saraswathi, L. S. and Natpracha, P. (1986) *Towards Shared Learning: an Approach to Nonformal Adult Education for Marine Fisherfolk of Tamil Nadu, India*, BOBP REP 29; *Towards Shared Learning*, trainer's manual and animator's guide, prepared by Dr L. S. Saraswathi, BOBP MAG 1, 2, Madras, 1985; *Learning for Participation: an*

Approach to Training for Adult Education, version of this manual published by Department of Adult Education, Government of India, Delhi, 1986; Tietze, U. (1983) *The Impact of Management Training on the Performance of Marketing Officers in State Fisheries*, BOBP WP 22.

(7)   See note 1 above; Bhasin, K. (1983) *Breaking Barriers: a South Asian Experience of Training for Participatory Development*, Rome: FAO; Staley, J. (1982) *People in Development: a Trainer's Manual for Groups*, Bangalore: Search.

(8)   McLaughlin, M. and Berman, P. (1977) Retooling staff development in a period of retrenchment, *Educational Leadership* **35** (December), cited by Gough, R. (1985) Staff development—as part of the continuing education of teachers, *British Journal of In-Service Education* **12**(1), 35.

Chapter 14

Barriers to Development

There is currently considerable, perhaps exaggerated, pessimism about the efficacy of Development as one of the tools for helping to solve some of the world's problems. I think the statements made are unnecessarily gloomy; but the criticisms must be faced squarely if we are honest, for they contain much truth.[1]

Some of the pessimism is based on a false concept of Development as input, seeing technical advance, growth and modernization as ends in themselves. But even those who see these as merely means to an end cannot be other than jaundiced at the results of all the interventions of recent years. As we have seen, Development is not simply the provision of amenities such as clinics, sanitation, wells, libraries, sewing machines, power stations, boats and fertilizers, but the use of these amenities for the improvement of the quality of life. And while the quality of life for some has undoubtedly improved, for the vast majority of the world's population it has not. What has gone wrong? What is preventing them from joining in? What is stopping Development from being effective?

TYPES OF BARRIERS

Participation studies have identified three main sorts of barriers:

(a) Those inherent in the programmes themselves—that there are not enough to them, for example, or that they are of the wrong kind, not relevant or not in the right format, not at the right location or time to facilitate participation.
(b) 'Situational' barriers which lie in the life-site of the target group—domestic, occupational or financial circumstances, for example, which prevent full participation.
(c) 'Attitudinal' barriers within the target group which stop them from taking action: what might be called the 'It's-all-right-for-them-but-it's-not-for-me' syndrome.

This three-fold distinction will be useful for our discussion of the barriers to Development.[2]

'Provision of programmes' barriers

The barriers most frequently and most easily identified are those which are seen to lie in the programmes which are being offered to the people.

Lack of resources

The most usual reason given for the failure of Development is the lack of resources. 'We need more . . . [more money or more technical knowledge, more skills or more equipment, etc.]' is the frequent plea. 'We cannot undertake this Development task until we are given the resources.'

The resources for Development are clearly not adequate: and many of the rich countries of the world, like the United Kingdom, stand condemned for their steadfast and selfish refusal to donate adequately to the world's needy populations. Resources need to be increased, and sacrificially, before Development can be fully effective. Nevertheless, we need to test the validity of this alleged barrier.

(a)   We should not see resources solely as money or skills or equipment. There are other resources. Indeed, the most valuable resource is people—their indigenous knowledge and existing skills (though we should never value people for what they possess), their willingness, their aspirations and intentions, their desires and their goals. The defeatist attitude of the Development worker who says that we can do nothing unless we are given money or other inputs is itself more of a barrier than the lack of resources.

(b)   Part of the planning and awareness stages of any Development programme will include the identification of what those other resources are. But planners rarely look closely enough at the resources already available, which can be mobilized, enhanced and harnessed to the Development task. Agricultural extension workers plan as if the solution of the world's food problems depend on them alone, as if no one else is concerned; health agencies work in isolation from other resources. Agencies need consciously to explore and to exploit all the possible aids which are available, to work with others to build up a supportive climate for their programme.

A recent health project, Heartbeat Wales, will illustrate this. In order to launch an effective campaign against the exercise and dietary habits which contribute to heart disease, the organizers (the equivalent to a Development agency) devised a broad strategy of health and nutrition programmes. They did not confine the target group to high-risk men aged between 40 and 50, smokers, and so on, but widened it to include all adults, men and women. They pressed others into helping them. Doctors were asked to advise all patients about heart disease risks, schoolteachers, employers, health advisers, government bodies and even the media were asked to promote the mission. Any agency which could help in building up a general atmosphere in which heart disease and its causes were discussed openly and commonly was mobilized; even commercial concerns like sports equipment manufacturers and shops were called upon with the message: 'If we are successful—and we intend to be successful—then you are likely to sell more of [this or that]', in return for which they were enlisted to help with the campaign. What is more, the campaign organizers identified some of the sources of the problem, those companies making and marketing products liable to induce heart disease, and approached them with much the same message: 'If we are successful—and we intend to be successful—then you will sell less . . . [high-fat milk or meat or butter, etc.]. It will therefore be in your own interest to manufacture and promote low fat . . . [milk, meat, butter, etc.].' In this way, even some of those who were part of the problem were helped to become part of the solution. The aim of the campaign was summed up in the slogan: 'Making the healthy choice the easy choice'.

There are plenty of resources scattered throughout the community, and one of the most neglected parts of Development planning is the identification and mobilization of those resources. Many Development agents suffer from resource myopia.

(c) My third point about resources is that we should ask ourselves why there are not enough resources of the kind we feel we need. The failure of governments and other donors to provide enough resources would seem to reflect a lack of commitment to Development, to reflect a set of attitudes towards other people and their needs. And the fault for this would seem to lie with those who see the need and the processes to meet those needs, and who have failed to convince the decision-makers to change those attitudes. The removal of the lack-of-resources barrier is an educational as much as a political task. Development workers should not always blame others for the lack of resources; some of the blame lies with themselves for not having made the case adequately. It must be stressed that this is not the same as Development agencies defending themselves and their particular role, a course of action to which many bodies, especially NGOs, devote much of their energies. It is a question of promoting the cause of Development itself.

(d) My final response to those who say that there are not enough resources is to point out that what we have had has on the whole failed to do much good. When a programme is ineffective, it can be argued that it makes no sense to give it more resources. No one can blame the decision-makers for being reluctant to assist Development programmes which have ultimately had harmful results. I quote from three recent critiques which speak of

the growth of impoverishment amongst the poor peasantry as a consequence of development policies being pursued at present. . .government development policies have increased rural poverty. . . .

the adoption of improved production techniques, land augmenting investment, etc. were mostly done by the rich and middle peasantry. . .the rural rich have managed to sabotage the land reform program, appropriated most of the public resources and hi-jacked the co-operative movement. . . .

Official statements confirm the fact that economic inequalities have increased, with the rich growing richer and the poor feeling more deprived in a relative sense even though they may be slightly better off than before.

This picture can be repeated: 'country after country reveals the same pattern of relatively high growth rates, combined with a failure to meet other major needs and with dramatic inequities in the distribution of economic and social benefits'; 'the so-called community assets created under the anti-poverty programmes proved beneficial only to the affluent sections of the village population'.[3]

Lack of resources in themselves then are not the main barrier to Development—for there are resources other than money and technical assistance, especially human resources, if only we could identify and mobilize them; and any lack of resources may largely be our fault, not others', for the results of what we have received are not always pleasant to see and we have failed to convince those who could help of the very real need.

Where then do the true barriers to Development lie?

Opposition to Development

It is easy, and usual, to blame others rather than ourselves for any failure in Development. And with a good deal of justification. We all know that there will be many opponents to Development in all societies. The rich will not welcome the poor becoming richer except to buy the rich people's goods. Politicians will not welcome the people becoming decision-makers and critics: 'opposition [to a women's programme] came from some of the men, particularly landed farmers wishing to maintain a status quo which was to their personal advantages'.[4] Those at the core of society will resist pressure from the marginalized to join them at the centre. And so we could go on.

Some of this opposition is on a grand scale. But much of it is at the micro-level: like the bus conductor in Tamil Nadu who was regularly defrauding illiterate villagers who used his bus to take vegetables to market, until an animator taught the villagers to read and thus to resist his cheating, so that now he refuses to pick up the villagers or the animator. Such stories can be multiplied many times—sometimes with more serious results. In one project in Orissa, an awareness programme for a Harijan colony led to an outbreak of violence between these people and the rest of the villagers, to two deaths and to the imprisonment of the animator on the grounds of stirring up communal hatred.

But opposition such as this is not a barrier to effective Development. Such hostility only comes into play once Development has begun to be felt; it shows something of the success of the programme. It is real and common; and steps need to be taken to identify the possible sources of such opposition and to nullify it. Many agencies ignore the reality of the opposition their programmes will arouse. Nevertheless, this is not the reason why programmes are in many cases ineffective. We must look elsewhere.

The design and execution of programmes

Most of those engaged in Development programmes blame workers in other parts of the Development structure for the barriers. The following ladder is typical of many programmes:

Planning agency (usually at central level)

|

Executive agency (including project officer and supervisor level)

|

Change-agent

|

Target group

And it all depends where you stand in this hierarchy who you blame.

Planning agency   To the executive agency, the planners are to blame. They do not allocate adequate resources; or they choose the wrong sort of programme. They set unrealistic targets, like eradicating illiteracy in a set number of years or suggesting that a literacy programme can be effective with little or no post-literacy materials. They are constantly changing policies, launching new programmes every two or three years without waiting for earlier programmes to mature. They are in too much of a hurry, calling for evaluation before the programme has had a chance to take hold, digging up the young plant to see how the roots are growing. They are inefficient, withholding money until the last minute and then expecting the immediate implementation of the programme planned many months before. The Development drives are fragmented, so that a constellation of different bodies—government ministries and departments, international and national aid agencies, official and voluntary organizations—deal with different aspects of an integrated plan; as with adult education, there is no system of provision, just chaos and competition. The list is endless. The resourcing, design and implementation of programmes are all wrong, so it is alleged, and the planners are to blame.

But even if such complaints are true (and not all of them are), we have to ask ourselves, why is this so? Part of the reason springs from the lack of experience on the part of administrators who have never worked in the field; so that they do not understand the problems of those trying to carry out the programmes at grass-roots level. But there is a deeper cause than this—an apparent lack of commitment on the part of politician and administrator alike. They seem to view Development as a tool to win votes or other advantage; and government officials frequently see their current role as simply one step in a career, a professional progression which will soon take them away from Development issues. So they press unrealistically for the sort of immediate statistical results which will ease their passage to promotion: they are in effect using the people for their own ends.

Executive agency   If you are a change-agent or planning agent, however, things will look different. The executive agency will be to blame—for corruption, for frequent changes of personnel (supervisors, for example, come and go), for inefficiency. They are open to all sorts of pressures from interest groups, political and economic. There is the District Adult Education Officer I met who admitted that he had taken the job because it would enable him to serve his last years before retirement with little or no work to do. There are the non-governmental bodies set up primarily to ensure their staff an assured income from Development funds drawn from governmental or aid agencies' programmes. There is the agency which adopted spurious evaluation techniques and in the search for statistics moved the programme to another centre at the first opportunity. The executive agency cannot be trusted by the planners to run the programme properly and so the planners devise new forms of red tape to keep the local executive agency trussed up; and they in their turn truss the change-agent and the target groups in their own variety of red tape. And again we have to ask ourselves why this is so. And the answer appears to be the same: an apparent lack of commitment to Development.

Change-agent But then again the real fault, so it is alleged, lies with the change-agents. They attend to their work, if at all, very irregularly. They are not innovative. They leave the programme at the first possible moment, abandoning the target group. They are themselves ignorant; they do not understand and cannot be made to understand. And the root cause of this is once again that they are not committed.

Such is the dismal picture which is often painted at conferences and seminars on the evaluation of Development programmes. The lack of commitment at various levels of workers within the programme negates the efforts of more well-intentioned workers elsewhere in the chain. But there is a logic gap here: if the main barrier to Development springs from a negative set of attitudes on the part of those who plan and/or carry out the programmes, then these attitudes can be changed by others within the programme. It may seem strange to suggest that Development programmes should be directed at Development workers themselves, but Development begins at home.

And in any case, the criticism is exaggerated. Not all the barriers spring from a lack of commitment. Those who plan or implement the programmes often make mistakes, not through a lack of commitment but through a lack of experience, especially through failure to understand the target group properly. So we must now turn to those barriers which have been identified as lying in the target group—those which spring from their life situation and those which arise from their attitudes. For even if with full commitment we were to provide more resources and more programmes, we may still find that they are ineffective, either because the target group could not participate or because they will not. We need to examine this more closely.

'Target group' barriers

One thing all three groups engaged in Development—planning agent, executive agent and change-agent—are often agreed on is that the people, the target group, are the main barrier to Development. They are thought to be ignorant: they lack proper knowledge, they have silly superstitions and they resist change. In 1967, for example, during the 'green revolution', many women resisted the new high yield variety rice seeds because they alleged the new crops would cause sterility; it took several years to overcome this false knowledge. In parts of central America, many campesinos (rural workers) think that to study paper closely after working in the fields all day will make them go blind, and for women, 'that it was unlucky for women to read or write for three months after childbirth'. But even when the people possess the correct knowledge, their attitudes are thought by those who work with them to constitute a substantial barrier; they do not wish to change their way of life.

Such criticisms of the target groups are common. The people are not aware and cannot be made aware. They are not motivated to their own Development. They are victims of their own making. Examples abound. In parts of India, brahmins are reluctant to plough and non-brahmins reluctant to breach the brahmin's monopoly of growing coconuts because of traditional patterns of culture. Farmers are reluctant to use bonemeal on their fields because of what it is thought to contain, or to grow particular vegetables because of a coincidental family tragedy which they attribute to this cause. A story from Karnataka will help to illustrate this view. In the late 1970s, I accompanied a commissioner for the release of bonded labour on a visit to a village where he 'liberated' 24 men from their bonded labour under the recent legislation. He gave them, as the law required, the choice of having some land allocated to them in another district or receiving some sheep to help them become economically independent where they were. They chose the sheep. When I asked him some months later what the outcome was, he replied: 'That was one of my failures: they ate the sheep in one great village feast and turned up to work again a day or two later.'

The people themselves, therefore, are often seen to be the main barrier to Development. They refuse to accept the innovations offered to them, preferring traditional ways. They quarrel among themselves over who should benefit from the Development interventions or allow old feuds to determine their allegiances towards the change-agents. They do not want to change; they prefer their poverty and squalor to the new life the Development agent has to offer to them. They prefer to shit on the pavements rather than use the toilet facilities provided for them. The people neither can nor will accept our Development programmes; their cultural patterns prevent them from responding to the challenge of Development. Or so it is alleged. In response to such views it is necessary to examine both contextual barriers and attitudinal barriers.

Contextual barriers

The first thing is that our programmes frequently fail to take account of the real-life situation of the people we are seeking to help, to address the issues which face them. We see so little.

Two instances will illustrate this. An experimental project in Tamil Nadu in 1962, which provided every house in a particular village with a toilet, found that these were not being used, particularly by women, who continued to walk long distances from their homes for toilet purposes. There were several reasons for this: for one thing, defecation was an activity which gave the women an opportunity for community news-sharing; for another, defecation was something which traditionally was done in the open, not in a confined space which made the women feel uneasy. These factors had not been 'seen' by the Development planners.[5]

The second example comes from the Andhra Pradesh oral rehydration therapy programme mentioned earlier (see p. 146). The women in this programme clearly knew about the need for ORT and possessed the skills and information required to carry it out, but they still failed to do it. The programme had not taken account of the other pressures on the mothers involved—pressures not only from the other older women in the family and village community but also from their inherited communal traditions and their own upbringing, which supplied powerful emotional barriers to the execution of the 'new-fangled' process. A two-fold strategy was devised. The pressure from others was to a large extent negated by widening the target group to include all the women and girls in the village (even, on an experimental basis, the men, though it was found that this made no difference to the effective implementation of the ORT programme). To overcome the weight of tradition, a group or 'club' was set up within each village to serve as a support network through which the mothers of very young children could encourage each other when an infant was afflicted; identity with a group broke down much of the hesitancy caused by the novelty of the remedy.

So, the barriers which arise from the life-site of the target group often spring from our perceptions and our planning. We cannot blame the people for our failure to take proper account of the very real disadvantages under which they live. To say that the people are too poor and tired and distracted by other concerns to take full advantage of the programmes we offer, that the struggle for living takes up most of their energies and motivation so that they are unable to profit from Development, is merely another way of saying that we have not taken these factors properly into account when devising the programme for them. Our programmes do not address their concerns or fit into their life patterns. It is asking too much to expect anyone to learn literacy or hygiene when they are worried about where the money for the next meal will come from. More time and care needs to be given in our planning to identifying the factors in the lives of the target group that create barriers to effective Development. And it is our responsibility, not theirs, to address these situational barriers; we cannot just accept these as something we can do nothing about.

In response then to the criticism that the people themselves are the greatest barrier because they neither care about nor are able to engage in Development, we need to assert that this picture of the people is not just incomplete, it is inaccurate. It is not true to say that the people are not aware. It is true that they do not see themselves and their social and physical environment in the same way as we see them. It is not true to suggest that they are not concerned, not motivated, have no aspirations. But it is true that they have priorities which are different from ours, which may relate to family or local community or some other factor we may have overlooked. And their 'failure' to change their patterns of behaviour, to utilize the facilities provided for them, may be due to the fact that they have these other priorities.

Attitudinal barriers

But beyond this, if we regard things from the viewpoint of the target group, we may receive a shock. The villagers and urban slum dwellers, the so-called backward classes and 'weaker sections' to whom our programmes are directed, see the same things as the Development agents see—inefficiency, blunders, corruption, politicians playing games with the lives of the people in the name of Development, frequent changes of policy, programmes coming to an end before the promises made are fulfilled. They are not blind: they see that some programmes in agriculture have resulted in heavy indebtedness for farmers who have had to pay both for the new seeds and fertilizers and also higher rents in crops and cash. And through it all, they see the same apparent lack of commitment.

Above all, they see the attitudes of the Development agents towards themselves. They are constantly reminded that those who claim to seek their welfare appear to believe that they (the people) cannot develop and do not want to develop, that they are unable and unmotivated to change their way of life. From the start, they are often treated as reluctant target groups, to be cajoled with the carrot or compelled with the stick. Motivational studies have shown that people tend to behave in the same way as they are regarded. If a person is treated as untrustworthy, unambitious, unmotivated, lazy and stupid, that person will increasingly respond in those ways: evaluations of prison regimes have shown this to be true. On the other hand, if people see that they are regarded as reliable, adventurous, hard-working, considerate and able, they will tend to behave more and more like this. These factors work in Development as well. It is no wonder that the people in our programmes, treated as failures and blamed for their own condition, or alternatively as people to be pitied and assisted by those who are superior in every way, will respond accordingly. For, as we have already seen, oppression takes the form of the people accepting the value placed upon them by the oppressing minorities, accepting their worth as perceived by others: accepting as inescapable

> the limits man imposes on himself through being unaware of his own potentialities . . . [Development] attempts to cure the person but does not realise his sickness may in fact be in his society whose dominating elements impose on the others the set of values meant to safeguard their own interests. The oppressed may internalise these values and build up a very low self-image, or there may be a conflict between the individual's awareness of the unjust situation or his craving for genuine freedom and the dominating values which he has internalised.[6]

The Development agency, in the attitudes which it adopts towards the target group, has the potential for becoming a demotivator more than a motivator of the people, of being an oppressor more than a liberator when it holds negative views of the target group.

IDENTIFYING AND COUNTERACTING THE BARRIERS

The barriers to Development then will be seen differently according to the way we look at the Development process. If viewed as a top-down programme, with assistance descending the chain, the main barriers will be seen to be administrative—lack of resources or bad design of programmes, unrealistic planning or instability of policies, inefficient execution of the programmes or corruption. But if viewed from the bottom up, what will be seen is an apparent lack of commitment all along the chain, seemingly caused by a fundamental belief that the people cannot act in their own Development and are unmotivated.

Faced with this enormous barrier set up by the agents themselves, the target groups begin to believe it of themselves—that they can do little or nothing to alter things, to take control of any part of their lives. Motivation depends on confidence, and since this essential confidence has been destroyed by the Development agencies themselves, the people appear to be unmotivated. Many target groups come to accept the values imposed on them by the agencies as inescapable.

These values held by both sides of the Development equation are surely the major barrier, for the administrative and programme barriers simply reflect the attitudes of the planners to Development and to the target groups. At bottom, the barriers to Development are not so much lack of resources or administrative matters or ignorance but negative attitudes towards the people held by the agencies and people alike.

Once we have identified these attitudinal barriers, it is possible to take steps to overcome them through a planned programme of education and training.

We have already seen that all programmes of Development need to include specific activities designed to change attitudes, to build up confidence and to increase motivation. But the Development agents will not be able to change these attitudes and build up this confidence and motivation in the participant group unless they themselves believe that the people in their programmes are basically able and willing to make these changes. The challenge of Development is to ourselves as Development agents: whether we believe in the people. We need to change our attitudes towards the people—in other words, to develop ourselves.

Development then is not just the provision of resources or the designing of programmes to supply new facilities and teach the people to use them—although inputs of new knowledge and new skills are important to successful Development. It is, rather, encouraging people to come to believe in themselves, to believe that they can make these changes for themselves. The biggest obstacle to Development lies in the attitudes and values of the Development agency towards the target group, and in the attitudes of the target group to the Development goals. Changing these attitudes and value systems is the essential role of the education and training stage in the Development process, the reason why no Development programme can be complete without a central core of education and training of adults.

NOTES TO CHAPTER 14

(1) Much of the material in this chapter comes from discussions in a workshop on the barriers to development organized by the University of Madras Department of Adult and Continuing Education late in 1987, and from subsequent discussions. See UNRISD (1979) for an analysis of obstacles to development; also Cohen and Uphoff (1977). See also for example Griffin, K. and Khan, A. R. (1978) Poverty in the Third World: ugly facts and fancy models, *World Development* **6**(3), 295–304; Farmer, B. H. (ed.) (1977) *Green Revolution?*, Macmillan; Resistance to change: its analysis and prevention, in Bennis *et al*. (1964); etc.

(2) Cross (1981), p. 54; ACACE (1982). For other analyses to barriers in AE see Jarvis (1983), pp. 61–5; Boshier, R. W. (1985) Adult education: motivation of participants, in Husen, T. and Postlethwaite, N. (eds) *International Encyclopedia of Education*, Pergamon.

(3) Grant, J. P. (1972) Accelerating progress through social justice, *International Development Review* **16**(3), 4; Grant, J. P. (1975) *Global Justice and Development*, Washington; Patnaik, U. (1987) *Peasant Class Differentiation*, Delhi; Rahman, A. (1987) *Peasants and Classes*, Delhi. See also Parmar (1975); Chenery, H. *et al*. (1974) *Redistribution with Growth*, Oxford: Oxford University Press, p. xiii. ILO reported that 'the sort of resources created in areas such as land reclamation and dryland development went to the landed gentry', *Poverty and Landlessness in Rural Asia*, ILO Report, Geneva, 1977. It is worth quoting the example of Mexico as given by Grant (1973) in full: 'In the sixties, Mexico's per capita income increased from $441 to $606, and GNP grew seven per cent each year. However, (i) the ratio of income between the top twenty per cent widened from 10 : 1 in 1950 to 16 : 1 in 1969; (ii) rural landless labourers increased in number by one million and their average number of work days dropped from 190 to 100 per annum; (iii) the income of landless labourers decreased by 30% while that of factory workers increased by 75–80% between 1967 and 1974; (iv) 80% of the increase in agricultural produce came from three per cent of the farms employing only six per cent of the workers; and (v) health and education programmes continued to neglect rural people's needs.'

(4) Lewis, C. (1988) Transformation through self-reliance, *Development Forum* **16**(5), 6.

(5) I owe many of the Indian examples to Professor Sundaram of Madras University. For South and Central America, see Archer, D. and Costello, P. (1990) *Literacy and Power: the Latin American Battleground*, London: Earthscan, p. 29.

(6) Fernandes (1980), p. xxix. See Hirst, P. H. (1974) *Knowledge and the Curriculum: a Collection of Philosophical Papers*, Routledge and Kegan Paul.

Bridge

We have noted in Part I of this book that there is a demand for a re-orientation of adult education in the West in the light of the great social and environmental problems which face the world today—problems which call for the mobilization of Adult Education agencies as well as other social tools. And we have suggested that the concept of Development as practised in Third World countries might become the basic principle for such a re-orientation. This led us to examine the theory and practice of Development.

Part II has contained this analysis. It has looked at the various approaches to Development, whether seen as a tool of government to achieve economic growth or to meet the needs of the people, or seen as an instrument of the people to achieve liberation, empowerment and participation. It has examined the stages in the Development process, the agencies involved, the change-agents and the barriers to Development. And it has argued that at the heart of all effective Development programmes, there lies the objective of changing attitudes so that the desired practices may be adopted by the participant groups. This process of attitudinal formation and change is itself an educational task: so that at the heart of all forms of Development lies a process of education and training of adults (ETA).

Development then is not distinct from ETA; and as such it is possible for Development to form the basis of adult education programmes. But there are some distinctive ways in which a Developmental model of adult education would approach its task, some different roles to be played. Part III looks at these differences.

Part III

Adult Education and Development: Re-orientation

Chapter 15

Seeking New Objectives

It is the argument of this book that adult education in the West needs to become re-oriented to a Developmental model. This will make sense out of its claims to be a critical and effective means of examining reality and social change, will justify its existing programmes, and enable it to help the work of the growing number of Development programmes, thus overcoming the marginality and apparent irrelevance from which much adult education as at present constituted suffers. For Development is now clearly central to Western societies in a way that adult education is not.

It is also the argument of this book that Development, in order to be effective, needs the experience which adult education can bring to the programmes of education and training for adults (ETA) that lie at the heart of all Development. Some Development workers are already looking for a 'Third Force', an approach to Development which lies somewhere between the imposition of predetermined goals and the directive approaches of the formal Development agencies on the one hand, and the mere facilitation of the wishes of the participant groups on the other hand. Adult education could provide this third force.

CONGRUENCE

The congruence of adult education and Development is clear. They speak the same language and have concern for the same groups. Both set for themselves purposes and goals. Both consist of planned interventions into the natural processes of social change and individual learning. Both share common approaches to the agents of development.

But there are differences. The voluntaryism of adult education can be seen as the antithesis of the more 'missionary' approach of Development. Adult education in the West (though not in the Third World) has traditionally been oriented more to individual than collective goals, while Development is mainly concerned with societal issues. Adult education, which claims to be open-ended, non-directive and holistic in its approach, is thus suspicious of Development, which is seen to be state-led, normative and concerned almost exclusively with economic progress. Such issues must be addressed if we are to pursue this re-orientation seriously.

It is true that there is much in the top-down model of Development which can be the enemy of participation. But there are other models. If Development is seen as a tool used by governments to manipulate the people, then many in adult education will rightly wish to remain aloof from it. But if Development is seen as the tool of the people to achieve their own betterment, to overcome their sense of exclusion and dependency, then adult education in almost all its forms must surely join in this struggle.

A coming together of Development and adult education will call for changes in both partners. For example, adult education will need to accept collective goals set by others as its own; and Development will need to pay more attention to education and training for adults (especially to attitudinal change) as an essential element of its programmes.

Adult education built upon Development models will thus call for considerable re-orientation in thinking. Perhaps the first and most challenging aspect of this lies in the area of objectives, the goals of its programmes.

Existing attitudes to objectives

There are mixed attitudes towards objectives in adult education. At one extreme are those who assert that the adult educator has and should have no prior (tutor- or agency-set) goals. The purpose of education and training for adults, they urge, is to meet the expressed needs of the learners, to do only what they wish. Learner-centred adult education demands that the learners set their own goals, plan their own learning. However, in practice this attitude is relatively rare and even more rarely carried through. Even in programmes which claim to be built on this principle, tutor/agency-set objectives in relation to the acquisition of knowledge and the development of skills or attitudes will form part of the course once the learners have set the direction and pattern of the learning process. These programmes distinguish between the long-term goals, which the participants set for themselves, and the shorter-term intermediate objectives needed to achieve these goals which are set by the tutor/agent.

But most adult educators set out with their own goals. Some of these are very general; Paulo Freire talks of the 'pursuit of full humanity', and there is a long tradition in Western education concerned with the pursuit of 'the good', 'what makes for human flourishing or well-being', a process which 'would encourage a person . . . to break a rule or convention if he/she judged that to act in accordance with it would not promote "the good", either generally or of the person involved. . . .' Such general aims imply more detailed personal objectives held by the tutor, though these may still be expressed in more or less general terms—to encourage personal growth or to widen horizons, to enhance choice, to increase critical awareness, to develop assertiveness, or to promote awareness—and the learners are persuaded to internalize these tutor/agency-set goals. Some programmes—the teaching of second language literacy or adult basic education (ABE), for example—have more specific objectives: in these the learners are still encouraged to determine much in the way of content, methods, pace of learning and so on, but the goals are set and evaluated by the tutor/agency and offered to the learners. There is (it is argued) a fundamental reason for this: many of the learners in these programmes cannot determine their course of action and even their needs until they have become more aware of the range of options available.

But beyond these programmes lies the bulk of adult education, which is based on tutor/ agency-set objectives—craft and skill courses, language tuition, even classes such as creative writing. 'Liberal adult education' so valiantly defended in current debates, with its fare of subjects including politics, literature, art appreciation and some science, is built on goals set by the tutor/agent such as 'to create independent free learners', or 'to induct [the learners] into a specific culture'. And even more narrowly based are some of the industrial training and professional development programmes for working and unemployed people.

Adult educators are then neither unaccustomed nor averse to setting goals and objectives for their learners. And it is also clear that an 'entry-point' philosophy is well-known, accepted and utilized, by which the aspirations of the learners are taken as a starting point and motivation for a pre-set programme of learning. Much adult education in the West starts with the learners' own goals and progresses from this point to the goals set by the tutor/agent.[1]

NATIONAL DEVELOPMENT GOALS

Sometimes tutor/agency-set goals relate directly to nationally set Development goals. The General Secretariat for Adult Education in Greece, for example, includes among its aims and objectives

> stamping out illiteracy and semi-literacy; contributing to socio-economic and cultural development, especially in the most disadvantaged regions, through integrated regional projects; encouraging local development initiatives and the participation of the population in community life; increasing vocational qualifications in the prospect of decreasing unemployment and underemployment; discouraging the exodus from the rural areas; vocational and social integration of persons with special needs (physically and mentally handicapped, minority groups and the most disadvantaged); providing equal employment opportunities for women and changing attitudes concerning the situation of women; protecting the environment by setting up alternative development projects and safeguarding the local and national cultural heritage.[2]

Multi-ethnic adult education in many countries is responding to a call for national integration and communal harmony. The adoption of social goals by adult educators is consistent with both tradition and contemporary understandings in adult education. Programmes aimed at overcoming educational and social disadvantage and directed at societal change have, as we have seen, a long and honourable history; and the current concern for equity in relation to education and other aspects of social and economic injustice suggests that social concern in adult education has increased during the 1980s.

But despite this, most adult education in the West is still dominated by objectives related to individual growth and personal achievement rather than to structural change. The dangers of 'colonizing people' (as Freire and others have put it) have been frequently rehearsed: adult educators must not become 'cultural workers . . . evangelical activists or parachuted experts'. Words like paternalism, patronage and tokenism abound in the literature; and warnings about social engineering and prescriptive change are still heard. Adult education, it is asserted, aims 'to provide understanding, not instil a given set of values'; it must 'avoid becoming a tool of the administration, "priesthood", "top management'' etc.'. Denmark reports its 'surprise [at] the success and explosive growth of courses of a more authoritarian kind . . . [incorporating] a simple message, a trivial observation and plenty of personal insults to course participants with a different view, . . . of training courses . . . for higher output and greater job satisfaction'. In the light of negative comments such as these, it is surprising that some countries can still report 'a governmental invitation to adult education to do . . . work . . . [in relation to] unemployment and social disintegration'.[3]

Even when a more positive approach is adopted, there is a reluctance to accept some national goals but not others. There seems to be an underlying assumption that conformist goals are inappropriate (except in basic education and second language teaching and one or two other programmes such as keep fit) but that goals leading to individual nonconformity and diversity are acceptable.

However, in the last ten years or so, the national agenda has become both wider and more concerned with issues which also concern adult educators—improved health, increased prosperity, the enhancement of work skills, urban renewal, conservation of the heritage and environmental resources among them. Why are these sometimes seen as inappropriate goals for adult educators, simply because they are state-set goals? To take two examples from the United Kingdom: the Tidy Britain campaign for environmental enhancement has been almost entirely ignored by adult education; while on the other hand, women's equal opportunities programmes are felt to be more appropriate.

Campaigns

One reason for the antagonism of some adult educators in the West to nationally-set goals is that most of these programmes are run on a 'campaign' model (AIDS is an example). These campaigns almost always bypass adult education; they very rarely seek to involve adult education agencies in their work. The government-inspired Heartbeat Wales and the non-governmental British Food and Farming Year 1989 (see pp. 170 and 65) demonstrate this: almost the only set of resources not mobilized in these campaigns was adult education. Programmes such as these try to undertake themselves what education and training of adults (ETA) they deem necessary. They rely on media coverage and direct contact to change the climate of opinion in favour of their desired behavioural modification. In Development terms, they tend to follow the 'direct action' route (see Figure 10.4 above, p. 121). And such a route, omitting the core element of ETA, makes the outcomes less permanent than they need be. Nationally launched programmes, whether they are run by government, para-statal or non-governmental bodies, need the co-operation of educational agencies, for their work lies as much in attitude change as in knowledge provision (for which campaigns and media coverage are suitable). Adult education has a role to play in the field of public enlightenment.[4]

Development goals in adult education

As these campaigns need the contribution which adult education can offer, so also adult education needs these new objectives to preserve its existing concerns and to end the marginalization from which it currently suffers in almost all countries in the West. So far, as we have seen, adult education has concentrated on individual–cultural and a few carefully selected social goals; and despite protestations, the social change philosophies which exist are still largely individualistic in character.[5] A wider acceptance of national Development goals now seems to be called for. Indeed, Development itself should come to be the determinant for the provision of all adult education; it should be the criterion by which the success or failure of the programmes should be judged.

I understand the fears that many Western adult educators have concerning economic Development, 'the imposition of a . . . skill centred "deficiency" model type of provision only offered to pre-selected groups of adults . . . [in a] one-dimensional vocationlism'.[6] But many Development workers are also aware of the dangers of economicism. A wider concept of Development as touching all aspects of life is now prevalent; and the involvement of adult education in Development will help to ensure that a narrow economic model does not reassert itself, that Development addresses itself to a wide programme of life-enhancing societal change. Adult education can and should be the guardian of wider values in regional and national Development by fully involving itself in these programmes.

But it will not be easy. Part of the problem lies in the fact that Development, like adult education, is sectoralized, divided up into fragments, each part addressing specific issues. Health and literacy and agriculture and skill training are all taught in separate compartments. Functional Development has never really worked. Integrated Rural Development programmes tried to overcome this problem but failed. Issue-based Development (as in adult education) seeks a more integrated approach but such programmes are limited to particular issues and tend to fade away quickly. There are some recent trends in Development towards new non-compartmentalized approaches, paying attention to creating a balanced programme, trying to overcome the imbalances which exist in society: and adult education could play a part in making sure that such programmes are rounded programmes.

This involvement in Development would enable adult education agencies to preserve the work they are already doing, which they are expert in, and which is currently under threat. It is not a call for a move away from the traditional concerns of adult education to a new nationally controlled programme. Rather it is fitting the existing work into a wider framework of social, economic, cultural and political Development, so that the true value of what is currently being done will become more apparent than at present. The existing social and cultural programmes offered by most adult education agencies in the West are of national significance; but they will only appear as such if they are located within a fully balanced Development programme. The adoption of Development—a full Development programme rather than a narrowly economic programme—as the main goal of all adult education will help to preserve and make sense of the existing cultural adult education programmes.

I do not want to overstate the position. Adult education agencies are not the only bodies engaged in Developmental work. Adult education has no monopoly over what the French call the *formation* of the adult population. Nor do I wish to exaggerate the newness of this approach: a good deal is already being done, in a piecemeal fashion; and current discussions of 'priorities', of 'target groups', of 'interventions' show that there is a trend in this direction. But the time has come to develop a coherent theory of adult education which will make sense of all these diverse and fragmented elements, old and new.

In this process, three issues are likely to feature. First, adult education will seek to justify its programmes in terms of national, regional or local Development as much as or even more than individual cultural enhancement. The concept of Development helps to make sense of the concern for personal growth which dominates most adult education. For we need to ask *why* adult education is seeking to promote individual development, if it is not for the sake of the health of society as a whole. This is not a polarized situation, adopting only the new or defending only the old, but an all-embracing logic frame which combines both in a creative and meaningful tension.

Secondly, adult education will plug itself into the various national and regional Development programmes, whether run by government or non-government bodies, using their resources, accepting their goals, yet bringing its own values, expertise and experience to bear on these programmes.

Thirdly, adult education will preserve its independence from these agencies in order to be able to add its special concerns and insights to these goals. By keeping its independence, it will be better able to ensure that a balance is struck between the diverse programmes, and so build a full programme of Development to meet the needs of the locality as it sees them.

Each of us will have our own views as to what that balance will comprise. Some will stress the value of the neighbourhood group in a regional context; others will assert the importance of the national and sectoral. But whether more locally or more centrally oriented, a balanced programme will embrace elements drawn from all aspects of Development:

Social development, promoting communal harmony and equity, the legitimation of all groups (especially women and other oppressed and marginalized sectors) in the community, equality of opportunity in educational provision (including adult education), health and welfare in all its aspects, the strengthening of indigenous social organizations, community welfare, the enhancement of the environment, etc.

Economic development, seeking the promotion of the economic welfare of the *whole* community, large-scale and small-scale, urban and rural, multinational and self-employed; the development of a dynamic and yet balanced economy; the overcoming of poverty; the encouragement of entrepreneurship and economic organization at all levels; and a concern for 'sustainable Development', conserving resources.

Cultural development, including the maintenance and promotion of the indigenous culture in all its aspects (including religion) and strengthening the various forms of cultural groups within the community; yet at the same time widening horizons to other forms of culture, preventing cultural expressions from becoming divisive.

Political development at local and national level, strengthening in some cases existing structures, yet persuading them to listen to marginalized groups, increasing opportunities for other voices to be heard, other hands to be felt on the wheel, other focuses and structures to emerge, to ensure a wider involvement in the planning, decision-making, implementation and evaluation of the community's affairs—to strive in short for an increase of pluralism and participation with equity and harmony.

Such a programme will seem over-ambitious and unrealistic to some, plain wrongheaded to others. But I am not suggesting that adult education can do all of this. Rather I am suggesting that adult education should be concerned to join with others in a balanced programme which will include elements drawn from all the facets of Development.[7]

Nor should a lack of consensus on what comprises a balanced Development programme for the region be regarded as a drawback. Rather it will free adult educators to use their own judgement. Nevertheless, the general picture remains clear. Adult education exists to promote the Development of the nation/region/locality, not just the welfare of the few self-selected individuals who currently come into its programmes. And to fulfil this aim, adult education agencies will need to do two things: to select relevant elements from the national Development programmes and apply them to the locality (however defined), and secondly to build up their own programmes.

Development planners have faced this issue. They recognize that they cannot do everything themselves. Some countries have prioritized Developmental needs: certain issues are seen to be more urgent than others. The fact that the priorities which Development has set for itself tend to be different from those chosen by adult education does not mean that adult education should remain separated from Development. We have already seen that some programmes of adult education are based on concepts of collective needs—the needs of community groups, of the disadvantaged, of minority and ethnic communities, of the economy, of employers and of other sectors. There will always be disagreement as to the nature of these needs; but in many areas (health and conservation, for example), the consensus is perhaps more remarkable than the disagreements. And in these debates, the voice of adult education needs to be heard, defining local, regional and national needs from its particular perspective.[8]

ESTABLISHING NEEDS IN ADULT EDUCATION

We have already seen some of the methods used by Development agencies to determine the needs of particular localities and sectors. The same procedures are open to adult education agencies. It is possible to start with a conceptual model such as Basic Human Needs or Maslow's hierarchy of needs and apply this to the region. Such models are useful tools to evaluate programmes but they do not always identify the felt needs of the people.

A second method is to accept the needs as determined by the national programmes and apply these to the neighbourhood. This too has merit; but it will be necessary to judge these needs by their perceived relevance to the local community. A third method, already being pursued by some agencies, though usually on a limited scale, is the preparation of their own needs surveys for the region. These can never be final, they will require revision as the programmes proceed.

Such surveys however have their dangers. Some have pointed to the patronizing airs of many of those engaged in needs surveys, caricaturing the relationship as a contrast 'between those with needs, mindless incompetents on the one hand, and the needs-meeters on the other, perceptive, enquiring, responsible, able to take a broad view and make prescriptions'. What is more, needs surveys alone cannot determine the wants or aspirations of the local community which will form the entry points for the programmes. Developmental adult education agencies need to become receptive and sensitive to felt needs. But feedback procedures from the local community are already a feature of most adult education programmes: in a case drawn from Turkey, for example, 'one of the essential roles of the university staff was, and still is, to make a detailed analysis of the community's resources, problems and needs on the spot and in consultation with those concerned'. The most effective way to avoid these patronizing attitudes and to identify felt needs is to enable the local community itself to assess and identify its own needs.[9]

Case study: Clones

A case study will illustrate this process. In 1984 a group of residents of Clones in Co. Monaghan, Ireland, approached Magee University College in Londonderry concerning the possibility of a needs survey of this small town situated right on the border whose economy had been badly affected by the troubles of Northern Ireland. For more than a year this group made a study of their own local community with the assistance of a member of staff from the college. They devised, sent out and processed a questionnaire to one in three of the town's adults and to all of the youth aged between 14 and 18 years; they surveyed the economic, social and cultural life of the town; they examined the voluntary organizations; they explored new possibilities ranging from mushroom growing to tourism. On the basis of this work they wrote and published their own needs survey and social, economic and cultural Development plan (which differed in many ways from the plan drawn up by the county experts in Monaghan and the national experts in Dublin). The change of attitudes experienced during this process was remarkable: negative feelings towards the town gave way to a sense of pride; and the determination and confidence with which the group approached the task of legitimizing the local community within the county and the nation were greatly increased. From this, a Clones Development Trust was launched and an ambitious programme for Clones— not just as a small (and somewhat undistinguished) market centre serving the immediate and diminished locality but as a place with a national role to play—has been drawn up and is being implemented by the people of the town in association with national and regional agencies. The arbitrary closure of the Institute of Continuing Education in Magee in 1985 broke the links between the town and the adult education agency but by then the essential educational and training tasks within the Development programme had been all but completed. In this way, an adult education agency fulfilled a Development role even though the role did not conform to the provision of a traditional adult education class.[10]

Such an example suggests some of the ways in which a Development model will differ from existing patterns of adult education. Developmental adult education will call for new formats of programmes to meet the needs of the local community. Perhaps the most important difference will be that the criteria for the mounting of any programme will not be so much whether there has been any local demand but whether it serves a balanced Development programme for the region. The expressed wishes of the local community will be a necessary part of the feedback systems involved in identifying the needs of the region; but these expressed needs (like the national objectives) will have to be evaluated. Adult education agencies will have full scope for the exercise of independent judgement, balancing the demands of the local against the national.

The aspirations and intentions of the local community will form the entry points leading to the fulfilment of goals set by the adult education agencies. A project in Portugal illustrates this well:

> the problem was . . . [the need] to reach a minimum level of development before adult education could contribute to any kind of development. For the village authorities . . ., the basic questions were the installation of a proper sanitary system (sewerage, drinking water, etc.) and an adequate communication network (e.g. a telephone box). Once these basic needs were met, adult education could then start to play its useful role for the community in question.[11]

CONCLUSION

My point is, I hope, a simple one. Adult education agencies in the West have not in the past been shy about setting objectives for themselves and for their learners. The needs of today suggest that a full and balanced Developmental programme will alone make sense of the currently limited and indeed elitist set of goals of most existing adult education programmes, which are aimed primarily at individual self-fulfilment. The Adult Education Institute or Centre, WEA, University Adult Education Department, community school, college or other institution should aim at the full Development of its region, using both the national campaigns such as health (diets, smoking, AIDS, drugs, alcoholism, etc.), energy conservation, environmental enhancement, workforce training and the like as far as they are relevant to the needs of the locality, and the expressed wants of the locality to set its objectives. The agency will hold a mediating position between these two sets of demands, and at the same time will itself have a positive role to play.

It is too easy to assert that in this process collective goals will have primacy over individualistic goals—that it is the collective 'good' rather than the individual 'good' which is being sought: for as Freire has argued, 'the pursuit of full humanity cannot be carried out in individualism but only in fellowship and solidarity. . . .'

To be 'authentically human' calls not for self-assertion but for community identity.[12] Community and individuality go together; and in Developmental adult education, the objectives set—because the programme of education and training that goes on within Development is primarily aimed at attitude change—will comprehend both individual as well as societal goals, and thus will fulfil the current search for a new synthesis of programmes which are of high utility to both society and to the individual.

NOTES TO CHAPTER 15

(1) For 'the good' in education, see Dewey, J. (1916) *Democracy and Education*, New York; Brown, A. (1986) *Modern Political Philosophy: Theories of the Just Society*, Penguin, cited in Jeffs, T. and Smith, M. (1990) *Using Informal Education*, Open University Press; Grundy, S. (1987) *Curriculum: Product or Praxis*, Falmer Press; Freire (1972). On objectives in education, see for example Knox (1977), chapter on 'Assessing learner needs and setting objectives'; Rogers, A. (1987), ch. 4; Tyler, R. W. (1950) *Basic Principles of Curriculum and Instruction*, Chicago; Mager, R. (1962) *Preparing Instructional Objectives*, California; Bloom, B. S. *et al.* (eds) (1956) *Taxonomy of Educational Objectives*, vol. 1, Longman; Krathwohl, D. R. *et al.* (eds) (1984) *Taxonomy of Educational Objectives*, vol. 2, New York.

(2) EBAE (1988) Greece, pp. 3–4.

(3) Kandrup (1988), pp. 1–2; Miliband, R. (1969) *The State in a Capitalist Society*, London: Weidenfield, p. 19; Fletcher (1980), pp. 73–5; Jackson (1970).

(4) Jacobsen, B. (1989) The concept and problem of public enlightenment, *IJLE* 8(2), 127–38; White, P. (1983) *Beyond Domination: an Essay in the Political Philosophy of Education*, Routledge and Kegan Paul.

(5) For the long tradition of this in the West, see National Council of Labour Colleges Report, *Education for Emancipation*, 1935.

(6) Harries-Jenkins (1983); *AE* 60(3) (1987), 277, 239.

(7) *AEF* 25(3) (1988), 6; Jobert (1988), pp. 1–2; see De Sanctis (1988), p. 4: 'the educational programme should not be limited strictly to the field of education but ought to reach out to areas which contain educational elements (production in factories, agriculture, artisans, the service sector, health and home)'. For an example of a balanced programme of regional

development through adult and continuing education (drawn up for Magee University College but never implemented because of the closure of the Institute of Continuing Education in that college in 1985 by the University of Ulster) see Rogers, A. (1982) and (1984).

(8) For an example of this in practice, see EBAE (1988) Greece, p. 5: 'These are alternative training and cultural projects . . . in support of local development initiatives based on the priorities of Prefectural Councils . . . e.g. aquaculture, fish breeding and oyster farming, development projects for women's co-operatives, training courses for local executive functions, the development of tourism, etc. The development projects follow closely the developmental objectives of the Prefecture as well as the Integrated Mediterranean Programmes.'

(9) On needs as the basis of AE programmes, see Marriott, S. (1984) *Extra-Mural Empires*, University of Nottingham, p. 123; McIlroy and Spencer (1988), pp. 101–3; Strategy Report (1980); Griffin, C. (1983) Social control, social policy and adult education, *IJLE* 2(3), 219, 226. For Turkey, see Council of Europe (1984), p. 26.

(10) *Clones: a Needs Survey*, Clones, Co. Monaghan: Clones Study Group, 1985.

(11) Council of Europe (1984), pp. 13, 26.

(12) Freire (1972), p. 58.

Chapter 16

Seeking New Target Groups

'Tell us, in your country do the learners come to you or do you go to the learners?'

We were a group of twelve, sitting in the YWCA in Madras. The others were women animators working in the slums of that city. We had just spent an exhausting two hours identifying what they had to do as part of their role as instructors of literacy—visiting the women who do not turn up to the classes, remonstrating with husbands who stop the learners coming, coping with drunken men who disrupt the class, negotiating with the 'village' headman over a meeting place and so on, as well as teaching literacy, awareness, craft skills, elementary health and other subjects. Theirs was a demanding task.

OUTREACH

The question gave me a jolt, for it suddenly related the work I was doing in India to my 'normal' life in England. I considered carefully. I remembered the days when, as a resident tutor in Lincolnshire, I went to the villages, sought out the equivalent to the 'headman' (Church of England vicar first, then the other ministers of religion, school-teacher next, president of the Women's Institute and other notables), explored whether a group of learners might be found: if so, in what subject? did we have a tutor for that (or another) subject available? and so on. Eventually some class was born, to survive for one, perhaps two winters while I passed on to other villages. But what a far cry all that was from the concerns of bodies like the YWCA in Madras who went into the slums, negotiated long and hard, fought bureaucracies for the resources, identified one or more animators, trained them and carefully monitored, supervised and supported them in their work over several years! Not all programmes in India are as conscientious as this one, but several of those run by voluntary bodies are.

In any case, those days in the West are gone. The earlier tradition of outreach through bodies like the Educational Settlements Association in urban areas and the Rural Community Councils in the 1920s and 1930s, and the network of WEA and University Extra-Mural resident tutors with classes meeting in schools, church halls and other community buildings, and sometimes even in private houses, hardly exists any longer.

WEA and EMDs alike have withdrawn into Centres where they plan and publish programmes of adult classes and wait for learners to come in response to their advertisements. Even the imaginative Community Educators established by the Inner London Education Authority have over the last few years retreated into the Adult Education Institutes. Innovative ways of informing the people of programmes and attempts at persuasion through the mass media are poor substitutes for 'going to the people'. In the large majority of instances, it is a case of the learners coming to adult education, not the reverse.[1]

No discrimination

We must be fair. There has been for years a struggle by adult educators against any form of discrimination. Increases in fees have been resisted by providers in government and non-government programmes alike, and the effects of such increases on the enrolment of adult students have been monitored and publicized.[2] Arguments in favour of positive discrimination on behalf of particular groups (the retired, the unemployed, women without independent incomes, those on state benefits, etc.) have been advanced, often successfully. There has been an equally persistent struggle against educational discrimination; the case for opening formal and non-formal education programmes to new groups of potential students or for providing access/preparatory/bridge/return-to-study courses to enable those without the necessary entry qualifications to enrol, or to reduce the number of programmes with age disqualifications (especially opening higher education to mature students)—all these are indicators of the long-standing concern of adult educators to ease entry paths into the programmes for disadvantaged potential student populations.

But the philosophy behind these initiatives is still one of 'coming in', of providing learning opportunities for those who select themselves. We can all think, in every country of the West, of the adult education centre (whatever title it gives itself) which prides itself and is publicly recognized and commended for pursuing an 'open door' policy; which seeks new ways of attracting new learners in, but which is nevertheless a central institution which expects the learners to take the first steps, to come to meet the teachers rather than the reverse.

Community involvement

Some new forms of outreach are emerging. The Each-One-Teach-One literacy schemes go to the learners, but these still tend to be responsive programmes, reacting only after the potential learners have made the first approach. There are Education Shops, taking adult education information into the high streets; stands at public exhibitions and in public libraries, stalls at agricultural shows, etc. There are new formats to reach out to the people, especially 'packs', often multimedia (packs have recently been issued on drugs and other health matters such as diet, exercise and AIDS, and on conservation, community action, unemployment, Plain English and many other subjects). Home learning materials covering subjects as disparate as dressmaking, gardening and learning a language are increasingly available. Distance education and open colleges are springing up, and learning materials and programmes are now widely available. There are those institutions—an increasing number—who are opening their doors more and more widely to the community, encouraging both individuals and groups to use their resources, who go out into the local community and exhort the unemployed, the exploited and the disadvantaged, ethnic minorities, residents' associations, women's groups—in short any voiceless sector—to take advantage of the facilities on offer.[3]

Adult education agencies are then reacting to the current situation in several ways: by persuading individuals and groups to come in; by launching wide campaigns for new learners; and by selecting and concentrating on special target groups. The Netherlands Council of Europe Experimental Project can stand for all the others: it chose for its programmes

> specific target groups: women, especially the wives of immigrant workers, immigrant work-ers and their families, (young) unemployed persons or persons in danger of losing their jobs; the illiterate; workers about to retire; and in general people with an inadequate educational background.

Other forms of community involvement in adult education activities are growing. Libraries and museums, art galleries and historic sites are reinterpreting their role in a Developmental context, reaching out to those who use them to touch them more deeply. Community radio stations provide structured learning opportunities. New forms of basic skills education are breaking through more and more barriers, independent of the adult education agencies. Community schools are becoming resource centres, collabo-rating with local groups. Community activities such as publishing newsheets are being pursued by associations, sometimes in conjunction with adult education agencies, some-times separately.[4]

But few of these activities have much in common with Development programmes in the Third World. Indeed, they are marked off from them in two ways. First, their learners are still *voluntary* learners, not a mass audience who need to be persuaded to learn. 'How do I motivate my learners?' was one of the first questions I had to face in India; and I had no answer, for I had no experience to draw upon; it was not a question I had had to face in adult education in the West. Secondly, few of these agencies are moved by a philosophy of Development. They are not active agents for Development. Instead they tend to be responsive to expressed needs. Most adult education bodies in the West do not exist to promote the Development of the region in which they stand; they exist to help those persons who feel that they need help to escape from their social environment rather than to change it. There is no fully fledged Development concept which inspires their work.

Thus even these newer activities still reach only a few in the community. In that sense they are divisive. They are not aimed at the Development of the local community as a whole but at the improvement of the standing of some within the community.

MASS ADULT EDUCATION

Current Development programmes, on the other hand, call for a mass approach in two ways:

(a) Development agencies are increasingly coming to recognize that programmes which concentrate on limited target groups are likely to be less effective than those aimed at wider audiences. Thus they aim at a mass impact in order to achieve more of their goals. 'It is imperative for *everyone* to be able to adjust and innovate, thus implying continuous learning and social mobilisation on a hitherto unprecedented scale . . . learning should enable *all* to play a full part in decisions which shape their future' [my italics].

(b) Secondly, Development seen as attitude and behavioural change calls for the identification and strengthening of those support systems (motivators) and for the identification and weakening of those hindrances (demotivators) which exist within the participant group's environment. To be effective, Development calls for the creation of a congenial milieu, a Development-literate society, just as adult education calls for the creation of a 'learning society' to surround and support the learners. And this demands a mass approach, not one involving just the few: Developmental adult education 'should enable each individual to become an active agent of development'.[5]

The new target group then for Development-oriented adult education is nothing less than the total neighbourhood in which it operates: the full community, not just sectors in it. The classical distinction between 'community' and 'association' is of value here, community being that group to which one belongs more or less involuntarily, primarily because of birth or residence, and association being that group to which one has attached oneself more or less by choice. Adult educators, even community educators, have on the whole concentrated on association more than community—on working with voluntary and interest groups and parts of the local or regional or national community rather than with the community as a whole. But structural change can only be brought about by means of a programme which touches and develops the whole community, not just one part of it.

Adult education and a total approach

Do adult educators in the West go out to the learners? Not in the same way as those engaged in Development in Third World countries. Adult educators do not on the whole launch a programme of (say) nutrition education and take it to the people, meeting wherever they can and going from door to door, persuading all men and women to healthy eating, exercise or environmental health. Perhaps this is felt to be someone else's job; or perhaps adult educators do not believe enough in the universal necessity of their own programmes. The principle of voluntaryism which lies at the heart of adult education in the West is seen to be the enemy of Development.

But some things are too important to be shared only with the 10–20 per cent of voluntary learners who come to adult education classes. Matters relating to poverty and health, to environmental enhancement and resource conservation, to peace and communal harmony must reach the widest possible groups. Such issues are of special relevance to adult educators for two reasons: they concern adults more than children; and they are educational matters.

The contrast with the mass campaigns is enlightening. Their task is persuasion—not just to attract some people to come in to listen but to promote behavioural change. Their aim is to create a popular movement in favour of the desired activity—to take exercise, to give up smoking, to support nuclear disarmament, for example. Their process is mass contact and the creation of local agents and groups. Many sales campaigns reach out to the people in general more effectively than adult education—often using a Development model of part-time trained local agents.[6]

These examples serve to highlight the fact that in the West adult education agencies reach only a few. In contrast to these campaigns, adult education programmes are marginal to the Development of the region in which they stand. If they were closed down tomorrow, the Development of the locality would hardly be affected. But such a limited approach is a denial of the very philosophy on which adult education in the West has been built. It will be instructive to look at some of the more common claims made by adult educators and their implications:

(a)   The need for changing society is so urgent that we cannot leave this to the schools, which will take time for their effects to be felt; we must educate the adult population.
But that surely means *all* the adult population, not just the few currently being taught.

(b)   Education cannot be limited to vocational training or socialization; it is all-round personal growth.
But such an important message surely applies to *all* adults, not just to the few.

(c)   Education is not (or should not be) a scramble for position within a set social structure but a means for changing that structure.
But structural change will hardly be brought about by educating the few.

(d)   The learning needs of adulthood demand the provision of lifelong learning opportunities.
But, since such adult learning needs are universal, so too should adult education be universal, not limited to the few.

Every philosophical basis for adult education implies the education of *all* adults, not just the few. The 1919 Report recognized this: 'Adult education is a permanent national necessity, an inseparable aspect of citizenship and therefore should be both universal and lifelong.' The Russell Report of 1973 repeated this, speaking of adult education 'as an integral part of total provision, not as something for the less fortunate or more studious but as something to be expected and experienced by the whole nation'.[7]

Implementing a mass approach

Can adult education in the West re-orientate itself to become a mass programme, to go to the people with its own message? How can it be done? The answer, I suggest, will include six main points:

1.   Learning programmes provided by adult education agencies need to be seen to be geared to generally agreed socially useful purposes, aimed at Developmental goals addressing real and contemporary problems, even though they may do this from a perspective of general principles rather than immediate local concerns alone.

2.   Such programmes (like Development programmes) should be located within the community, not within the institute. To create a learning society, we need to develop

the ability of the learners to learn where they live and work rather than come to rely upon a dedicated learning institution, however valuable that may be for specific purposes. It is true that the relatively few experiments made with work-based learning programmes have not been a resounding success; but it may have been the application rather than the principle which was the cause of this failure, and new initiatives in this area are now being made. The withdrawal of adult learners from their life-site into learning institutions, which currently characterizes adult education (for financial rather than educational reasons), denies the principle of life-related learning for immediate rather than future application.

Some of this is already being done. But to take an adult class to a village or suburb is quite a different thing from launching a mass Development programme. To identify a few within the town or local area who wish to study or practise a particular subject is not the same as trying to persuade the whole community to internalize desirable goals and change their way of life, and in the process build a better community.

3. It would seem necessary, as many Development models suggest, to work as far as possible through existing structures rather than to set up new structures. These may be formal or non-formal, statutory or alternative—but if we are to aim at the Development of the region/locality/community, it can be argued that it is better to work within and to change existing channels so that the community can influence them and take control of its own Development processes.

4. In order to do this, it will be necessary to start with the aspirations and intentions of the local community, when these can be discovered and articulated, and to proceed beyond these towards the goals of the Development programme. It is not enough just to meet local aspirations unless these lead on to a full and continuing Development process for the region. A programme run by the Women's Institutes in the UK is revealing in this respect:

the initial objective was very specific: to improve the education of women in the country in matters of hygiene and family economics: it rapidly expanded however to include the positions of local, regional and national bodies in the formulation of social, educational and economic policy.[8]

Issue-based adult education: there are examples in all countries of adult education programmes which begin with local issues: the earlier work of Highlander in the USA and Antigonish in Canada, and of various projects in the UK, such as the Coin Street conservation project, the Popular Planning Pilot project at Clapham (London), the Dearne Valley Project, to name but a few. But there are major differences between issue-based and Development-based adult learning programmes. For one thing, issue-based programmes face an immediate crisis situation and fade away once the issue ceases to grip the local community; Developmental adult education on the other hand not only continues but gathers momentum as more and more goals are achieved. It may be possible for long-term Development-based programmes to emerge out of issue-based programmes, but experience suggests that this is rare. And issue-based programmes, because they take sides, necessarily involve certain sectors of the whole community and exclude others, those who disagree or who do not feel strongly about the issue under debate, for example. Development programmes on the whole involve the total community; they unite more than they divide.

5. In this context, Development-based mass adult learning programmes need to join forces with and utilize the resources of the other state and voluntary Development programmes. Hitherto, adult educators have tended to keep aloof from such campaigns, to work in isolation—and thus have been accused (sometimes justly, sometimes unjustly) of being parochial.

    Both adult education and Development in the West have been characterized by 'little overall planning' (Scotland), 'a scattered intervention, inconsistent from area to area, in some places too casual even if generous, limited by sector to a cultural area, split by working problems' (Italy). The time would seem to have come for adult education agencies to adopt a co-operative role based on a policy of promoting regional Development: 'public institutions, special bodies and cultural associations [are all] called upon to contribute to the realization of a plan which will result in a real movement'.[9]

6. Much of the work will be non-course activities. Traditional forms of adult education classes are already being supplemented by community festivals (like the Victorian Week in Ilfracombe run in 1988 by the local Community College as a learning experience for the whole town), advice centres and counselling, library provision, community newspapers and the like. But the 'class' still holds sway. Long ago, the Russell Report exhorted UK adult education to be more flexible:

> insistence upon regular times of meeting, the routines of enrolment and registration of attendance, minimum numbers, the charging of fees in advance (or at all), and formal class teaching will often destroy any chance of successful educational penetration into these sectors of the population. Whatever the providing body, it must be imaginative and flexible in approach, it must recognise that progress will often be slow and difficult to evaluate, it must be prepared to support its staff in discouragements and false starts, and it must allow for the inevitable expense (para. 284)

Until agencies become willing to work in new ways, to take workshops and 'clinics' out to the learners as Development does, they will find it hard to participate in the work of other Developmental bodies.

Can it work in the West?

There are some indications that a Developmental adult education can be built in Western societies today. The 'Look After Yourself' programme is one such example. In this project, the UK Health Education Council (as it then was) called for volunteers (mostly women) from the local community, trained and enthused them both in health and exercise matters and in techniques of communication, and let them loose on an unsuspecting public. Their target group was the whole population, and their aims were clearly stated: to build up both the physical and psychological factors which help to determine a person's health 'through the acquisition of knowledge, understanding and skills' and 'through a process of self-awareness and self-decision . . . to promote good health in a positive way . . . a highly innovative approach in community and adult education that offers people from all walks of life and all ages a practical, safe and individually adaptable guide to a healthy lifestyle'—language redolent of both adult education and Development.

Currently over 1500 trained adult tutors promote and run basic ten week courses for adults in a variety of settings—adult education centres and colleges of Further Education, health centres, sports centres, private social agencies, and increasingly in industry and business, the 'workplace'. . . . It is conservatively estimated that there have been in excess of 100,000 adult participants in basic LAY courses, not allowing for 'extension' courses or those held within the NHS and other agencies.

Among the innovative features of this 'national provision of . . . a radical approach to health education', it was noted that 'the syllabus had broken with the usual single-subject approach . . . and combined a number of disciplines into a unified programme'; that the project 'produced a number of people highly committed to the holistic approach to health [with] vision, dedication and ability to implement the basic concept . . . people from different backgrounds . . . prepared to work together to advance a common belief'.

From our point of view, the programme had a number of interesting features. First, it is one of the few campaigns which built in from the start close links with adult education agencies. Secondly, as much as 65 per cent of the programme's budget was spent on training the 'animators'; one of the primary objectives was to create a specially trained and committed cadre of local change-agents. The movement died away, not so much because the original goals had been met but more because the volunteers were not given enough continuing support; they were to a large extent left on their own, so that confidence and commitment declined. And the programme was too large, based and organized nationally rather than locally. The support of adult education agencies to these volunteers on a local basis might have made the programme longer lasting.[10]

There have been other moves in the same direction. A contrasting one because it was small-scale and local rather than national in its approach was that run by ACRE (Action for Communities in Rural England), in association with the University of Bristol Extra-Mural Department, in three counties: Dorset, Somerset and Wiltshire. This 'fused two hitherto . . . separate processes—village-based adult education and rural community development. Groups of village people learned to identify their community's problems, resources and aspirations and then girded themselves for action.' The process was one of providing courses

designed to make the participants think about their communities and the future of their communities. They were also designed to develop practical skills amongst the course members to help communities to grow—to grow not just in population but also in community strength and in richness of opportunities . . . to make the participants feel confident in their own research and planning. . . .

From the initial three centres, the programme grew to involve 17 centres, nine county councils, three universities, two WEA districts and other bodies. Among the needs identified and the action programmes commenced were rural bus schemes, oral history projects, youth clubs, village halls and playing fields, conservation schemes and interpretation of local history, village newsletters, health groups, tourism promotion, day centres, local resources centres, community and amenity associations, transport for the elderly, summer playschemes and local libraries. Such examples of long-term involvement with the local community through the co-operation of agencies suggest that the re-orientation of adult education towards Development models is already taking place.[11]

Throughout the adult education world, then, examples which approach a Developmental model can be found. The WEA in the UK, for instance, has reported programmes with both rural and industrial groups, and courses directed at, and sometimes planned in association with, unemployed groups, black and ethnic minority communities and especially women can be found with many agencies. Health and safety at work training, and some significant role education (local councillors, school managers, work with police and prison staff, etc.) can be found in some places. Several of the innovative projects under the REPLAN scheme in the UK (such as the Horwich Unemployed Support Group's access programme and the Sunderland Reach Out project) had elements of regional Development in them. Scotland's Adult Learning Project and the Number Shop may be matched in Northern Ireland by the work formerly done by the Institute of Continuing Education at Magee University College for which a regional Developmental programme was drawn up shortly before its closure, and to a certain extent more recently by the People's College in Belfast. It is significant that the writings of Third World Development practitioners like Thomas La Belle and Torres which (apart from the publications of Freire) have been largely unknown in the West are now being used as models for new approaches. The papers presented to the European Bureau of Adult Education Conference in Madrid in September 1988 and the Council of Europe's Adult Education and Community Development Project reveal case after case from countries as far apart as Portugal (the Radial project in the Algarve) and Greece, from Italy (the Women at School programme in Turin) to Finland (adult vocational training); and in the west of Ireland, the work of such bodies as University College of Galway shows the way adult education agencies are grappling with local Developmental problems.[12]

Nevertheless, most of these programmes are on a limited scale and still use traditional formats. The LAY and ACRE programmes consisted of set courses of 10 or 24 weeks' duration for small groups of self-selected learners in each centre, and once the courses were ended, the assistance of the adult education agency was withdrawn except informally. The Charleroi Open University project in Belgium comprised 'catching-up *courses . . . courses* related to projects aimed at environmental change', again for small groups; and in Sweden, the Landskrona experiment comprised 'many training *courses*' [my italics]. Adult educators are more accustomed to dealing with a changing clientele than to working in a long-term continuing programme. They are used to meeting the immediate learning needs of one small group of learners and then passing on to new learners. Development, on the other hand, calls for long-term continued mass programmes as well as shorter-term projects to test methodologies and strategies.[13]

It has been left to agencies outside of adult education to pursue Development programmes in the West: to Rural Development Boards or inner city renewal agencies. And these bodies on the whole ignore the possible contribution of adult education agencies to their Development goals and as a result their programmes often represent unacceptable and ineffective models of Development.[14]

Development needs adult education

Agencies involved in Development programmes in the West need the contribution which adult education can bring. An example of this may be drawn from the work of one of the EEC-funded Integrated Development Programmes of the Highlands and Islands Development Board in the Western Isles of Scotland.

The stated objective of this programme was 'to improve the working and living conditions' of the residents of these islands. The order of these goals would seem to indicate the priority of economic over social matters: certainly, although the programme was called 'integrated', its main thrusts were economic (agriculture, tourism, fishing).

The programme was an outsider-led one, based on external judgements such as 'agriculture alone would not provide the population with a reasonable [*sic*] standard of living . . . [though] the maintenance and development of agriculture is an important part of the programme'. The programme was planned and run by outsiders, project officers and other government bodies: 'the administration of the various schemes under the Programme is the responsibility of a number of [already existing] public agencies and forms an addition to their existing activities. . . .' Despite the fact that it was recognized that earlier projects had failed 'because they were not locally led', this programme was a set of externally prepared and offered schemes: 'it is now up to the local people to take full advantage of the opportunities now available to them'. The only decision-making available to the local population was whether or not to join in an already pre-packaged programme.

The residents of the Islands were only marginally involved in drawing up the list of needs: 'a series of consultative meetings were . . . held throughout the area to seek local views before the Programme was drawn up [by the EEC agents]: and local opinion will continue to be sounded as the Programme proceeds'. 'The Project Team [note the capital letters] mounted a substantial campaign to ensure that the people of the Western Isles were made fully aware of the opportunities available to them under the Programme.' The local adult education agencies were not involved. The programme itself consisted almost entirely of knowledge and technical inputs provided by outsiders, mainly the extension staff who 'are undertaking training in nature conservation' and who 'are encouraged to learn the local language and customs of the region: also to take part in local activities'.

This project is a warning of the dangers of Development without adult education. It is arguable that the involvement of adult education agencies in the planning of such programmes, their purposeful identification with Development goals drawing upon their experience and insights in participatory action, would have prevented such an economically dominated top-down arrogant and dehumanizing input model of Development from being framed. Development agencies *need* adult education to learn that Development (like adult education) is a two-way, not a one-way, process, that local people *can* plan and carry out their own Development tasks and not rely on outsiders.[15]

Development needs adult education for other reasons. There are many Development programmes and they are frequently separated from each other. Housing and health in inner cities, for example, are handled by different agencies. Voluntary and statutory bodies alike launch programmes of aid and welfare. The possibility that adult education could fulfil the role of co-ordinating agency for these programmes is not an impractical proposition. And there are signs that, although some organizations are hesitant about what they see as the exclusively educational dimension of adult education, a number are stretching out their hands to adult education for help. The National Federation of Women's Institutes in the UK and the clergy of many churches are examples of this trend.

An example of a co-ordinating role being provided by an adult education agency, in contrast to the EEC Development project in Scotland, is the University College of Swansea's Valleys Initiative for Adult Education (VIAE). Through this two-and-a-half year programme

> community needs can be met without duplicating provision, resources are efficiently and imaginatively used and good practice is promoted . . . [through] a coherent strategy of adult education for the 1990s which takes into account the needs of disadvantaged groups such as the unemployed, the disabled and single parents . . . a means of encouraging community development and socio-economic regeneration . . . will respond to demands from the community by providing what they want rather than telling them what they should have. It is a forum where all groups—statutory, voluntary and community—meet on equal terms free of the traditional provider–client relationship.

Vocational education is a VIAE priority but it also has a cultural dimension: thus a certificated training course in 'machine-knitting for women considering working in the garment industry' has a fashion design element funded by the Welsh Arts Association. Welsh language classes for English newcomers are provided to promote integration, communal harmony and cultural enrichment. Apart from 'new skills training . . . in electronics and computing . . . there will also be a need for confidence boosting pro-grammes to enable locals to consider and implement alternatives to unemployment'. There is an element of outsider–insider relationships in these references to 'locals', and many of the programmes are formal-type adult education courses, but the balanced approach to Development (economic, social, cultural and political) in an integrated project built by a university adult education agency in association with other bodies shows it can be done.

Co-ordination is not an inappropriate role for an adult education agency. It is already being undertaken in many parts of the West—in the Coria Experiment in Spain ('an integrated project co-ordinating services which originate in several ministries') and in Portugal's Integrated Regional Project ('the project associates a number of services, i.e. government departments or institutions working in the region') and elsewhere; and programmes such as the ILEA Education Community Officers, the Frobisher Institute in London and some rural programmes have clearly shown that this role is an acceptable one to some adult education agencies.[16]

Adult education needs Development

There is a final compelling reason why adult education should move to an integrated regional Development model. Adult education will never again—on its present perfor-mance—reach out to the people *where they are* unless it links up with these Development programmes. It is inconceivable that village classes on the older models will be run again. Even now, courses for the unemployed rarely, and usually only on a short-term basis, extend to rural areas. The only way adult education will be felt in the urban slums and in the villages of the West today is if it joins hands with national Development programmes, bringing with it its value and belief systems, abandoning nothing but joyfully espousing new Developmental goals and using the resources at the disposal of these programmes. There is nothing to suggest that adult education will suffer from this marriage. There is nothing to suggest that these Development programmes will reject the offer of support from adult education agencies. And it is the only way that adult education can move more centrally to socially purposive activities, acquire adequate resources, and take its message of 'people power' to all the people, not just to a few.

But such an analysis suggests that it is adult education which needs to take the first move to join up with these national campaigns and programmes. For it is unlikely that many of the Development agencies will approach adult education: it still appears to them to be too entrenched in its individualistic and voluntaryist liberal traditions to share the concerns of the Development agencies. This is not true.

NOTES TO CHAPTER 16

(1) Newman (1979); Thornton and Stephens (1977).
(2) Daines, J., Elsey, B. and Gibbs, M. (1982) *Changes in Student Participation in Adult Education*, University of Nottingham.
(3) For access into the formal system, see Squires, G. (1978) *Patterns of Entry to Adult and Continuing Education*, OECD; Lambert, P. (1988) *Mature Student Entry to Higher Education*; Mature students in Lancaster University, *AE* **58**(2) (1985); Jones, H.A. and Williams, K.E. (1979) *Adult Students and Higher Education*, ACACE; Roderick, G.W. *et al.* (1981) *Mature Students in Further and Higher Education: a Study in Sheffield*, University of Sheffield; Rogers, A. (1982) People power in adult education, *Aontas Review* 3(2), 11–24. For other groups coming in to adult education, see for example Lieven, M. (1987) Adult liberal education: a case study in ambivalence, *AE* **60**(3), 225–30: 'community groups, adult education centres, unemployed people, access courses, women's groups and the like were invited to work with tutors [at Fircroft College] to set up new programmes'; see Scribbens, J. (1987) Political education: working with the local community, *AE* **60**(3), 245–49.
(4) Council Europe (1984), p. 22; Dadswell, G. (1978) The adult independent learner and public libraries, *AE* **51**, 5–11; Dale, S. (1979) The adult independent learning project: work with adult self-directed learners in public libraries, *Journal of Librarianship* **11**, 83–106; Dale, S. (1980) Another way forward for adult learners: the public library and independent study, *Studies in Adult Education* **12**, 29–38; Groombridge, B. Adult education and broadcasting: open education, in Rogers, A. (1976); Brookfield (1983), pp. 60–89, 159–62.
(5) Council of Europe (1986b), pp. 3, 5.
(6) One thinks in the UK and the USA of the 'Avon ladies' and the 'Tupperware parties', etc.
(7) 1919 Report, p. 5; Russell Report, p. 16.
(8) Council of Europe (1984), p. 25; Hall (1988).
(9) Gerver (1988), p. 1; De Sanctis (1988), p. 3; Newman (1979); Alexander, T. Adult education for popular planning, in ILSCAE (1986), pp. 81–7; *Value for People: Adult Education and Popular Planning: Strategies for Meeting Economic, Social and Technological Change*, London: Popular Planning Project, 1986.
(10) Daines, J. *et al.* (n.d.) *Look After Yourself 1978–86: Innovations and Outcomes*, University of Nottingham.
(11) ACRE Reports: ACRE (1985), pp. 4–6; ACRE (1988), p. ii; *REPLAN Rural Needs Bulletin* **1** (1987), 8–9.
(12) See Fryer, P. (1983) Education from below: the Oxford industrial branch and the WEA, *Trade Union Studies Journal* **7** (Summer); Connor, D. Some developments in the Workers' Educational Association, in Costello and Richardson (1982); Groombridge, J. (ed.) (1987) *Learning for a Change*, REPLAN, Leicester: NIACE; Thompson (1984); Taylor and Ward (1986); Spencer, B. (ed.) (1986) *Adult Education and the Unemployed*, University of Leeds; Gerver (1988); Rogers, A. (1984); De Wit, P. (ed.), (1989) *Innovative Projects in Extra-Mural Education 1985–89*, Leicester: UCACE; La Belle, T. (1982) Formal, nonformal and informal education; a holistic perspective on lifelong learning, *International Review of Education* **28**(2), 159–75. La Belle was cited in Thompson (1980),

and his work is increasingly becoming known, see e.g. Jarvis (1987). But in the extensive literature cited in McIlroy and Spencer (1988) there is no Third World writer listed. See Melo (1988). See EBAE (1988), Italy 3; EBAE (1988), Finland; University College of Galway Annual Reports of the Department of Adult Education.

(13) Council of Europe (1984), pp. 16–17, 19.

(14) For Ireland, see Scott, I. (1985) *The Periphery is the Centre*, Arkleton Trust; for inner city renewal, see Urban Regeneration programmes of Civic Trust (UK).

(15) The project was described in *The Times*, 16 December 1985. This account is based on papers from the Highland and Islands Development Board, especially *An Interim Assessment of the IDP for Agriculture and Fish-farming in the Western Isles* prepared by Professor George Houston, to whom I am grateful for sight of these papers.

(16) *Times Higher Education Supplement*, 13 January 1989; Council of Europe (1984), pp. 10, 11–12; Mee (1980), pp. 80–81.

Chapter 17

Changing the Role of the Change-Agents

The re-orientation of adult education to a Developmental model is likely to call for fewer changes in terms of staffing and staff roles than in other areas of work. Indeed, in this field adult education would seem to have much to offer to its Development colleagues. For its ideals are closer to emancipatory Development than are those of, for instance, agricultural and other forms of extension. It is significant that some trainers of extension workers now cite authorities (Paulo Freire, for example) and talk in terms (participation, etc.) which are similar to those used by adult educators. Nevertheless, some changes will be called for on the part of adult education staff, in attitudes and approaches if not in structures.

THE EXISTING PATTERN

There is currently a two-tier staffing pattern in adult education in the West. Except in the USA, where much adult education is located in or offered through universities and colleges, most of the face-to-face teaching of adults is done by part-timers, though there is a growing number of full-time professionals based in adult education institutions.

The UK model may be taken for closer analysis. There, part-time teachers ('tutors') are usually volunteers. Many are untrained and unqualified to teach: the dictum that one needs to be both trained and qualified in order to teach children, that one needs to be qualified but not trained in order to teach college and university students, but that one does not need to be either trained or qualified to teach adults, still holds good. I think of one organizer who told his colleagues during a discussion of tutor recruitment: 'I have no difficulty finding part-time tutors; I get them out of the Yellow Pages [of the telephone directory]'. For him, demand for an upholstery course was met by persuading a practising upholsterer over the phone to extend his/her activities to include serving as a part-time tutor without any further training. But things are changing. The need for opportunities of systematic training of tutors is seen as a priority for many providers, and voluntary training programmes are increasing. Several agencies have introduced qualifications as well, at the instance (so they aver) of the part-time tutors themselves.[1]

These part-time volunteer teachers, although often locally based, are not, however, chosen by the community. In many cases they come in from the outside as visiting 'experts', like the older adult education extension lecturers. They are selected by educational administrators for their experience and expertise as much as for their willingness to teach and their proximity to the location of the course. They normally serve for only a short time (the turnover rate of part-time adult teachers is very high; one recent survey suggested 30 per cent per annum); and like their counterparts, the change-agents in Development programmes, they are paid but a pittance.[2]

There is growing concern about these part-timers by professional adult educators. These full-timers are more likely to be organizers or teachers than supervisors of the part-timers. The supervisory role is normally exercised by an administrator, because supervision in much adult education, as in Development, is seen as a control mechanism rather than as an educational support system. Full-timers are more usually than not trained, and some are qualified teachers as well. Increasingly they are building up a career pattern for themselves, although promotional prospects are becoming more prescribed rather than more open.

The picture then is one in which the adult education agency, sometimes within but not of the local community, selects many part-time para-professional and a few full-time teachers of adults for small groups of self-selected voluntary learners. The pattern varies in other countries with more full-time career adult educators; but even in these countries, part-time instructors form a large part of the total cohort of adult educators.[3]

THE DEVELOPMENT MODEL

In order to re-orientate adult education to locality Development, there is no need for a radical realignment of professionals and non-professionals. Indeed, in its employment of part-timers, adult education is markedly better than some Development models which send in full-time visiting 'experts' (extension workers) to teach the locals. Nevertheless, some changes of roles and procedures will be necessary.

The part-time tutor as change-agent

Since the Development model of adult education seeks to work with all members of the local community and not just with a small 'class', and since it seeks to work over a long span of time rather than just for the term of one course, the part-time Developmental adult education workers need to come from within the local community itself and to continue to live within it. Grass-roots adult educators should be insiders, permanent resource persons for community needs. Nor is there any reason why there should be only one such worker chosen in any subject area; a team or group may be both more efficient and more personally rewarding for the part-timers. 'No body which programmes and organizes from the outside [should] be set up'; rather 'the en masse establishment of local educational agents (at the collective or individual level, professional or voluntary)' is the way forward. If possible (and in many sectors of the local community, structures exist which will permit this, for example ethnic groups), these 'animators' might be chosen by or in association with the community. They must certainly be acceptable to the community rather than simply self-selected.

Such persons, however chosen (whether volunteers in response to general appeals or invited from within the neighbourhood), would then be given initial and in-service training, in which the Development goals would be internalized, and continuing support by the full-time staff. The training would cover the content of the Development programme—the necessary knowledge, understandings and skills needed to be a local resource person (for 'programming in adult education is based on the reality inherent within its agents'); but it would also help to develop the attitudes (especially confidence and commitment) needed to promote the mission of the programme to the whole community. The part-timer would work within the community, not just as tutor but as promoter, with regular two-way links to the full-time professionals, constantly supported by them and building bridges with other agencies who can provide access to resources which may be needed for the Development of the locality.[4]

It is important that these new-style resident part-time adult education tutors (Development change-agents) should not be unthinking implementers of someone else's programme but should themselves be innovative and responsive to the needs of the community in which they reside and work. And they need to be conscious that support for such innovative approaches will be constantly available. This calls for careful selection of the part-time workers (avoiding the reluctant change-agent) and for careful and continuing support. Above all, Developmental adult education must be wary of using change-agents merely for the sake of the programme; they are members of a local community whose own needs are being met.

But in the end such resident part-time workers need to be willing to make themselves redundant in promoting the Development programme and not to create dependence upon themselves. Their aim will be to build up a learning community, perhaps through self-learning groups; to see themselves as one of many resources and one of many links to outside resources, as a servant-for-the-time-being of the community. Careful training as well as selection is required for these local change-agents.

One or two examples will help to illustrate the sort of programme I have in mind. The Development of the Western Isles of Scotland (see p. 204) could have been better provided for if the communities involved had chosen local farmers (some of whom were already under-employed, as the EEC survey revealed) who, given short and continuing periods of training, worked among their own community in a part-time capacity, doing the tasks that the full-time interventionists were in fact doing, and supported by visits from the agricultural extension worker. Such an approach would have been more acceptable and more productive than outside experts coming in and giving lecture/demonstrations. Similarly, health education programmes in inner-city areas could be provided by the careful choice of local part-time workers (men as well as women) who receive training and work within the whole community with ongoing support from outside full-time helpers. The switch in emphasis is from a model of adult education consisting of part-timers persuaded to serve as tutors to volunteer learners, to a model consisting of part-time volunteers teaching non-voluntary learners.

Local community history

The way that this model could be adapted to the traditional work of adult education can be seen in the discipline of local community history. At the moment, local history is taught to adults at several different levels, ranging from lectures and slide shows (with some visits) given to relatively small audiences of passive voluntary learners to more active programmes of research and field work to even smaller groups. It is regarded as primarily a matter of developing personal interest; the rest of the local community are not involved 'because they aren't interested'. But local community history can be not just an academic pursuit or personal hobby but a community activity leading to an increase in a communal sense of the past, to a feeling of belonging to a community with a unique and relevant past, and to a concern for the conservation and enhancement of the built environment. As such, local history is important not just for a small band of enthusiasts but for all members of the community; it should reach the widest possible audience. Local history needs to be taken to all the people and be built up *with* them rather than granted to a few who come to the fount of knowledge.

Adult education agencies should, therefore, encourage some persons (if possible chosen by the community and certainly acceptable to them) to become part-time local history 'workers' in their own community. This can be built on to the existing pro-gramme relatively easily: students can be encouraged to share their new insights with others. But beyond this, new groups of learners can be recruited specifically as 'animators' to engage in outreach work in their own local communities. The budget currently spent on paying an external lecturer to come in and give a series of lectures or run a class could instead be used to support the efforts of these indigenous local history workers. Part of their task would be to promote an interest in and understanding of the local community's past throughout the whole community, to make it a mass move-ment, not just for a self-selected elite. These local history animators would need train-ing, teaching–learning materials and constant support; and this would be the role not just of local history specialists like the county archivists, museum staff, local history librarians, etc., but also of the full-time local history tutor on the staff of the adult education agency.

Various projects show that it can be done. The La Guardia Community History Project in Astoria, New York City, run by the Community College is one example of the way the local people can work in their own local history and in return can receive much by way of a greater awareness and understanding of their own past. New York State has statutory full-time or part-time local historians in each township and county, paid on the rates, some of them serving on the 'expert' model, others on the 'animator' model. In East Tennessee, local history agents in each of the counties of the region have been given training and support by the East Tennessee Local History Society to encourage their whole community to engage in related local history studies, and useful comparative reports have been published on the Great Depression (*Hard Times Remembered*) and other topics. A project designed for County Offaly, Ireland, had each of the ten small towns in that county appoint local residents to build up teams of people to work in concert on a related theme, with training provided by the county adult education agency. In Le Creusot, France, local community history was used as the basis for training for new and compatible forms of Development for this severely damaged region. In Liverpool, local history activities lie at the core of community development programmes seen as social action. All these are examples of recent projects which demonstrate new approaches to mass local history on a Developmental model. What makes the Le Creusot example different is that it was intended to lead to new forms of economic activities building on the past skills available in the community (in the end it was ineffective in this respect). It can be done; and if local history has any social value at all, it needs to be done. We cannot justify a voluntary elitism any longer.[5]

The same is true for other areas in traditional adult education programmes. If the study of literature, science, art or politics, for example, has any value, then it has value for everyone, not just for the few. The creation and support of a cadre of part-time trained promotional agents (animators) *within* the locality rather than full-time or part-time adult education lecturers for art, music, literature, science, politics and economics coming in from outside will enhance the interest in and understanding of these subjects to the benefit of the whole community.

This re-orientation is already taking place. The ACRE project mentioned above (see p. 202) aims to train community workers in rural areas who are volunteers from their villages or towns. The National Federation of Women's Institutes in the UK conducts training courses for people who are already elected or appointed leaders in local community voluntary bodies or action groups; most of these are professionals in some field or other. The Institute of Adult Education in Guildford is running SCALP (the Surrey Community Action Learning Programme)—'a scheme of helping volunteers to work locally with adults in order to develop their skills, knowledge, confidence and potential'; among the areas for which volunteer workers are being trained are programmes for 'the unemployed, older people, drug users and abusers, mentally handicapped, family relationships, health and retirement, mothers and infants, parents and teenagers etc.'.[6]

But this is still some way from a fully Developmental model. A contrast can be seen with the Sarvodaya movement in Sri Lanka. When a local community approaches that organization for help and training, it insists that those sent for training should be acceptable to and if possible appointed by that local community. There are some signs of this approach in the West: in the Le Creusot project, 'an overall approach was necessary to forming a group of new social agents'; while in the USA, 'local facilitators' are being developed with the slogan 'Anybody can teach'. The Council of Europe Community Development project in Switzerland 'employed regional animateurs'. But there is still some way to go in exploring forms of local community animators appropriate to the traditions and conditions in the West.[7]

The full-timer as supervisor

The Developmental model also calls for changes in the agreed roles and activities of the full-time adult education staff; these will become 'supervisors' (not in terms of control but in terms of continuing help) of the part-time Development workers. To do this, they need to be experienced practitioners as much as subject specialists. They must be carefully selected and trained, not least in the meaning of Development itself. Their activities will be more in the promotion of their subject area within the community and the identification, support, training and counselling of the field workers than in direct teaching of small groups.[8]

Warnings about the dangers of this becoming a 'top-down' model need to be heeded. 'The future of an adult education operation should not depend on one or two irreplaceable organisers.' It is not a case of the full-timer directing the part-timer. Part-time change-agents can contribute to, and sometimes even control, their own training. Networks of self-learning groups of change-agents in specific subject areas (agriculture and health are good instances of this, but there are others) have been usefully established, just as local subject tutor groups have been established for part-time adult education tutors with profit. Through these means, the full-timer can receive constant feedback which will be necessary for the fulfilment of their role.

This new role for the full-timer cannot be undertaken in isolation from other local Development agencies. Instead of keeping aloof from such programmes and campaigns, the provision of inter-agency training events and regional support networks will promote an effective Development programme for the region and at the same time overcome the marginalization of the adult education agencies.

The role of the full-time adult education worker in a Development model of adult education will thus be as supporter of the change-agents and as trainer.

Supporter

The full-timers would, in association with the local community and where appropriate with other bodies concerned with the programme (e.g. vocational training, health, etc.) recruit the part-time workers. There is already much experience of this in the process of appointing part-time tutors; but the criteria for the part-time resident Development change-agent, whose role is to promote their programme on a long-term basis throughout the whole community, will be different from those used to select a part-time tutor to teach his/her subject for a short period to a few, often some distance away from their own home. And having appointed the resident workers, the full-timer will be charged with supporting them with moral encouragement and confidence building, with training programmes and resource allocations and regular (participatory) evaluations.

In this the preparation and provision of teaching–learning materials will form an essential part of the activities of the full-timer. Immediately I can hear the chorus of protests. Years of discussions among local history tutors will be repeated in every subject area. Resistance to a core curriculum and to standardized syllabuses (although in the UK the Further Education Unit and other bodies have been advocating such strategies, and the Open University has been using such materials for many years); the necessity of meeting the individualized needs of the learners—all the traditional arguments against mass adult education will be rehearsed with energy. It is surprising how resistant to change are those very people who most vociferously advocate the need for constant learning changes in others! But recent work in distance education, in self-learning ideologies and practices and in the provision of learning packs, has taught us not only that it is possible to prepare and produce teaching–learning materials while yet retaining flexibility, but also that it is possible, given suitable training, for part-time teachers of adults to use these materials creatively. Some part-timers are already calling for such help from their full-time subject colleagues.

Training

This brings us to the full-time tutor's role in training. A great deal has been written on this subject and I do not propose to repeat it here. In this field, adult education is ahead of most Development programmes, whose training is largely devoted to the subject matter of the programme with elements of communication skills and relatively little if any attention being given to self-knowledge, personal growth and attitude-change. Adult educators, for instance, have become aware of the necessity to use in training the same active teaching–learning methods which they advocate for the adult learners, whereas many extension training programmes use more formal methods to advocate non-formal practices. Most adult education training is designed to develop initiative, innovative approaches to teaching adults, responsiveness and sensitivity to the learners rather than conformity to set models.[9]

Nevertheless, adult education trainers can learn from the Development process, for training is a form of Development. Starting from the existing state of the trainees, with all their potential, aspirations and intentions, the training programme will seek to enhance awareness—of self, of the programme goals, of the relevance of the subject to the community within which they will be working, of the needs and hopes of the local community and of particular groups within that community. It will help the trainees to acquire the knowledge, understandings and skills needed for the task—not just techniques but full personal development including values and belief systems; and it will encourage the trainees to decide upon, plan, execute and evaluate programmes of action. In other words, the full-timers will be engaged in a Development programme with a participant group of part-time community workers, just as the latter will themselves be involved in a Development programme aimed at the whole of the population within the community. Both will have experienced for themselves the process they hope to promote with others.

The objectives of this change-agent Development programme will be three-fold. First, it will seek to develop within the change-agent a sense of confidence and a commitment to the programme goals and to the people in the community. This concern to bring together the people and the Development programme will be the well-spring for all the actions of the local part-time resident change-agent. Secondly, it will seek to develop the necessary competencies, knowledge and understandings to implement this Development programme—both the subject matter (health or local history, for example) and the methodologies needed to engage in community (mass) education and training for adults. This will on occasion call for a team approach rather than a polymath approach; but a wider-ranging training programme rather than narrow specialisms is likely to be more effective in the long run. And thirdly, it will seek to develop in the trainees a willingness and an openness to learn, a sense of the need for continuing education for themselves and for those they work with.

It is these objectives, these attitudes, which the part-time community Development workers are most likely to 'catch' from the full-time professional adult educators. But this will call for some radical rethinking about the full-time and part-time teachers in adult education and their relationship, and for the training of the full-timers into the goals of the Development programme. This is where it will all begin; and this is one of the greatest challenges of the Development model of adult education. The changes need to commence with the adult education agencies and their staff.

The time is ripe for such changes. Recent alterations in funding arrangements in the UK and calls elsewhere in the West for relevant, work- and life-related adult education concerned with national goals mean that there is for the first time in many years a greater flexibility in relation to the way adult education providers can use their financial and human resources. It is possible, given goodwill, to change these roles; and if adult education is to be redirected towards socially useful goals, such re-orientation needs to be done now.

NOTES TO CHAPTER 17

(1) See Lowe (1975), ch. 7; Hetherington, J. (1980) Professionalism and part-time staff in AE, *AE* **52**(5), 324–8. For the USA, see Willie, R., Copeland, H. and Williams, H. (1985) The adult education professoriat in the US and Canada, *IJLE* **4**(1), 55–68; Brookfield (1988).

(2) UCACE (1983), *The Role of the Part-time Lecturer in University Adult Education*. For a survey of the part-time teachers in adult education, see *Learning to Teach, Teaching to Learn*, report of Northern Ireland Working Party on the training of teachers in continuing education, Northern Ireland Council for Continuing Education, 1985.

(3) For Europe, see *Adult Education and Voluntary Action*, EBAE Newsletter **2** (1987): for USA, see Johnstone, J. W. C. and Rivera, R. J. (1965) *Volunteers for Learning*, Chicago; and note 1 above.

(4) De Sanctis (1988); for change-agents in the West, see Franklin, R. (1969) *Toward the Style of the Community Change Educator*, Washington: National Training Laboratory.

(5) La Guardia project: details can be obtained from Dr Richard Lieberman, La Guardia Community College, 31–10 Thomson Avenue, Long Island City, New York 11101. For East Tennessee, contact Dr Mark Wetherington, East Tennessee Historical Society, 500 West Church Ave, Knoxville, Tennessee 37902. For Le Creusot, see Arocena (1986); Arocena, J. (1986) *Le développement par l'initiative locale: le cas français*, Paris, pp. 75–84. For Liverpool, see Yarnit (1980a). The County Offaly project has not yet been written up.

(6) For the NFWI project, see Hall (1988), pp. 247–9. For SCALP, see papers of the Guildford Institute of Adult Education (University of Surrey). See also Jackson (1970); Thompson, N. (1980) Training for bridge building, in Fletcher, C. and Thompson, N. (eds) *Issues in Community Education*, Falmer Press. For Europe, see Arocena (1986), p. 6; Titmus (1981).

(7) For the USA, see Fessler, D. R. (1976) *Facilitating Community Change: a Basic Guide*, California; Alinsky, S. D. (1971) *Rules for Radicals: a Practical Primer for Realistic Radicals*, New York. For general discussions, see Kidd, J. R. Adult education, the community and the animateur, and Blondin, M. Animation sociale, both in Draper, J. A. (ed.) (1971) *Citizen Participation: Canada*, Toronto; Brookfield (1983), pp. 179–83, and Brookfield (1988); Berridge, R. A., Stark, S. and West, P. T. (1977) *Training the Community Educator: a Case-Study Approach*, Michigan; Hiemstra, R. (1980) Adult and community education: mobilising the resources of the city, in Franklin, S. W. (ed.) *The University and the Inner City: a Redefinition of Relationships*, Mass. For Le Creusot, see note 5 above; Switzerland, see Council of Europe (1984), p. 28.

(8) Council of Europe (1984), p. 14. Much of the writing on the role of the adult educator is concerned with the full-time rather than the part-time tutor. See works cited above and Jackson (1971).

(9) On training, see Elsdon, K. T. (1975) *Training for Adult Education*, University of Nottingham; Advisory Council for the Supply and Training of Teachers (1978) *Training of Adult Education and Part-time Further Education Teachers* (Haycocks Report II); Graham, T. B. *et al.* (1982) *Training of Part-time Teachers of Adults*, University of Nottingham; ACACE (1983) *Teachers of Adults: Voluntary Specialist Training and Evaluating Training Courses*, Leicester: ACACE; Daines, J. *et al. The Training of LAY Tutors*, University of Nottingham; Daines, J. *et al.* (1984) *Final Report Supplement on the Look After Yourself Tutor Training Programme*, University of Nottingham. For the USA, see Grabowski, S. M. *et al.* (1981) *Preparing Educators of Adults*, Jossey Bass; special edition of *Convergence* **18**(3–4) (edited by R. Boshier, 1985); Brookfield (1988). For Europe, see EBAE, *Training and Further Training of Adult Educators* (1982); *The Trainers*, CEDEFOP Vocational Training Bulletin 13 (December 1983). See Chapter 13, notes 5, 6 and 7.

Chapter 18

Achievements and Outcomes

The re-orientation of traditional adult education in the West towards a Developmental model will cause some major reassessment of the process of evaluating achievements. And in this, adult educators will have much to learn from Development workers.

THE LACK OF EVALUATION IN ADULT EDUCATION

Adult educators have a poor record in evaluation. There are many reasons for this. They do not often set the objectives of their programmes very clearly, except perhaps in craft classes, and therefore they are not used to evaluating in any credible way whether anything has been achieved in the course of their work. It is unusual for an adult education agency to evaluate itself except in terms of numbers of learners, consistency of attendance or rate of drop-out, or the coverage of subjects in the programme as a whole. It is unusual for any tutor (full-time or part-time) to assess their achievements except in terms of the immediate product of the class or attendance of the learners. A good deal is talked about evaluation and the need for feedback in adult education but little is done in practice. When defenders of liberal adult education say that the aim of their courses is to develop independent judgement or to increase powers of decision-making, they never test whether these aims are being achieved; they are unable to present to their critics or to their friends any convincing evidence that these worthy objectives are being satisfactorily fulfilled. Such statements are typical of the sloppy thinking which characterizes much of the current debate on adult education in the West.[1]

As for indicators of success, most tutors will provide statements like 'the learners participated in discussion' (as if the goal of the exercise was to get as many people as possible to say something, on the grounds that discussion is a good thing in itself) or 'the learners produced this item or that written report' (without any clear indication as to whether the product was an end in itself or a means for learning, whether the object was a desirable one or of an acceptable standard or not). In practice very little systematic comparable evaluation of their work is undertaken by adult education teachers, largely because they are not precise enough in what they are seeking to achieve.

There is another more understandable reason: the fear of traditional assessment procedures, such as examinations, which are on the whole designed to create failures rather than successes has led to a reluctance to evaluate adult education at all.[2] Such thinking results in a good deal of laxness on the part of adult educators in judging their own and their students' performances. Standard norms are despised; few peer group evaluations are employed. Individual progress reports barely exist except in one or two specialized areas. Learner satisfaction (expressed in a very vague way) and enrolment in further courses seem to be the main criteria of evaluation—which has led commentators to suggest that adult education in the West is nothing more than 'entertainment' for the already educated.

EVALUATION IN DEVELOPMENT

Development workers, in contrast, are accustomed to setting very clear goals and with them the measures, processes and instruments by which the attainment of those goals may be judged. Relief of poverty, or failure to relieve poverty, can be demonstrated; improvements in health, increased output for agriculture or crafts or industry, literacy and numeracy skills, the establishment of co-operatives, better housing standards, even signs of increased involvement in decision-making or the improved status of women, can all be felt and seen and demonstrated to others in actions, and even to some extent measured. It is not just a case of quantity: qualitative betterment can be measured against regional, national and international norms.

Evaluation in Development often runs beyond the achievement of targets to an assessment of *impact*—the effects a programme has on the community in general. Many agencies find the concept of 'impact assessment' of greater usefulness than 'evaluation'. It is thought to be more precise and can be subdivided into different kinds—the social impact or the economic impact of the intervention, for example; and it can comprehend both positive and negative impacts. Not all Development programmes use impact assessment as a tool of evaluation, but most try to weigh the consequences of their actions on the communities with which they are dealing in a way that adult education workers do not.[3]

Nevertheless even in those evaluations which speak of impact, there is often a tendency to use general terms rather than search for particular impacts. They look for the reduction of inequalities, for overall increased prosperity. They fail to look at the unique results of their programmes. And this means that such evaluations miss a great deal; for the Development intervention in each locality will react with the previous experience of the community in a unique 'chemistry', creating unique outcomes in each case. All programmes will have different outcomes, even where the objectives are the same (for example, in literacy programmes); and it is the task of evaluation to identify and to judge these specific outcomes.

THE NEED FOR EVALUATION IN ADULT EDUCATION

Those engaged in adult education have traditionally rejected setpiece evaluation. But the necessity to change and improve upon what they are doing in order to become more effective, the need to build on success and to learn from failure, the need to justify to others what they are doing, the need to help the learners to move on to new programmes—all these and other reasons will increasingly bring adult educators to evaluate their work more rigorously. Already there are signs that it is happening.

It is therefore necessary to consider how this should be done. I do not mean whether we shall use examinations or not. Rather I am here concerned about what it is that we are looking for in assessing Development-based adult education, what are the measures of success or failure which we can use. The methods of evaluation will follow from decisions on matters such as these.

OBJECTIVES AND OUTCOMES IN EVALUATION

Here we need to remind ourselves of the distinction which exists between objectives and outcomes (see p. 89). All adult education and all Development is aimed at certain objectives—i.e. the purposes of the programme. There can be no education and no Development without goals. But equally all adult education and Development programmes bring with them certain other results, unplanned by-products. Some of these spin-offs can be anticipated, but others cannot be foreseen at all. Any evaluation of adult education directed towards local or regional Development must not just assess the level of achievement of the identified objectives of the programme but also weigh carefully the other outcomes of the intervention (see Figure 18.1).

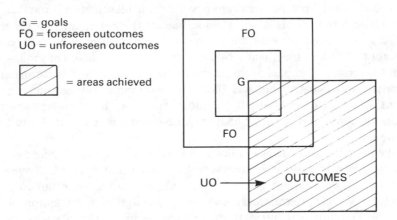

Figure 18.1   Evaluation of goal achievement and outcomes

Achievement of objectives

The first measure of whether programmes are effective is whether they achieve the goals which they set for themselves. But unless these goals and objectives are set out clearly, neither agents, teachers nor learners will be able to determine whether they are on the right course or whether they are making any progress.

In doing this, it is necessary to prescribe the conditions attached to those goals and objectives—the standard and the context within which the task will be performed. This is well understood in some literacy programmes which set out to help learners acquire not just the ability to read and write but to read some set piece with fluency and with understanding and to write some message with a set measure of proficiency. It is also true of other programmes. In health education, measurable changes in mortality and illness rates can be used; while in nutrition, scales of weights and heights and the reduction of deficiency diseases serve as indicators of achievement. In the Look After Yourself programme, the measures were clearly set out and regularly monitored.[4] In other programmes, assessments will be measured in terms of income levels or the improvement of housing. Some of these indicators will be quantitative, others will be qualitative—for example, increased awareness in the community at large or the level of participation by various marginal groups in the community's affairs.

I can imagine the horror with which some adult education colleagues are likely to receive these suggestions. But are these unworthy goals? If so, why? Can liberal adult educators explain why adult education should not strive (along with other concerned agencies) to improve the lot of the community in which it is set and by which it is supported? Are goals which can be quantified (in health, for instance) any worse than those which are subject only to qualitative judgements—for example, an increase in identity with and concern for the local community, or changes from negative to more positive attitudes, or increases in artistic appreciation?

Such factors, related as they are to the goals defined for the programme, provide more or less precise measures of the achievements of Developmental adult education programmes—more or better local amenities, greater influence in local decision-making, more jobs or higher income levels through increased agricultural yields or industrial productivity, the declining number of AIDS cases, an improved environment, reduced waste, etc. And these measures will be judged not solely through the changes in the lives of the immediate participants but by their impact on the whole community. For adult education is not located on a desert island; it belongs to and is part of the local scene. The impact of these programmes on that local scene needs to be assessed from time to time.

Objections to evaluation

Let us face squarely some of the objections to such evaluation. How, it will be argued, can one measure enrichment of soul, the cultural Development which comes from literature, art or music, for example? The answer to this must be that because it is difficult, that is no reason not to make the attempt. In any case, most teachers of adults in these and other subjects will already be looking for *indicators* of such learning changes, both for their own sense of achievement (necessary for motivation to continue with the teaching) and for the sake of the learners themselves. Unless such an enrichment manifests itself in some form of changed behaviour (for example, more frequent engagement in activities which call into play the enhanced aesthetic appreciation or spiritual qualities, increased use of artistic facilities—attendance at concerts or visits to art galleries—more insightful contributions to discussion, or wider and deeper listening and reading), then we have no sign at all that any learning is taking place. Feedback of this sort is essential in all forms of education; without it, we shall be teaching in a vacuum. So the answer to this question must be: how do those who teach in such areas know whether or not they are 'winning' in relation to the tasks they have set for them-selves and for their learners? How can they and the learners tell whether the learners are making any progress in the subject? Many tutors either do not clarify for themselves what their goals are or, if they do, are satisfied with less than informative indicators of progress on the part of their students.

But how, it will be argued, can such measures of achievement allow for the individual learners setting and achieving their own goals? The answer must be that in the Develop-mental model of adult education, the main objective of the programme will be to meet a community need or aspiration; the attaining of individual learner goals will be 'other outcomes', by-products, not the primary programme objective. So that the evaluation of any programme will be made on the basis of its success or failure in meeting commu-nity needs as much as in terms of its success in fulfilling individually set goals.

Some may see such goal achievement measures as too mechanistic. But value judgements are not excluded, even when quantitative assessments form the basis of the evaluation. Indeed, they are inevitably involved in all forms of Developmental adult education; for the first question to be asked about any goal is whether this is the *right* goal for that community. For example, are we teaching the right subjects? are we promoting the right purposes, the right sort of economic activities? are we helping the right organizations within the community? In the end, all forms of Development and adult education intervention are a matter of values, even when these are unspoken.

In any case, Development, whether national or local, has multiple goals, and some-times goals have a habit of getting in the way of each other. Is contentment 'better' than improved health, for example? Is the provision of large dams and artificial lakes, with all their potential for power, irrigation, flood control and tourism, worth the displace-ment of hundreds of families? Even on the smaller scale of Developmental adult education, judgements are called into play in the setting of priorities. With limited resources, decisions have to be made as to whether to support this particular objective or that one—whether to go for the short-term AIDS campaign or the longer-term nutrition programme; whether to assist with tidying up a spoiled physical environment or promoting further industrial development; whether to work for improved housing through local authorities or through private enterprise; and so on. In all cases, value judgements are involved, even when efforts are made to quantify some of these aspects, for example by using cost-benefit analysis. What we cannot get away from is the chal-lenge which the urgent necessities of today's world present to adult education and its providers that they do something rather than do nothing.

Failed or delayed achievements

Two further aspects of this process of assessing goal achievement need to be mentioned. The first is the necessity to scrutinize carefully the goals which were *not* achieved and as far as possible the reasons for that failure, for rarely will all Developmental goals be achieved. And secondly, there is need to assess the *delayed* achievements. Some of the results will only appear after the end of the programme, sometimes after a long period of time. Adult education, with its emphasis on short-term courses and temporary inter-ventions, usually ignores those achievements which mature subsequently; they are more frequently evaluated in Development programmes.

Other outcomes

Beyond the planned outcomes of the programme, the purpose for which it was established, there will be other outcomes which are not among the primary goals of the programme. We have seen above an example of such a situation in Development; the same will be true of Developmental adult education. Such spin-offs may be as important for the learners and for the local community as the set objectives.

Foreseen outcomes

Some of these by-products can be foreseen. It is possible to anticipate that a co-operative training programme, for example, will have results within the community in the provision of particular services, or that a small business management course may lead to the establishment of new local credit facilities. Many local history classes have as one of their intended (spin-off) outcomes the rescue of local sites or records of historical value. These are not the objectives of the programme, even though foreseen; for had they been the primary goals, the programme would have been devised differently.

Such 'side' outcomes may be assessed and evaluated in the same way as the objectives. Are they felt to be desirable outcomes in terms of the Development of the locality? A literacy programme may lead to wider job and income possibilities or increased political participation, which will usually be considered as desirable outcomes. On the other hand, an adult training course in an income-generating programme which leads to greater inequalities and an increase in social conflict can hardly be described as having beneficial outcomes in the community as a whole, whatever the goal achievement of the participants. Whether the main results of any programme outweigh such by-products is a matter for judgement by the adult education agency and the community concerned.

Not all the foreseen outcomes will be achieved in the course of the programme. For, as with the main objectives, some of the anticipated by-products will fail to materialize, either in full or at all, and others will be delayed in appearing. In any evaluation of the impact of Developmental adult education, we need to assess the nature and effectiveness of the unplanned but foreseen outcomes.

Unforeseen outcomes

There will be unexpected results of the programme. These, more than the other two sets of outcomes, will tend to have a longer-term aspect to them: they can only be seen after the event. One example will suffice. A local history class concerned with early photographs and ephemeral records of a small market town resulted in two persons setting up what they called a local 'Archive Unit' to buy up such items for their own personal gain. This stopped the flow of this kind of material to the local museum and record office, an entirely unforeseen and regrettable outcome of this programme. Other instances can be envisaged: one can imagine a programme in which unexpectedly bad relations between the change-agent and the participants resulted in the programme of learning being put back by several years, and for some individuals for the rest of their lives. Things like this have happened frequently at school and college and are not unknown in adult education.

Attempts to assess the impact adult education programmes have on the learners and on the community of which they form a part will necessarily include some evaluation of these unexpected outcomes. As we have seen (p. 171), the long-term and unexpected outcomes of many input programmes of Development have included increased inequalities of wealth, so that however effectively the programme may have achieved its set goals (increased productivity or marketing, economic growth, etc.), the ultimate and unforeseen outcomes outweighed the immediate beneficial gains. We need to see if the same is true of our adult education programmes.

Evaluation in adult education has almost always ignored these other outcomes. I once asked a group of learners about these outcomes and received the response from one of the participants: 'I got married'. This certainly was not the objective of the course; I am not even sure that it could have been a foreseen outcome. In terms of personal and perhaps even community enrichment, it may be regarded as a desirable outcome, but one might have hesitations about a programme where such an outcome became common! Certainly there is not the systematic investigation of the total impact adult education courses are having on the community in which they are set in the same way as this occurs in Development. Agencies rarely ask themselves what they are doing to the local or regional community. Adult educators need to come to know not only their learners but also the community, to watch what is happening and to continue to relate to the whole community, not just the class, on a long-term basis so as to assess the delayed outcomes of their programmes. This can be achieved through continued contact with the local change-agents who will be their main agents for the provision of Developmental programmes. The short-term courses currently offered by most adult education providers may not be the best mode of promoting the long-term all-round Development of the locality (see Figure 18.2).

	Immediate achievement	Delayed achievement	Non-achievement
Planned objectives			
Foreseen outcomes			
Unforeseen outcomes			——

Figure 18.2 Outline schedule of impact evaluation

Nor should we just *assess* what is happening; we need to *evaluate* these outcomes as well, to judge them. Are they desirable or not? Do they contribute to the welfare of the neighbourhood? 'Policies, programmes and projects must be analysed in terms of who benefits, how, when, where and why, and future programmes adjusted accordingly.'[5] (See Figure 18.3.)

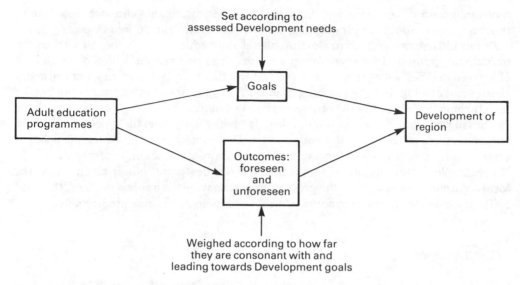

Figure 18.3 Summary of evaluation of achievement in Developmental adult education.

The process of evaluation

Perception evaluation

In the assessment and evaluation of the longer-term outcomes, there lies a problem: how can we distinguish between those changes in the local community which are the results of the programme and those changes which are already taking place independently? Change is occurring all the time, sometimes rapidly, sometimes slowly. Some of these changes are caused, diverted, hastened or slowed down by the intervention, but some are not.

As we have seen, Developmental adult education is not an intervention into a static situation; it does not commence a process of change. Rather it is stepping into the life of an individual, group or community while it is already in a process of change. Can we determine those changes that are directly attributable to the intervention? It is probably never going to be possible to do this with any measure of certainty, especially as we shall be unable to use a control group!

Shall we then abandon all hopes of assessing and evaluating outcomes? This would be very damaging to our understanding of the effects of our programmes. Perhaps the best way to undertake this task is to ask the participants and the wider community which changes *they* attribute to the adult education intervention and which changes they attribute to other factors. Where this has been done, experience suggests that they are likely to overestimate the impact of the programme rather than to underestimate it.

There is an important reason why we should trust the judgement of the participant group and the local community as to the outcomes arising from a particular programme. If the participants and the local community react positively towards the programme, believe that it is yielding valuable fruit, 'feel good' about it, then they will be receptive, motivated towards openness and change. But if the participants and local community think negatively about the programme, then they will resist the desired changes.

For as in Development, so in Developmental adult education it is the attitudes of the participant group and local community towards the programme which determine its effectiveness—not whether we teach well but whether they feel that they can learn and change and develop through our programmes. The value of our programmes can best be seen through their belief in the programme and its outcomes.

The true evaluation of programmes, then, is whether they meet the expectations of the community or not. In short, the evaluation of Developmental adult education is based on *their* values, not ours. For however effective our programmes may seem to us to be in (for example) increasing literacy or reducing birth, death and illness rates, unless the local community believes that the programmes are having desirable outcomes, they will resist or ignore all efforts to encourage them to participate in these programmes.

CONCLUSIONS

This chapter has argued that the test of the worth of adult education today should no longer be whether the programmes satisfy individual learning needs but whether they contribute to the full social, economic, cultural and political Development of the community and neighbourhood within which they take place. Moreover, the measure of this contribution is to be seen not in terms of demand from individuals or the achievement of personal growth and satisfactions, but in the impact these programmes have on the community as a whole—not just in terms of goal achievement but also in terms of the foreseen and unforeseen, immediate and delayed outcomes, i.e. the spin-offs from these programmes.

The programmes we plan and execute can no longer be seen as free-standing, solely in the domain of the private. To believe this is to delude ourselves, for they have never been purely private in their outcomes. We need to recognize that adult education, like Development, forms part of the public domain, is accountable to the national and local community and can and will be judged by whether it contributes to the general good both in its specified goals and in its outcomes.

In response to those adult educators who will regret this proposed re-orientation of the evaluation of the effectiveness of adult education away from the primacy of the individual to the community, we would wish to remind ourselves that the main element in all Development programmes is not collective knowledge transfer but attitudinal and behavioural change. Attitudinal and behavioural education lie at the heart of the Development process and this essentially calls for individual learning. In this way, it would seem, the needs of the individual learner and the needs of the community as a whole can be reconciled, and the tension between the individual and collective role of adult education resolved.

NOTES TO CHAPTER 18

(1) Elsdon, K.T. (1972) Evaluating teaching and learning, in Rogers, J. (ed.) *Adults in Education*, BBC; Knox, A. (1980) *Developing, Administering and Evaluating Adult*

Education, Jossey Bass; Guba, E.G. and Lincoln, Y.S. (1983) *Effective Evaluation*, Jossey Bass; Alkin, M., Daillak, R. and White, P. (1979) *Using Evaluation—Does Evaluation Make a Difference?*, Sage; Eisner, E. (1985) *Educational Evaluation—a Personal View*, Falmer; Feek, W. (1988) *Working Effectively: a Guide to Evaluation Techniques*, London: Bedford Square Press.

(2) For example, De Sanctis (1988), p. 4: 'programming of targets should not even hint at a scholastic programme complete with final diploma tied to a pre-set curriculum' [but what if this is what the learners want?].

(3) Hicks, N. and Streeten, P. (1981) Indicators of development, the search for a Basic Needs yardstick, in Streeten, P. and Jolly, R. (eds) *Recent Issues in World Development*, Pergamon; Oakley, P. (1982) The evaluation of social development, *RRDC Bulletin* **14**; Seers, D. (1972) What are we trying to measure? *Journal of Development Studies* **8**(3) (April), 21–36. The almost complete lack of evaluation in non-formal education is revealed by *Participation, Learning and Change*, report of the Commonwealth Conference in Delhi, Commonwealth Secretariat, 1980, ch. 4.

(4) Charnley, A.H. and Jones, H.A. (1979) *The Concept of Success in Adult Literacy*, Cambridge; see also Look After Yourself report cited in Chapter 16, note 10.

(5) Green (1977), p. 39; Council of Europe (1984), p. 20.

Chapter 19

Sharing in Development

Adult education agencies have over the years built up appropriate strategies and considerable competence in helping groups of motivated learners to learn, and this expertise is growing as experience widens and increases. But Development-based adult education will seek to bring into its field new audiences, some of whom will be reluctant learners. Does this call for new strategies, and does adult education have anything to learn from Development in this respect? For the traditional partnership between teacher and taught which currently exists in adult education in the West will to some extent disappear, to be replaced by a 'them and us' approach.

The problem is not solved by saying that adult education agencies are part of the communities which they are trying to serve and that therefore adult education is not outsider-intervention but insider-self-help. For in practice the problem will still remain. Even within Development-based adult education, agencies need to choose whether to continue to focus their attention (as in the ACRE example referred to above, p. 202) on voluntary self-selected learners or whether to turn their attention towards the larger numbers of the population who do not attend traditional adult education classes. There is no way out from what has been called 'this paternal trap. A decision not to act is itself an action.' All Development and all adult education is an intervention; and an assessment of strategies in relation to target groups is called for.[1]

It is to participatory methods that we need to turn for the answer. 'Participation' and 'participatory' are the 'in' words of both adult education and Development at the moment. It is at this point that the separate paths of Development (including Extension) and adult education cross; it is on this topic that the practitioners of both can talk to each other in language which both can understand. Adult educators have for long insisted that student/learner participation is necessary for effective learning; and Development workers have (rather more recently) come to aver that participation is essential for effective Development.

PARTICIPATION IN THEORY

It is relatively easy to sit in the study and write a textbook about participation; it is easy to review case studies drawn from many countries, showing how in each case this one was or was not 'participatory'. Over the last ten years or so, such books have proliferated; the romanticization of participatory approaches as the cure-all for adult education and Development problems has increased. But it is harder to do it in practice and it rarely fully works. Some writers have the grace to admit this, but others do not.

I can think of some striking failures. One was a workshop on monitoring and evaluation of adult literacy programmes in Delhi where we found ourselves engaged more of the time in training than in participatory problem-solving, largely because the gap between the understandings and experience of the various participants was too wide; we were often speaking different languages and calling upon different memories, and the views of what was involved in the issues under discussion were clearer in the minds of one set of participants than in the minds of the others. Another was the participatory evaluation of outcomes programme with a group of village-based literacy animators in Tamil Nadu. This failed because the local participants were not accustomed to looking at themselves and what they were doing any more than they were used to working in a team. There were, however, some successes: a series of participatory 'camps' with village women in south India which explored the 'self-image' rural women held of themselves—a programme which took three workshops spread over six months before the pattern of activities became clear. It would seem that fully participatory activities in Development and adult education involve great care, long preparation and frequently a considerable sense of frustration.[2]

In this respect, adult educators tend to be rather more advanced in concept construction and in the practice of participation than Development workers. There are several reasons for this. The philosophy of adult education as two-way learning leads more easily to participation than the one-way process of 'persuasion' which underlies most Development and extension today (however much some leaders in Development attempt to redefine extension). The rejection of hierarchy and the desirability of negotiating learning, of sharing in decision-making, of equality in learning—all these feature in adult education and point in the same direction. Again, the concentration by adult educators on active learning methods, the recognition of the relative ineffectiveness of the lecture-demonstration as a tool for learning (except with some limited audiences), the need to encourage the learners to do as much as possible for themselves, particularly so that planned learning may continue once the class has come to an end and the tutor is no longer present, all these lead to participatory work in adult education programmes.[3]

Development too is increasingly aiming at participation—at agencies 'not "doing" development but working with people towards development', at people planning and executing their own Development. The awareness that Development interventions have in many cases actually deprived people of control over their communities' responses to natural events such as drought or deforestation which they once possessed has led in some circles to an insistence on people's full involvement in Development. Many factors have pressed Development workers to urge more and more participatory approaches. They include: the necessity for the Development process to continue when the intervention has ceased and the change-agent has withdrawn; the problem of securing the wholehearted support of the local community behind the Development goals; and the need to ensure that the techniques and technology are appropriate to the indigenous knowledge and experience of the target group and are thus accepted and adopted.[4]

We must not, of course, overstate this. In both adult education and Development we need to be wary of excessive claims and the way words are used. The term 'participatory' is attached to many programmes which show no signs of the target group joining in the decision-making and implementation stages of the programme; indeed, which manifest no participatory element at all. A 'participatory' family planning camp kept 30 women sitting on the floor listening to lectures and demonstrations for one-and-a-half hours, and when I asked what was participatory about it, the organizer responded: 'Well, they listened.' There was not even participation in discussion. The same can be seen in many other programmes: I quote from one such statement:

> 'People's participation' is an important component of [the programme]. As part of this component, a consultant will conduct a socio-economic survey of the villages . . . she will investigate the current economic activities. . . . Mechanisms for involving the people in [the programme] will be identified. . . . Youth associations, co-operatives, panchayats [local government councils] and private groups will be studied for this purpose. Marketing channels for [the programme's] projects will be investigated. Major constraints to people's participation will be identified . . .[5]

It would seem that little of this activity was to be done by the people; the consultant would run the show. Such top-down attitudes suggest that the consultant may herself become a major constraint to the people's participation.

The reasons for this failure to comprehend the implications of calling a programme 'participatory' are hard to find. In part they seem to lie in the formal education which most Development workers have received and which they pass on to the change agents. But there are other possible reasons: the philosophy of the aid agencies, for example, or the expectations of the target group or the confusion which still surrounds the term 'participation' in many people's minds.

What do we mean by 'participation'?

Essentially 'participation' must carry with it some notion of sharing, joining in. To have any valid meaning at all, 'participation' cannot mean target groups 'working on their own',[6] even though that may be the eventual aim of the adult education or Development programme.

Sharing in what?

The uses of the word 'participation' in many adult education and Development contexts fall into two main clusters of ideas:

(a) They may refer to *people's participation in government*—sharing in decision-making, in running their own affairs, in the planning, execution and evaluation of affairs after the end of the programme. In other words, 'participation' in this sense is the *result* of adult education or Development. That participation is the end of the process can be seen from the fact that when the people have fully taken control of their own learning-Development, they no longer need interventions.

(b) More normally they refer to *participation in the adult education or Development process* itself: sharing in the programme, in decision-making and implementation of activities.

Both of these senses of the word are closely connected, for (b) is seen to lead to (a). It is clear that one cannot prepare for 'participation in government' without engaging in 'participation in the programme'. Nevertheless, it is useful to distinguish between 'participation' used to mean sharing in running the affairs of the community and the same word used to mean joining in the adult education or Development process.

For the moment, our concern must be with participation in the process. Three main views present themselves.

Being present

'Joining in' may of course merely imply 'presence' rather than involvement in activities and some measure of control over the programme.[7] Studies of 'participation' in adult education courses normally refer to 'attendance at classes'. They concentrate on why non-attenders fail to 'participate'; they are not concerned with the exercise of control, with the measure to which the participants share in the planning and running of the adult education programme itself.[8] But the concept of 'participation' normally goes much further than just being present; it implies various levels of 'sharing' in the programme.

Helping with other people's tasks

Participation can simply mean joining in activities determined by others—the Development or adult education agency: collecting information, for example, or surveying the resources of the neighbourhood. Several recent reports of 'participatory evaluation' programmes show the evaluators, even when they are drawn from other neighbouring agencies rather than outside experts, simply asking questions and receiving answers, so that 'participation' is seen as the people 'providing . . . input in the form of information during a survey . . . [or] carrying out orders in implementing an activity'.[9] But this must surely be the minimum range of activities that can in any meaningful way be called participation. Carrying out other people's instructions or just providing information for another person's survey has been likened to 'the bullock's participation in ploughing'.[10]

Taking responsibility

Participation must mean more than just collaboration: but how much more is a matter of debate. To 'participate' can include the participant group undertaking the activities of the programme with assistance and guidance, helping to decide on the adult

education programme or the Development plans, helping in the evaluation of the programme, choosing between different alternatives and sharing in the responsibilities. The
amount of participation is usually a matter of choice on the part of the adult education
or Development agency.

Whose programme?

Participation thus implies one group of people joining in someone else's programme.
But whose programme? Normally it means the target group joining in the Development
worker's or adult educator's programme. But aspiration-led Development and 'needs-
based' adult education will start with the agency joining in the programme of the target
group and proceed from this entry point towards the agency's goals.

Changing patterns of participation

In both of these cases, the level and nature of participation will change as the programme progresses. In the first case, the agency sets out the programme and invites the
target group to join in. Participation will tend to evolve from a situation where the
agency will serve as leader and the target group as followers, through a stage where both
partners will be more or less equal, to a final stage where the wishes and decisions of the
participants will take precedence. A reverse process will characterize those aspiration-
led programmes where the agency begins with the intentions of the target group and
moves towards the Development goals. In this case, the wishes and decisions of the
participants will at first predominate, then will come a stage of sharing on a more or less
equal level, passing to a pattern of change-agent-led Development or adult education.

Persuasion and negotiation

Both of these models involve an element of persuasion. The change-agent will need to
persuade the target group to adopt certain practices, while on the other hand the participant group will seek to convince the agency that what it intends to do is worthy of
acceptance. But persuasion is not the same as participation; it is not a process of sharing.
   Participation-as-sharing does not imply the abandonment by either the target group
or the agency of its own commitment, of deferring entirely to the other party. Belief and
commitment, 'a willingness to be partisan but open to debate', are essential to true
Developmental programmes. 'A sceptical tradition which is sceptical and nothing else'
will never achieve participatory adult education or Development. 'Let us be as partial as
we like to our own views, provided we expound as faithfully as we can the views of
others' was part of the war cry of an earlier generation of adult educators; and that may
be modified to include a willingness to listen and to enter into debate when challenged.[11]

PARTICIPATION IN PRACTICE

Such is the theory of participation. While we need to look closely at the practice of both adult education and Development programmes before we accept their claims to be participatory, at least their claims are praiseworthy, and on occasions their practice too is participatory. Interestingly some of the best participatory work has been done by adult education agencies in the West—in women's groups, for example, or creative writing, theatre workshops for the deaf, and the like—rather than by Development agencies in the Third World.

Participation in local community history

My example comes from the field I know best, local community history. From the late 1960s local history research classes in the UK were established. In these, groups of adults examined, wrote up and published the history of their own communities. The process went through four main stages, representing the main activities of historical research:

- determining the theme
- collecting the data
- analysing the material
- presenting the findings to the audience

(a) At first those who led these study groups were tentative. We started in the middle— with the *analysis of local history material*, which was found and often presented to the class members in 'predigested' form (with all the Latin and the difficult hand-writing taken out, for example). We asked the learners to join with us in tasks which we identified—to process documents which we discovered, to find answers to questions we posed; then we wrote up the results of all this work. The learners became convenient groups of workers, like 'gang-labourers', learning techniques and working under our supervision, and we justified this on the grounds (1) that a group can cover more territory (academically speaking) and process more data than a single worker, even the tutor; and (2) that active teaching methods were more effective in adult learning than passively listening to illustrated lectures. Thus we allowed the learners to help to analyse the material—to engage in parish register counts to arrive at graphs of population natural increase or family reconstitution, for example, or to survey in depth collections of probate inventories. We chose the subject; we identified the source material.

(b) Later we became bolder: we encouraged our student learners to *write up the material* for themselves. Of course we kept a close eye on it, to ensure its academic acceptability. It was our (academic) standards by which their work was to be judged. But as they became more confident and more experienced, they began to take control of the presentation of the findings: they chose an exhibition format or radio play instead of the academic work. Or they decided to write for the general public in newspaper articles or booklets, or to prepare pageants or (rather later) a film or video. They experimented, when we were tied to more traditional forms of presenting local history.

(c) It was with oral history that the next major breakthrough came: with the participants *identifying the source material* (the reminiscences of older residents, early photo-graphs, newspaper clippings and the older buildings in the local community). Trained now in the techniques of locating and collecting local history material, they also analysed it and presented the material in appropriate formats, doing three of the major tasks of the historian.

(d)   But we retained until last the *choice of the subject matter*. It was with the History Workshop programmes at Ruskin College, Oxford, that local history became truly local. The participants chose topics to study which seemed to them to be important. They became participatory decision-makers in all the stages of the local history process, free to select the theme, identify the sources, collect the data, analyse the material and decide on the appropriate formats of presentation. It was their history after all.

Thus local history study groups determined for themselves what they wished to look at, what they considered most interesting and significant rather than relying on our judgement. They chose the period and the subject, using the tutor as a sounding board to assess whether the topic selected was viable or not. They sought out the material, asking us to help them locate relevant sources, often long distances from the learning centres. They processed the data, using us as a library catalogue to find parallel studies for comparison and as an evaluator against which their findings could be tested. And they took decisions (sometimes against our advice) on how the newly won knowledge was to be made available to the rest of the local community: they chose the target audience, the format and the style of the public presentation. They even wrote books! After acting as a catalyst to get the project started, our role was as consultants. Indeed, often that was too grand a term: we were one resource among many consulted by the group—library, archives office, museum, local specialists, local authority planning department, govern-ment experts, the older members of the local community, and so on. It was very humbling for a so-called academic expert to be put in that role, but it was also very rewarding.[12]

But these were groups of adult learners which could be called 'developed'. They were often few and well educated; in several cases, some members of a larger quiescent local history lecture course would have left before the small band of active 'workers' emerged. And they formed a relatively low percentage (say 10 per cent) of all local history classes provided in adult education throughout the country. And in many cases the members had worked together over a long period of time before they arrived at a fully participatory mode. The Stamford Survey Group which originated in 1965 in a conservation crisis in that fine Lincolnshire town worked together for eleven years, becoming more and more independent until it was able to stand on its own feet. None of the members could be expected at the start to do all that they now do; it took a good deal of training before they took full control of their own learning.[13]

Preparing for participation

While it is rewarding to work with such groups, the challenge must remain: what about those who do not work in this participatory way? The same dilemma faces those of us who work in Development: how to get groups who do not have the necessary skills and attitudes to act in a participatory way. Participation calls for many competencies: 'wide bases of perception, skills, an ability to analyse, means to communicate, high levels of consciousness'.[14] We cannot expect our groups to possess all of these to start with, to be able to plan and execute a programme from the beginning, for if a group has the capabilities of acting in a self-determining way, that group does not need Development help from us. But if our groups cannot take decisions or carry them out except with our help, how can we expect them to join with us in a participatory way?

Some of the strongest advocates of participation in Development have recognized this dilemma and thus have spoken about 'preparation for participation' as a pre-participation stage. But there is a logic-fault in this: for what is this 'preparation' for participation but the Development process itself? It is unacceptable to say that Development must be participatory but that in order to get the target groups to a participatory level, we need a prior stage of training. Either there are two stages, a pre-Development (non-participatory preparation for participation) and a participatory Development phase; or Development is non-participatory preparation for participation, and participation is the goal of the Development process, in which case Development ceases when 'participation' begins.

The question then is whether 'participation' is the goal of the Development (and adult education) process or whether it is the process itself. There are differing views of this.

PARTICIPATION AS THE GOAL

Participation-in-government is seen by many as one of the goals of adult education or Development programmes; indeed, some urge that it is *the* primary goal. It is one of the basic human needs, a good in itself: so that 'the quest for participation' becomes a process by which groups and interests seek to legitimize themselves in society as a whole.[15]

I have some hesitations about 'participation' as an end goal. First, stated like this, participation becomes a normative goal. And normative goals are intermediate goals, not end goals. End goals are always a matter of choice, not a matter of prescription for the target group. So participation is more truly an intermediate goal than an end goal. To make 'participation' an end goal and at the same time normative is to deny choice, not to increase choice.

But, in fact, participation in society at large is not a universal pattern of behaviour. In every form of association, only a few participate fully. In local history societies, out of every hundred members, five to ten serve on the committee, another twenty are volunteer helpers, 30–40 attend lectures or go on outings more or less passively, and the rest pay their subscription, receive the publications and do nothing else. The same is true of other bodies. Studies of groups like the churches and political parties reveal similar patterns: few members are initiators, a larger number are responsive activists, a larger number still are passive members, and beyond them lies a stratum comprising 'the sympathetic constituency'. And these are voluntary associations which members choose to join. For communities which we do not join voluntarily, the number of active participants is smaller; in practice the *right* to participate is more commonly accepted than the *responsibility* to participate. This may not be a good thing but it is true even in societies which we call healthy democracies. Freedom must surely include the freedom to choose whether or not to participate and at what level; we can hardly be prescriptive about participation. To try to change these attitudes towards greater participation is to impose our standards and values about participation onto others.[16]

My other hesitation about participation as the end goal of adult education or Development springs from the fact that, apart from the attitudes mentioned above, the barriers to participation are political and can only be removed by political action of some sort. All adult education and Development programmes have a political aspect to them but they are not the same as political action. Adult education and Development can play their part—in creating awareness, in equipping the target group for taking political action—but it is unnecessary and unhelpful, indeed positively confusing, to equate adult education and Development with the political action which springs from adult education or Development. The two activities often go together, but that does not make them the same. There is much in the way of political action which is not adult education and which is not Development.

Empowerment

Here we need to help ourselves by distinguishing between 'participation' and 'empowerment'. They are not the same thing, if language means anything. Empowerment means many things—helping the target group to equip themselves; the removal of obstacles to the exercise of power, and so on. Some people argue that empowerment is needed before participation is possible; others that participation leads to empowerment. Clearly the two are related to each other; but whichever view we take of these two concepts, we must not confuse the route with the goal.[17]

Participation as an intermediate goal

If participation is a goal of adult education and Development, it must surely be an intermediate rather than an end goal: that is, it is a goal which in its turn leads on to ultimate goals. Exactly what it leads to is uncertain. It can lead to an improvement in the quality of life, though the experience of those who participated in the revolutions of several South American countries or in other political upheavals suggest that those who participate are not always necessarily better off in the long run than those who do not. It is hard to imagine any improvement in the quality of life without increases in opportunities to participate; but whether the reverse is true is debatable. Again, whether participation will lead to the alleviation of poverty is not clear: for example, many fishing communities with co-operatives remain poor. It is arguable that 'participation in government' is one of the keys to a more equitable and peaceful society, that without participation there can be no communal stability or harmony. So that permanence and peace may be the end goals for which participation is an essential prerequisite. But equally in some circumstances, participation can lead to increased conflicts, not to greater peace. And participation in some form or other would seem to be a necessary antecedent for self-reliance.

PARTICIPATION AS PROCESS

If participation is seen as an intermediate goal leading to ultimate goals, then it can also be seen as part of the process. In this, adult education has a good deal to contribute both to the understanding of participation as process and to the practice of participation. For one of the basic tenets of adult education is that adult learners 'learn best by doing', that in the process of learning they should practise the activity which is the desired end of the learning process; that instead of learning *about* something, they should learn by engaging in the desired activity itself. Adult learners are not treated as if they are learning for future application (as in the training of doctors or accountants) but as learning for now; for adult education springs from the learners' immediate needs and therefore enables the learners during the educational process to pursue the desired activity (suitably broken down into manageable steps) during the course, not just after the course has ended. One does not learn to become a local historian and then subsequently practise it: one learns to be a local historian by being a local historian.

So it is with participation. We treat the people in our programmes from the start as if they can participate (at least in stages). The aim is to reduce dependency on the change-agent progressively, so that even if at the beginning there is relatively little participation, gradually more and more participation will be built up. In most programmes, there will normally be two stages. At first the change-agent will lay out the path to be followed, point to the necessary steps to be taken and encourage the participant group to join in. Even the most participatory of agencies do this under the guise of preparing for participation. This will then be followed by a stage during which the participants will increasingly take control of the activities themselves.

There is in this a fine judgement to be made, a double danger to avoid. At worst, we can ask the participants to do too little—to use the learners as cheap labour for *our* tasks, to limit their functions by underrating their abilities and their commitment. This is what occurred at first with the participatory local history projects: the students were used as assistants to make surveys: to hold the end of tape measures in industrial archaeology or vernacular architecture, for instance, when surveying old buildings or sites, or to collect oral memories, to count parish register entries or to analyse census records on forms which had been devised for them. All this may be useful: but it can only serve as the first stage in a participatory process.

On the other hand, we may go to the opposite extreme and expect too much of the participants too early. We forget that over many years and through a wide range of experiences and considerable training we as tutor/change-agents have built up bodies of knowledge, banks of concepts and shorthand jargon, understandings of relationships, groups of skills, sets of attitudes and values, all of which will be different from the knowledge, concepts, terminology, understanding, skills, attitudes and values of those we are working with. So that the possibilities of confusion, the slow pace of coming to agreement, the difficulties of finding meeting places with complete understanding—in short the barriers in the way of genuine participation—may well cause frustration to both sides. We must not expect too little of those we work with, but equally we must not expect too much.

The words of a distance learning course on Rural Development sum this up well. Drawing a distinction between the 'paternalistic approach' (input-Development) and the 'populistic' approach (participatory Development), it suggests that both approaches derive from unreal stereotypes of rural people who are neither as inert and ignorant as the paternalistic view assumes, nor as virtuous and wise as the populistic view assumes. Each community is likely to be heterogeneous. . . . Many studies across countries and communities have indicated that the rural people are considerably more capable and responsive than the paternalistic view suggests but generally less able to change their lives autonomously than the populistic approach presumes . . . if the rural people as supposed in the paternalistic approach are inert and passive, how can one expect them to become active and responsible agents of change within a short time? . . . The populistic approach on the other hand neglects the common fact that deeply entrenched local interests dominate at the community level and unless there are some rules and regulations from higher authorities, local organisations are likely to serve the interest of the dominant minority rather than the majority. . . . Therefore we must look at the strategy of rural development in terms of a system which is neither top-down nor bottom-up, nor exclusively governmental . . . it should be based on a network of decision-making . . .[18]

The same is true for adult education also.

Three possible approaches

There are then three possible approaches to this question of participation in Developmental adult education programmes.

Agency-designed

We may start with programmes leading to agency or nationally set goals—health or housing or environmental enhancement or other programmes—and lead on to more participatory activities. This is what most Development programmes do at the moment and what adult education does in regard to its cultural and personal growth programmes. Both set out goals determined by the agency and tutor and invite particular groups to join in these tasks: to learn about family planning or health or craft skills, for example, or alternatively to study literature or to develop assertiveness or to learn how to make a dress. To extend this process to Developmental adult education would be a natural progression. But problems frequently arise when this route to participatory adult education or Development is followed, as the Delhi and Tamil Nadu experiences related at the start of this chapter show: for in these two cases, the goals had not been properly understood or internalized by the participants; we had not all accepted the importance of the task, or even the length of time we were prepared to devote to it. And in relation to the wider and more unmotivated audiences Developmental adult education will seek to address, it will be even more difficult to persuade them to accept the goals and the programmes which go with these goals.

Participant-requested

We can go to the other extreme, asking the local community to set the agenda. Some adult education and Development programmes already follow this route; they invite the participant group to determine the goals and to use the change-agent as a resource to help with the process. This 'facilitation' is regarded by some as a later and more advanced form of participation. But equally it may be the starting point for our journey into Development; as we have seen, it is sometimes (often?) easier and more profitable to start with *their* aspirations and intentions rather than with those of the change-agent, to make the programme chosen by the local community the entry point to the Development process. It may in fact be harder to achieve participation when we ask the participants to join in our tasks than when we join in theirs. It may be easier for us to help them to solve their problems than for them to help us to solve problems which we have identified.

Some have gone further, to suggest that 'participant-designed' programmes are more appropriate models to draw on rather than just 'participant-requested' programmes. But such a procedure demands much of the participant group: and on the whole it seems to be best pursued with groups which are already motivated and reasonably equipped in terms of knowledge, skills and understanding, in other words, with groups which no longer need Development because they can manage to a large extent on their own. These are very similar to the adult education research or study groups of self-selecting elites. So that while Development will generally tend towards the first route, using persuasion as its main tool, adult education will on the whole tend towards the second because it is accustomed to working with small groups of voluntary, interested and able groups of learners.

Negotiation

There is a third way which may in the end prove to be more effective than either of the other two: the way of negotiation which, using the experience and expertise which the participant group will bring with it, will determine jointly the programme to be undertaken, the goals to be pursued, the types of knowledge, skills and attitudes which need to be developed. In short, it will be a process of joint decision-making and planning.

Adult education is more experienced than Development in negotiation. Adult educators, at least in theory, are used to negotiating with their learners the subject of the adult education programme, the format, the timing, the pace of learning and so on. These are not determined by the agency/tutor/instructor alone as they usually are in extension. Nor are they determined by the learner group alone: they are mutually agreed. So in Developmental adult education, on equal terms, the change-agent and the target group negotiate until they come to agreement concerning the programme; the decision-making is equally shared, the learning is on both sides.

In practice, however, true negotiation between equals is (despite the rhetoric) a rare animal in adult education. But when dealing with new target groups, with communities not accustomed to engaging with adult education or Development agencies, it may be the right road. And the process of negotiation itself amounts to the first step in the Development programme itself, the awareness-enhancing stage. When we start negotiating, we shall already have started on our new Development-based adult education.

Exactly which of these routes will be followed will be decided by each adult education–Development agency on a day-to-day basis. The decision will clearly vary according to the underlying philosophy which directs the programme, the particular goals being pursued and the willingness of the participant group to join in. All of them, given the intention of both parties to go in this direction, will lead to participation.

NOTES TO CHAPTER 19

(1)   Chambers (1983), p. 141.
(2)   Oakley (1984); Rahman, A. (1982) *Theory and Practice of Participatory Action Research*, Geneva: ILO; Fernandes, W. and Tandon, R. (eds) (1981) *Participatory Research and Evaluation*, Delhi; *Strength of a Song: Participation in Rural Development*, special issue of *RRDC Bulletin* **21** (1987); Pearse, A. and Stiefel, M. (1979) *Inquiry into Participation: a Research Approach*, Geneva: UNRISD. I wish to record my thanks to Dr L. S. Saraswathi of Madras for inviting me to participate, however marginally, in these programmes.
(3)   Participatory research, training and evaluation are the keywords of the International Council for Adult Education.
(4)   For an example of a development agency exploring the implications of the concept of participation for its practice, see *Bay of Bengal Programme News* **27** (September 1987).
(5)   This project proposal crossed my desk while in India: it must remain anonymous.
(6)   *RRDC Bulletin* **21** (1987), p. 7.
(7)   Bagnall, R. G. (1989) Participation by adults, *Adult Education and Development* **32**, 23–28.
(8)   For participation as 'presence', see for example Percy, K. Adult participation in learning activities, in Costello and Richardson (1982); the studies cited in Chapter 4, note 27. For a more general approach, see Norris, C. (1985) Towards a theory of participation in adult education, *AE* **58**(2), 122–7.
(9)   *Bay of Bengal Programme News*, cited in note 4 above.
(10) Fernandes (1980), p. xxix.
(11) Jackson (1980), p. 17; see Cole, G. D. H. *Students' Bulletin*, April 1925, cited in Thompson (1980), p. 124; Wootton, B. (1937) A plea for constructive teaching, *AE* **10**(2) (December), 91–105.
(12) Rogers, A. (1977); Rogers, A. The university and local studies: local history, in Thornton and Stephens (1977), pp. 137–42; Rogers, A. (1973) *This Was Their World*, BBC (reprinted as *Approaches to Local History*, Longman, 1977); Thompson (1978); Yarnit (1980a), pp. 185–7; publications of History Workshop, Ruskin College, Oxford; *Stability and Change: Some Aspects of North and South Rauceby in the Nineteenth Century*, Rauceby Local History Group, edited by A. Rogers (University of Nottingham, 1969); *History of Nidderdale*, Pateley Bridge Local History Tutorial Class, ed. B. Jennings (Huddersfield, 1967).
(13) Rogers, A. (1971) Stamford Survey Group, *Bulletin of Local History East Midlands Region* **13**, 71.
(14) Green (1977), p. 37.
(15) Habermas, J. (1976) Problems of legitimation in late capitalism, in Connerton, P. (ed.) *Critical Sociology*, Penguin.
(16) Currie, R., Gilbert, A. and Horsley, L. (1977) *Churches and Churchgoers: Patterns of Church Growth in the British Isles since 1700*, Oxford University Press, pp. 6–9—one of the clearest expressions of this theory of growth and participation.
(17) See Kindervatter (1979); Oakley, P. (1987) State or process, means or end? the concept of participation in rural development, *RRDC Bulletin* **21**, 3–9.
(18) Indira Gandhi National Open University course on *Rural Development* (Block 1, Rural Development—the Indian Context: Unit 2, Rural Development—Precepts and Practices, 1987), p. 28. I am grateful to Dr Ram Reddy the former Vice-Chancellor of IGNOU for permission to quote this and for giving me the opportunity to work in that new establishment for a short time, 1987–88.

Chapter 20

CONCLUSION: 'So you think you know better . . .?'

We must finally face the issue which has been underlying all the discussion in this book, the legitimacy of adult education agents adopting and holding goals of their own. Here lies the nub of the problem. How can the adult educator work for local or regional or national Development? How far can we use adult education as a tool for what some will see as mass persuasion? Is this a just way to treat the learners?

It is of course an ambitious task to seek for such an answer, but it must be attempted. What is clear is that the first stage of the search must be to define the issue itself as precisely as possible. So, what is the question?

It is, I think, this: can I legitimately go to a group of adult equals and say, 'I want you to learn this, even if you don't want to learn it—or at least don't want to learn it yet'. Will not such an approach deny their adulthood?

I hope that is the right question, because if it is, then I think I see a glimmer of an answer. Yes, I can do this because of the phrase 'a group of adult equals'. I too am an adult equal, and I too possess hopes and aspirations, beliefs and experiences which I wish to share. If I as an adult educator need to take the intentions and aspirations of the learners seriously and seek to meet them, they too need to take my aspirations seriously, should meet me as well. We have to appreciate to the full that phrase 'teaching on equal terms'. If adult education is teaching on equal terms, then it surely follows that the adult educator, the teacher, the one who helps the other to learn, has the right and even the duty to share his/her own goals and objectives, aspirations, intentions, insights, experiences, hopes and even dreams with the learners, and has the right to expect that these will be taken seriously. For teachers of adults are not 'non-persons': they are fully human and have their own contribution to make to the teaching–learning equation.

The answer to our question then must lie in the attitudes of the adult educator towards the learners and towards the subject matter of the programme. A deep concern for the participant group, and a belief in the importance of the task in hand coupled with a willingness to share on an equal basis—in other words, holding both a conviction of the truth and at the same time an openness to learn: in this double approach will lie the justification for Developmental adult education. And if we display this attitude of sharing, then there should be no problem in our groups considering in depth what is being shared. We are not engaged merely in educating people to agree with the Development or adult education agency; we *are* engaged in a process of sharing, in the course of which both sides will take each other seriously; and both sides will inevitably move their position.

This surely is my justification.

*   *   *

As I sit in my room looking over the Madras beach, with the heat well into the hundreds, I think of what I have seen and experienced. Yesterday (it seems ages ago) I spent the afternoon in a group of villages round Madurantakkam, some 75 kilometres outside Madras. For the third year in a row, the rains have been inadequate; the north-east monsoon came but the south-east monsoon failed almost completely. There is enough water to last the farmers for a few months, but the flight from the villages to the towns has begun; the drought is biting deeper.

I think of the city I am now in—of the dirt and the slums, the disease and the poverty in Triplicane just behind this University Guest House, where the 'cut' is a stinking open sewer, where the women cook their meals on open fires on the pavement surrounded by the shit of human beings and animals alike, where the cattle roam the streets, where the mosquitoes breed and the crows eat the dead rats in the open and people die of cholera in large numbers while politicians squabble over trifles—and I feel angry. I remember the adult education class held there every evening when the women return from their work as domestic and office cleaners and walk along a road which is more often than not under two or three inches of polluted water and sewage slime to reach a school building which has no electric light and meet with a literacy animator willing to talk with them and to teach them.

And then I think of the neat rich village in Norfolk where I have my home; where there are two or three adult education classes each winter—a WEA group which attracts some 25–30 well-educated and relatively wealthy persons to a series of lectures on topics like The Railways of East Anglia or The Plays of Ibsen—self-fulfilling and enriching programmes of adult learning, and one or two local authority classes in the village school on practical subjects. And I think, what of the other 900 or so persons in this village: does adult education have nothing to say to them?

Now this is the dilemma which faces every Development worker and every adult educator, whatever his or her context. But we need to remember, first, that it is easy to exaggerate. As we have so often reminded ourselves, adult education is not the only agency for the education and training of adults or for Development. It is one among many. And adult education is not a religion; it is one means to a common end—the betterment of the life of human beings.

Nevertheless, it is one such tool, and as such we have to take its goal seriously. And it happens to be the one tool that I know anything about, having served it for more than thirty years. I have seen adult education change lives—not of the masses, it is true, but of one or two persons, giving them a second (or in some cases, a first) chance. And I wonder: does it not have something to offer to other people? Why do we have to be content to offer courses just to those who come forward of their own volition? And why do we have to offer to these few self-selecting adult learners just the subjects they want to learn about rather than the things I think are important for the betterment of life—

things like health and income-generation or the plight of three-quarters of the world's population or the selfish waste of the world's natural resources? Why can't I share with the people the things I believe will help to change their lives as they have changed mine?

'So you think you know better . . .?' In one sense, yes. I think I know myself better after writing these pages. I certainly know a lot more about the two main subjects of this book, Development and adult education. I think I understand some of the problems of the Third World better, thanks to the generosity of friends like Chandra and Saraswathi and Rathindra and Elias and Ranjanidoss who introduced me to so many men and women in the towns and villages around Madras, as well as to so many ideas; and thanks to people like Philomena and Jhansi and Om and Ginny and Anita and . . . the list is endless over the years since I first came to India. Yes, I think I know some things better.

'So you think you know better . . . than me?' No, I don't. I know what I know. All I want is a chance to share. I no longer want one-way learning, even if it is learner-centred, learner-dominated learning. I want two-way learning: I too want to be taken seriously. And I no longer want an adult education which reaches only the few but the many; I want an adult education which has become a mass movement for the betterment of the whole as well as for the benefit of the individual. Like the Ancient Mariner, I want to share my experiences—not just with 'one in three' but with all three! Yes, I'm greedy: but perhaps it's because I believe.

But equally I want to listen, to carry on learning. I've learned so much over the last thirty or so years in adult education, so much over the last twenty years of visiting India and other Third World countries, so much over the last few months writing this book which has released the pent-up learnings of these years. And I want to go on learning; I don't want to stop. This book is not intended to be an end but the beginning of further learning in both adult education and Development.

Alan Rogers
Madras
January 1989

Bibliography

Note: this list contains works cited more than once in the notes or text. Works mentioned once only are not repeated here.

ACACE (1979) *Strategy for the Basic Education of Adults*. Leicester: ACACE.

ACACE (1982) *Adults: their Educational Experience and Needs*. Leicester: ACACE.

ACRE (1985) Report 1. Ian Scott: *Developing Your Community: Pilot Programme Report*. Fairford, Glos: Action with Communities for Rural England.

ACRE (1988) Report 2. Ian Scott: *Rural Community Development through Adult Education, Final Report*. Stable Yard, Fairford Park, Fairford, Glos: ACRE.

Armstrong, P.F. (1982) The 'needs-meeting' ideology in liberal education. *IJLE* 1(4), 293–321.

Arocena, J. (1986) From culture to the economy: new local social agents. In EBAE (1988), see below.

Batten, T.R. (1959) *School and Community in the Tropics*. Oxford University Press.

Batten, T.R. (1967) *Non-Directive Approach in Group and Community Work*. London: Oxford University Press.

Bennis, W., Benne, K. and Chin, R. (eds) (1964) *The Planning of Change*, 2nd edn. New York (3rd edn, 1976).

Bock, J.C. and Papagiannis, G.J. (1982) *Nonformal Education and National Development: a Critical Assessment of Policy, Research and Practice*. New York.

Bowles, H. and Gintis, S. (1976) *Schooling in Capitalist America*. Routledge and Kegan Paul.

Bown, L. and Okedara, J.T. (1981) *An Introduction to the Study of Adult Education*. Ibadan University Press.

Brookfield, S. (1983) *Adult Learners, Adult Education and the Community*. Open University Press.

Brookfield, S. (ed.) (1988) *Training Educators of Adults*. Routledge.

Brundtland (1987) *Our Common Future: Report of the Brundtland Commission*.

Chambers, R. (1983) *Rural Development: Putting the Last First*. Longman.

Chickering, A. (ed.) (1981) *The Modern American College*. Jossey Bass.

Clyne, P. (1972) *The Disadvantaged Adult*. Longman.

Cohen, J.M. and Uphoff, N.T. (1977) *Rural Development Participation: Concepts for Measuring Participation for Project Design, Implementation and Evaluation*. Cornell.

Coombs, P.H. and Ahmed, M. (1974) *Attacking World Poverty: How Nonformal Education Can Help*. Baltimore.

Costello, N. and Richardson, M. (eds) (1982) *Continuing Education for the Post-Industrial Society*. Open University Press.

Council of Europe (1984) *Adult Education and Community Development*, secretariat paper, Council of Europe CDCC Project CC-CG9 (84) 28, Strasbourg.
Council of Europe (1986a) *Challenge and Response*, CDCC Project CC-GP9 (86) 1, Strasbourg.
Council of Europe (1986b) *Final Conference Summary Report*, CDCC (86) 29, Strasbourg.
Crombie, A. D. and Harries-Jenkins, G. (1983) *The Demise of the Liberal Tradition*. University of Leeds.
Cross, K. P. (1981) *Adults as Learners*. Jossey Bass.
Dave, R. H. (ed.) (1976) *Foundations of Lifelong Education*. Oxford: Pergamon.
De Sanctis, F. M. (1988) Educational aims for the year 2000. In EBAE (1988).
DES (1972) *Education: a Framework for Expansion* (White Paper). London: HMSO.
DES (1978) *Higher Education into the 1990s* (DES discussion document). DES.
DES (1980) *Continuing Education: Post Experience Vocational Provision for Those in Employment*. DES.
DES (1985) *The Development of Higher Education into the 1990s*. London: HMSO.
EBAE (1988) Papers prepared for EBAE Conference on Adult Education and Social Development, Madrid, September 1988; available from EBAE.
Education Throughout Life (1986) Labour Party (UK) Policy Document.
Erb, G. F. and Kallab, V. (eds) (1975) *Beyond Dependency: the Developing World Speaks Out*. Washington.
Fernandes, W. (1980) *People's Participation in Development: Approaches to Nonformal Education*. Delhi: Indian Social Institute.
Fletcher, C. (1980) The theory of community education and its relation to adult education. In Thompson (1980), see below.
Fordham, P., Poulton, G. and Randle, L. (1979) *Learning Networks in Adult Education: Nonformal Education on a new Housing Estate*. Routledge and Kegan Paul.
Freire, P. (1972) *Pedagogy of the Oppressed*. Penguin.
Gerver, E. (1988) Trends in adult education in Scotland. In EBAE (1988).
Goulet, D. (1975) *The Cruel Choice: a New Concept in the Theory of Development*. New York.
Goulet, D. and Hudson, M. (1971) *The Myth of Aid*. New York.
Grant, J. P. (1973) *Growth from Below: a People-Oriented Development Strategy*. Washington.
Green, R. H. (1977) *Adult Education in National Development Planning: Notes Toward an Integrated Approach*. ICAE and DVV.
Griffin, C. (1983) *Curriculum Theory in Adult and Continuing Education*. Croom Helm.
Habermas, J. (1972) *Communication and the Evolution of Society*. Boston.
Habermas, J. (1978) *Knowledge and Human Interests*. Heinemann.
Hall, D. (1988) Training as an agent for rural development: the NFWI [National Federation of Women's Institutes] community action training scheme. *AE* **61**(3), 247–9.
Halsey, A. H., Floud, J. and Anderson, C. (1961) *Education, Economy and Society: a Reader in the Sociology of Education*. New York.
Harbison, F. H. and Myers, C. A. (1964) *Education, Manpower and Economic Growth*. New York.
Harries-Jenkins, G. (1983) University adult education into the 1990s. In Crombie and Harries-Jenkins (1983).
Harrison, J. F. C. (1961) *Learning and Living 1790–1960*. Routledge and Kegan Paul.
Hirschman, A. (1970) *Exit, Voice and Loyalty*. Cambridge, Mass.
Houle, C. O. (1961/64) *The Inquiring Mind: a Study of the Adult who Continues to Learn*. Madison, Wisconsin.
Hutchinson, E. and Hutchinson, E. (1978) *Learning Later: Fresh Horizons in English Adult Education*. Routledge and Kegan Paul.
Illich, I. (1970) *De-Schooling Society*. New York: (Penguin, 1973).
ILSCAE (1986) *About a Week in Nottingham: Themes from the 1986 Conference of the International League for Social Commitment in Adult Education*. ILSCAE (1987).
Jackson, K. (1970) Adult education and community development. *Studies in Adult Education* **2**(2), 156–79.
Jackson, K. (1971) Community adult education: the role of the professional adult educator. *AE* **44**, 165–72.

Jackson, K. (1980) Foreword to Thompson (1980).

Jarvis, P. (1983) *Adult and Continuing Education: Theory and Practice*. Croom Helm.

Jarvis, P. (1987) *Adult Education in the Social Context*. Croom Helm.

Jobert, G. (1988) Teachers and adult educators: the same struggle for development. In EBAE (1988).

Kandrup, P. (1988) Some recent trends in adult education in Denmark. In EBAE (1988).

Keddie, N. (1980) Adult education: an ideology of individualism. In Thompson (1980).

Kidd, J. R. (1959) *How Adults Learn*. New York (repr. 1973).

Kindervatter, S. (1979) *Nonformal Education as an Empowerment Process*. Amherst, Mass.

Kirkwood, C. (1978) Adult education and the concept of community. *AE* 51(3).

Knowles, M. S. (ed.) (1973) *The Adult Learner: a Neglected Species*. Houston.

Knowles, M. S. (1980) *The Modern Practice of Adult Education: from Pedagogy to Andragogy*, 2nd edn. Chicago.

Knox, A. (1977) *Adult Development and Learning*. Jossey Bass.

Lawson, K. H. (1977) Community education: a critical assessment. *AE* 50(1).

Lawson, K. H. (1979) *Philosophical Concepts and Values in Adult Education* (rev. edn). Open University Press.

Leirman, W. (1987) Adult education: movement and discipline between the golden sixties and the iron eighties. In Leirman, W. and Kulich, J., *Adult Education and the Challenge of the 1990s*. Croom Helm.

Lengrand, P. (1975) *Introduction of Lifelong Education*. Croom Helm.

Lindeman, E. C. (1926) *The Meaning of Adult Education*. New York.

Lindeman, E. C. (1938) Preparing leaders in adult education. Reprinted in Brookfield (1988).

Lovett, T. (1971) Community adult education. *Studies in Adult Education* 5, 2–14.

Lovett, T. (1975) *Adult Education, Community Development and the Working Class*. Ward Lock; repr. University of Nottingham.

Lovett, T. (1980) Adult education and community action. In Thompson (1980).

Lowe, J. (1975) *The Education of Adults: a World Perspective*. Paris: UNESCO.

Luna, J. L. A. (1988) Universidades Populares in Spain. In EBAE (1988).

McIlroy, J. and Spencer, B. (1988) *University Adult Education in Crisis*. University of Leeds.

Maslow, A. (1962) *Towards a Psychology of Being*. New York (new edn, 1968).

Mee, G. (1980) *Organization for Adult Education*. Longman.

Melo, A. (1988) The Radial Project: a support network for participatory development in the Algarve. In EBAE (1988).

Mengin, J. (1988) Models of local development. In EBAE (1988).

Midwinter, E. (1972) *Priority Education: an Account of the Liverpool Project*. Penguin.

Miller, H. L. (1964) *Teaching and Learning in Adult Education*. New York.

NAB (1984) *Report on Continuing Education*. National Advisory Board for Polytechnics and Colleges of Higher Education, UK.

Nerfin, M. (1977) *Another Development: Approaches and Strategies*. Uppsala.

Newman, M. (1979) *The Poor Cousin: a Study of Adult Education*. London: Allen and Unwin.

Oakley, P. and Marsden, D. (1984) *Approaches to Participation in Rural Development*. Geneva: ILO.

OECD (1973) *Recurrent Education: a Strategy for Lifelong Education*. Paris: Organisation for Economic Co-operation and Development.

OECD (1975) *Framework for a Comprehensive Policy for Adult Education*. Paris: OECD.

OECD (1979) *Learning Opportunities for Adults*. Paris: OECD.

Parmar, S. L. (1975) Self-reliant development in an interdependent world. In Erb and Kallab (1975).

Paterson, R. W. K. (1979) *Values, Education and the Adult*. Routledge and Kegan Paul.

Petersen, R. E., Gaff, S. S., Helmick, J. S., Feldmesser, R. A., Valley, J. R. and Nielsen, H. D. (eds) (1982) *Adult Education and Training in Nine Industrialized Countries*. New York.

REPLAN *Rural Needs Bulletin*. Cardiff: REPLAN Wales.

1909 Report *Oxford and Working Class Education*. Oxford.

1919 Report *Report of Ministry of Reconstruction Adult Education Committee 1919*. Ed. H.C. Wiltshire. University of Nottingham, 1980.

Rogers, A. (ed.) (1976) *The Spirit and the Form: Essays by and in Honour of H.C. Wiltshire.* University of Nottingham.

Rogers, A. (ed.) (1977) *Group Projects in Local History.* Dawson.

Rogers, A. (1980) *Knowledge and the People.* New University of Ulster.

Rogers, A. (ed.) (1981) *University Continuing Education: into the 1990s.* New University of Ulster.

Rogers, A. (1982) New lamps for old: the Institute of Continuing Education in Magee University College, Londonderry. *Aontas Review* (Dublin) 3(1), 52–6.

Rogers, A. (ed.) (1984) *Adult Education and Development in Great Britain and Ireland.* New University of Ulster.

Rogers, A. (1986) *Teaching Adults.* Open University Press.

Rogers, J. (1979) *Adults Learning.* Open University Press.

Russell Report (1973) *Adult Education: a Plan for Development.* Report of the Russell Committee. London: HMSO.

Ryan, W. (1971) *Blaming the Victim.* New York.

Seers, D. (1969) The meaning of development. *International Development Review* 11(4), 2–6.

Simpson, J. (1970) Permanent education and community development. In *Permanent Education.* Strasbourg: Council of Europe.

Sockett, H. (ed.) (1981) *Educational Analysis* 3(3): special edition on *Continuing Education.* Falmer Press.

Strategy Report (1980) *Continuing Education in Northern Ireland: Strategy for Development.* Northern Ireland Council for Continuing Education.

Szentes, T. (1976) *The Political Economy of Underdevelopment.* Budapest.

Taylor, R. and Ward, K. (1986) *Adult Education and the Working Class: Education for the Missing Millions.* Croom Helm.

Thomas, A. and Ploman, E.W. (1985) *Learning and Development: a Global Perspective.* Toronto.

Thompson, J. (ed.) (1980) *Adult Education for a Change.* Hutchinson.

Thompson, J. (ed.) (1984) *Learning Liberation.* Croom Helm.

Thompson, P. (1978) *The Voice of the Past.* Opus.

Thornton, A.H. and Stephens, M.D. (eds) (1977) *The University in its Region.* University of Nottingham.

Titmus, C. (1981) *Strategies for Adult Education: Practices in Western Europe.* Chicago.

UGC (1984) *Report on Continuing Education.* Universities Grants Committee (UK). London: HMSO.

UNRISD (1979) *Approach to Development Research.* Geneva: United Nations Research Institute for Social Development.

van Nieuwenhuijze, C.A.O (1982) *Development Begins at Home: Problems and Prospects of Sociology of Development.* Pergamon.

Wignaraja, P. (1976) A new strategy for development, *International Development Review* 18(3) 2–7.

Wilber, C.K. (ed.) (1973) *The Political Economy of Development and Underdevelopment.* New York.

Yarnit, M. (1980a) Second chance to learn, Liverpool. In Thompson (1980).

Yarnit, M. (1980b) Italy's 150 hours. In Thompson (1980).

Index

ACACE 37, 52
access 2, 40, 196, 206
accidental learning 10, 11
ACRE programme (UK) 202, 203, 212, 226
action learning 13
adult colleges 30
adult education
  centres 202
  institutes 30, 36, 55, 70, 71, 193, 196, 199
  methods 70
  in Third World 72–3, 76
adulthood 22, 42, 239
agencies 3, 4, 29
Agricultural Training Board (UK) 55
agriculture, agricultural extension 19, 30, 72, 85, 120, 131, 142, 156, 176, 189, 193, 204, 210, 217, 219
AIDS 60, 64, 142, 188, 193, 196, 219, 220
amenity groups 41
andragogy 45
animators 160ff., 195, 209, 212
Antigonish (Canada) 200
Aristotle 35
Aron, Raymond 93
Ashridge Conference 96
aspirations 151, 230
assertiveness 186, 236
attitudes 3, 122, 123, 139–40, 176–7, 193, 198, 224
Australasia 5
Australia 42, 155
Austria 46
awareness 111, 124, 133–7, 186–7, 219, 234

Bangladesh 103, 112
banking concept of education 35
barriers to learning 3
basic education 59, 186, 188, 197
Basic Human Needs (BHN) 98–100, 101, 102, 103, 104, 111–12, 147, 149, 191
Batten, T. R. 97
Bay of Bengal Programme (FAO, India) 128–9, 163
behavioural learning 12, 21
Belfast (Northern Ireland) 203
Belgium 203
Bombay 112
Boshier, R. 60
bottom-up Development 93, 156
  see also top-down
British Food and Farming Year 65, 188
Brundtland Report 97

bureaucratic route to Development 119

Cambridge (UK) 54, 55
Campaign for Nuclear Disarmament 49
campaigns 10, 64, 121, 188, 193, 197, 198, 201, 202, 220
Canada 42, 200
Central America 174
certification 40, 56, 72, 225
change-agents 3, 4, 41, 156, 159–68, 199, 202, 208–15, 222
Chipko movement (India) 128
churches 30
CIA test 135–6
Clapham (London) Popular Planning Project 200
clinics 87
Clones, Co. Monaghan (Ireland) 192
Club of Rome 48
Coady, M. 59
cognitive learning 12
Coin Street adult education programme (London, UK) 200
colonialism 91, 101
communicative learning 12, 15, 138
community 29, 198
  associations 41
  colleges 29–31, 35, 40, 201
  development 39, 67, 96, 97
  education 35, 47, 66–8, 73, 77
  mapping 134
  schools 193, 197
compulsory adult education 25
concept distance in learning 16–17, 140
conservation 189–91, 196, 198, 202
consumer education 76
continuing education 19, 24–5, 29, 31, 35, 37, 38, 53, 57, 58, 59, 62, 69
co-operatives 143, 217, 221, 228
correspondence education 30
Council of Europe 35, 197, 203, 212
  Community Education Programme 5
Cuba 101
cultural adult education, Development 187, 190, 205
curriculum 32, 46

dams 111
Dearne Valley adult education programme (UK) 200
decision-making 15, 123–8, 142–3, 204, 228–9
definitions 19, 28
Delhi (India) 227, 236

de-linking 94
Denmark 42, 52, 61, 188
Department of Education and Science (DES) (UK) 51
dependency 91–2, 101, 111
Development
  cycle 144
  definition 83–4
  goals 85–90
    see also goals
Dewey, John 66
dialogue 14
direct action route to Development 121–2, 188
disadvantaged 39, 48, 49, 96, 187, 191, 197, 205
distance education 196, 213
domains of learning 12, 21
Dorset (UK) 202
Dublin (Ireland) 192
Duncan, Alan 155

Each One Teach One adult education programme 196
economic growth
  Development 92ff., 97, 108, 189
  problems 97–8
education
  definition 5, 20, 21
  and the economy 51, 52, 57, 61–2
  purpose 33
  role 49
  and training of adults in development (ETA) 137–41, 185–6, 188
éducation permanente 36
éducation populaire 19, 20, 35
Education Shops 196
educational guidance 66
Educational Priority Areas (EPA) (UK) 39, 43
Educational Priority Groups (EPGs) (UK) 39
Educational Settlements Association 195
educational system 20
elderly in adult education 39, 50
elitism 42, 212
emancipatory learning 12, 15, 41, 138
empowerment in Development 103–4, 234
England 52, 53, 77, 195
English as a Second Language (ESL) 39, 55, 56, 186, 188, 196
entryism 155, 187, 192, 237
environmental adult education, Development 2, 29, 49, 66, 71, 75,

77, 89, 98, 187, 188, 190, 193, 198,
219, 220, 236
ethnic adult education 191, 197, 203, 209
Europe 57
European Bureau of Adult Education
(EBAE) 5, 203
European Commission (EC) 49, 204, 205,
210
evaluation 216–25
examinations 217
expectations 23
experience 9, 13, 14, 23
extension 4, 29, 30, 162, 163, 209, 214
see also agriculture
Extra-Mural Departments, universities
(EMDs) 30, 31, 52–3, 55, 56, 139,
193, 195, 196, 202

facilitation 155, 236–7
family planning 72, 73, 87, 88, 97, 120,
121, 136, 228, 236
farmers 89, 138
see also agriculture
Farmers Functional Literacy Programme
(FFLP) (India) 159
Fauré report (UNESCO) 48, 61
Finland 42, 52, 53, 58, 203
fishing boats 128–9
Folk High Schools 31, 36
Food and Agriculture Organization (FAO)
154
see also Bay of Bengal Programme
forestry 29
formal education, learning 10, 11, 24,
25–8, 29, 32, 35, 36, 40, 51, 68, 70,
72, 196, 228
see also educational system
formation (France) 189
France 42, 52, 53, 61, 66, 189, 211
Freire, Paulo 13, 39, 43, 186, 187, 193,
203, 208
Frobisher Institute (London, UK) 205
Further Education colleges 202
Further Education Unit (FEU) (UK) 213

Galway (Ireland) 203
Gandhi 87
Gelpi, Ettore 65
Germany 42, 52
Ghana 160
goals (objectives) in adult education and
Development 1, 3, 15, 21, 34, 58,
59, 69–70, 73, 74, 75–6, 91ff., 99,
114, 154–5, 156, 185, 186–93, 198,
199, 204, 210, 214, 218, 219, 220,
222, 233–4, 236, 239
Goulet, D. 99
governments and adult education 30
Greece 66, 74, 187, 194, 203
Green, R. H. 65
green revolution 174
Greenham Common (UK) 128
Guildford (UK) 212

Habermas, J. 40
handicapped 187
health adult education and Development
19, 29, 49, 54, 56, 64, 71, 72, 73, 85,
97, 98, 113, 138, 140, 156, 188, 189,
190, 191, 193, 195, 196, 198, 200,
201, 203, 204, 210, 213, 214, 217,
219, 224, 236
see also Look After Yourself
Heartbeat Wales (adult education
programme) 170–1, 188
heritage 188
Highlander (USA) 200
Highlands and Islands development 204
Horton, M. 59
Horwich (UK) 203
Human Resource Development (HRD)
94–5, 97, 101, 102, 112, 160
Hunstanton (UK) 55
hydro-electric projects 83, 85, 129, 220

Ilfracombe (UK) 201
Illich, Ivan 39, 74
immigrants and adult education 39, 49
impact evaluation 217
income-generating 19, 29, 54, 88, 112,
221
India 4, 5, 96, 103, 111, 112, 128, 129,
146, 149, 151, 159, 160, 162, 164,
172, 195, 197, 227, 240, 241
individualism in adult education and
Development 9, 34, 37–41, 43, 44,
45, 47, 59–60, 63, 67, 87–8, 89, 185,
187, 189, 190, 193, 206
individualization 1, 38
Indonesia 96
informal learning 10, 11
initial education 19, 25, 34
Inner London Education Authority (ILEA)
(London, UK) 196, 205
input Development 110, 157
input learning 13, 14
insider–outsider in Development 84, 86,
114, 160, 209, 226
insightful learning 15
instrumental learning 12, 15, 138
Integrated Rural Development (IRD) 97,
189
intentions 152–3
interests 12
internalization of values (oppression) 177
International Council of Adult Education
(ICAE) 48
Ireland 42, 52, 192, 203, 211
issue-based adult education 189, 200
Italy 66, 74, 201, 203

justice, adult education for 2, 47, 48, 52,
66, 73, 75, 77, 234

Karnataka (India) 175
KASUB 12, 17, 21
Kenya 95, 97, 129
Kerala (India) 89
Khan, Akhteer Hamid 97
Kolb, David 14

La Belle, Thomas 203
La Guardia local history project (New
York, USA) 211
Labour Party (UK) 38
languages in adult education 54, 56, 187,
196, 205
Le Creusot (France) 66, 211–12
learner-centred adult education 37, 42
learning 9, 20, 21, 137
contract 38
cycle 13, 14
episodes 10, 11
maps 16, 17
society 198–200
styles 13–15, 23, 24
legislation on adult education 120
leisure adult education 29, 41, 54–5
liberal adult education 24, 31, 34, 37, 41,
44, 47, 53, 57, 58, 60, 62, 68, 75,
187, 216
liberation Development 100, 101, 102–3,
104, 113–14
libraries 30, 65, 196, 197, 201, 202
lifelong learning 9–11, 19, 34, 35, 37, 199
Lincolnshire (UK) 195, 232
literacy 2, 19, 20, 24, 29, 39, 49, 72, 73,
87, 103, 115–16, 120, 138, 140, 143,
148, 156, 159, 160, 161, 164, 186,
187, 189, 195, 196, 217, 219, 224,
240
Liverpool (UK) 43, 211
Livingstone, Sir Richard 35
local education authorities (LEAs) (UK)
54–5
local history 59, 65, 202, 210–12, 214,
221, 231–2, 233, 235
London 42, 55–6, 196, 200, 205
see also Clapham; Inner London
Education Authority; Wandsworth
Londonderry (Northern Ireland) 192

Look After Yourself programme 201–2,
203, 219

McCleavy, Sister Catherine 149
Madras (India) 149, 195, 240, 241
Madrid (Spain) 203
Magee University College, Londonderry,
Northern Ireland 192, 194, 203
Mahaveli Dam Project, Sri Lanka 129
Mahbubnagar Experiment (India) 140,
161–2
Malawi 96
management 29
mandatory adult education 25
see also compulsory adult education
Manpower Services Commission (Training
Agency) (UK) 52, 55
manpower training 2, 3, 41, 51, 52, 64
Mansbridge, Albert 38
marathon 26
marginalization of adult education 40,
41, 52, 59, 68, 101, 185, 188, 199
Maslow, Abraham 38, 99, 147, 191
mass adult education 2, 197–8, 200–1,
203, 214
see also campaigns
Mauritius 114
Mbeere tribe (Africa) 138
Mechanics Institutes 34
media and adult education 10, 14, 21, 49,
65, 188, 196
memory 15
Mexico 178
Midwinter, Eric 67
Ministry of Reconstruction (UK), report on
adult education (1919) 56, 199
modernization in Development 91–2, 97,
100–2, 104
Monaghan, Co. (Ireland) 192
moratorium movement (India) 112
Morris, Henry 66
multi-ethnic adult education 187
museums 30, 65, 197, 221
Mwea Dam Project (Kenya) 129

Nairobi Declaration on Adult Education
48
Narayan, R. K. 136
National Council of Labour Colleges
(NCLC) (UK) 43
National Institute of Adult Continuing
Education (NIACE) (UK) 46
needs in adult education and Development
38, 45, 55, 98, 147–9, 191
negotiation in adult education 38, 237
neo-colonialism 112, 154
Netherlands 52, 197, 205, 206
networks 40
New Communities Project (UK) 39
New York (USA) 211
Nicaragua 112
Nirmada Dam Project (India) 129
non-formal learning, education 10–11,
19, 25–8, 31, 32, 44, 47, 72, 196
non-formal methods 27–8
non-governmental organizations (NGOs)
49, 56, 57–8, 65, 72, 73, 74, 86, 173,
187, 188, 193, 199, 204, 205, 233
non-vocational adult education 36, 41, 70
Norfolk (UK) 54, 55, 56, 240
North America 57, 59
Northern Ireland 4, 70, 192, 194, 203
Norway 42, 43, 52
nutrition education and Development 29,
89, 120, 131, 138, 143, 198, 220
Nyerere, President Julius 101

objectives *see* goals
OECD 36, 51, 55
Offaly, Co. (Ireland) 211
one world 4, 5
open colleges 196
open learning 30
Open University (UK) 40, 203, 213
opposition to Development 172
oral history 202, 231–2

oral rehydration therapy (ORT)   89, 142, 146–7, 175–6
Orissa (India)   172
outcomes of Development   171, 178, 218–22
outsiders in Development   146, 148–9, 156, 204, 205
    see also insider–outsider
Oxford (UK)   37, 232
Oxford and Working Class Education, report (UK, 1909)   38

paid educational leave   36
Palme, Olof   36
paradigm transformation   13
participation   37, 40, 42, 59, 73, 77, 85, 88, 89, 97, 101, 103–5, 113–14, 142–3, 187, 190, 204, 208, 213, 217, 226–38
peace, adult education for   2, 52, 66, 75, 77, 198, 234
people's universities   66
perception evaluation   223–4
personal development, growth, in adult education   28, 36, 38, 39, 45, 47, 49, 51, 186, 190, 199, 214, 224
persuasion   230, 237
Philippines   96
PICKUP adult education programme (UK)   41
playgroups   39, 56, 202
Plowden Report   66
political adult education   59, 73, 190
population   2, 49, 52, 98
    see also family planning
Portugal   66, 192, 203, 205
post-experience vocational education (PEVE)   41
poverty and adult education, Development   50, 71, 73, 91–2, 97, 188, 198, 217, 234
pre-school programmes   39
prison education   203
professional development programmes   11, 19, 24, 29, 47, 53, 187
programmes   85
projects   85
propaganda   10, 11
public enlightenment adult education   188
Putney (London)   55–6

radio   197
Rajasthan (India)   114
Reagan, President Ronald   112
Recurrent Education   19, 36, 37, 51
reflexive observation   13, 14, 15
religious adult education   71, 190, 204
remedial adult education   19, 34, 72
REPLAN (adult education programme) (UK)   55, 203
residents' groups   41
retirement education   39, 197
return to study   40
Rogers, Carl   38
rural adult education, Development   50, 187, 190, 202, 203, 205, 236
    see also ACRE
Rural Community Councils (UK)   55, 195
Ruskin College, Oxford (UK)   232
Russell Report on Adult Education (UK)   37–8, 43, 57, 199, 201

Sarvodaya Shramadana (Sri Lanka)   88, 99, 166, 212
SCALP (Guildford, UK)   212
Scandinavia   42
    see also Palme
schooling   20, 35, 51
Scotland   46, 51, 52, 58, 201, 203, 204, 205
second chance adult education   27, 30, 54, 56
self-help groups   30, 40
smoking   121, 193, 199
social action Development   59, 90, 113–16, 157
social change in adult education, Development   1, 37, 39, 43, 47, 51, 57, 59, 60, 62–3, 74, 90, 94, 185, 189, 199
social goals   60–1
social learning theories   12
social planning in Development   94
social responsibility   2
social roles education   11
Somerset (UK)   202
South Africa   102
South America   234
Soviet Union   40, 42
Spain   51, 61, 65, 85, 205
special needs adult education   39
    see also disadvantaged
Sri Lanka   88, 129, 166, 212
Stamford Survey Group (UK)   232
stimulus–response learning theories   12
study circles   36
Sunday Schools (UK)   34
Sunderland (UK)   203
supervisors   164, 212
surveys   132–3, 148–9
sustainable Development   50, 97, 190
Sutton-in-Ashfield (Notts, UK)   67
Swansea Valleys Initiative for adult education   205
Sweden   42, 203
Switzerland   212
Sydney (Australia)   155

Tamil Nadu (India)   128–9, 172, 175, 227, 236
Tanzania   101, 105, 140
target groups   85, 102, 146–7, 174–5, 189, 197, 201, 228, 234
Tawney, R. H.   56
taxonomy of Development   92, 106–7
teachers in adult education   30
    see also change-agents; tutors-in-residence
technocratic route to Development   120–1
Ten Have, T.   40
Tennessee Local History Project (USA)   211
Thailand   96
third force   185
Third World   5
Tidy Britain campaign   188
top-down model of adult education, Development   156, 186, 204, 212
Torres, C. A.   203
traditionalism   91–2
training   21, 24, 29, 31
    definition   5

of trainers   42, 163–6, 202, 208, 210, 213–14
Training and Visit system (agricultural extension)   160
transformation, goal of Development   105
trees   87, 113
trickle down theory of Development   93
Turkey   191
tutors *see* change-agents
tutors-in-residence   59

UK *see* United Kingdom
Ukai Dam Project (India)   129
unemployed, adult education, Development programmes   11, 25, 41, 49, 52, 55, 57, 62, 66, 70, 95, 115, 187, 188, 190, 196, 197, 203, 205, 206
UNESCO   19, 22, 35, 48, 65, 96
    Declaration on Adult Education   61
UNICEF   140
United Kingdom, adult education, Development in   42, 64, 65, 74, 188, 200, 201, 203, 204, 212, 213, 231
United Nations   97
universities in adult education, Development   25, 29, 30, 31, 36, 51, 52–3, 54, 61–2, 86, 97, 162, 191, 193, 203, 205, 208
Universities Grants Committee (UK)   51
University of the Third Age   40
USA   37, 42, 48, 52, 96, 200, 208, 212
USSR *see* Soviet Union

village colleges   66
vocational education and training   11, 19, 24, 29, 36, 38, 51, 53, 56, 57–8, 72, 73, 95, 187, 193, 199, 205, 213
voluntaryism in adult education, Development   1, 25, 34, 41–2, 43, 73, 185, 197, 198, 204, 206, 210, 237
von Freyhold, M.   140

Wales   170–1, 205
    see also Heartbeat Wales; Swansea
Wandsworth (London, UK)   55–6
wants   149–51
water   129–30
Western Isles Development Board (Scotland)   204, 210
Williams, Raymond   38, 59
Wiltshire (UK)   202
Wiltshire, H. C.   20, 24, 38
women's programmes in adult education and Development   29, 39, 49, 56, 66, 72, 86, 97, 98, 103, 112, 115, 153, 187, 188, 190, 197, 203, 206, 217, 231
Women's Institutes (WI) (UK)   55
Workers' Educational Association (WEA)   30, 37, 43, 47, 54, 55, 56, 76, 193, 195, 196, 202, 203, 240
workers' universities   36
working-class education   42, 43, 57, 59, 68
World Bank   112, 149, 154, 160
World Health Organization (WHO)   154